The Bluing of
Cooper Greens

Hugh McClintock

The best medicine

Roommates Hack Murtaugh and Aaron Blodgett join forces in raising hell at tranquil Cooper Greens, a retirement "depot" where elders, expecting to comfortably live out their lives, gather to catch their last train ride.

The announced presentation for a new, permanent cure for senior erectile dysfunction never happens. On the other hand, the disappearance of a cranky resident's brand new recliner does happen. The hell-raising of Murtaugh and Blodgett never ends – except when a resident's death gloms up the plan.

The characters of Cooper Greens infiltrate the plot in the same indifferent way dandelions invade a lawn. Although, their utterances are usually lighthearted, most of the characters are anything but chaste, scrubbed, one-time boy and girl scouts.

In short, Cooper Greens is not a feel-good story about cardigan-wearing elders stalwartly awaiting the appearance of the bearded scythe-wielder. It is the sifting and winnowing of two years of Hack's mostly humorous, mostly blue, hand-written notes, which I was privileged to maintain – and, as you will later see – that ends when the broadax of cancer cuts Hack down

.

Copyright © 2014 Hugh McClintock

Disclaimer
Any resemblance to actual locales or to persons living or dead is entirely coincidental.

All rights reserved
No part of this book may be used or reproduced in any manner whatsoever without written permission of the author except for brief quotations embodied in critical articles and reviews.

ISBN 10: 0615997155
ISBN 13: 978-0615997155

Printed in the United States of America.

A preliminary, draft version of *Cooper Greens* was published in 2009 as *Old Bones*.

[1]

A caregiver has straightened and smoothed the quilt on Hack's bed. Dressed, except for shoes, he is lying on top browsing the sports' pages of a day-old *Morning Beacon*.

"C'mon, Hack," Joe Luoma orders loudly from the doorway of Hack's room. "Off your bum. Let's go!"

"Go where?" Hack says, pretending that he doesn't know the destination Luoma has in mind.

Luoma is an out-and-out clod, a cesspit of vulgarity, and Hack wishes the hell he'd leave him alone. Only, at Cooper Greens, where insularity is non-existent, residents cannot "pretend" they don't hear the doorbell.

Besides, in time, Hack expects to create a little elation throughout his stay at Cooper Greens – for which collective behavioral upgrade, Joe Luoma might unwittingly play a minor part – "unwittingly" because Luoma is singularly ill-suited to participate in any collective therapy meant to flush Cooper Green's of its all-pervasive gloom.

"You know where," Luoma answers bristly. "Elm Street. I'm feelin' goatish as Paul Bunyan's ox."

Luoma had once before used that wisecrack on Hack, compared himself to the size and sexuality of that fictional draft animal. He does not know that oxen are fallow beasts, and Hack has never bothered to explain. Moreover, Hack suspects there is irony in Luoma comparing himself to an impotent ox, as he now and then lets slip a remark about his own insufficient virility.

"Feeling goatish!" Hack says, exaggerating a squint of skepticism. "Hell, you can't even remember the last time it got up."

"You keepin' track?" Luoma says, smirking.

Louma's voice is usually strong and raspy but this morning it is gravelly: he has yet to shake the grippe that has nagged him for three days; he unintentionally pronounced "goatish" as two wholly separate words, as "goat ish." His straight, unmanageable hair is an uncombed, disarranged mess, as usual, and he has not shaved since becoming racked with the flu. He is wearing a clean white T-shirt tucked into jeans, his one concession to the insinuation of haberdashery. A brawler all his life, Luoma is missing an upper incisor that was punched out years ago in a bar fight. A faded pink ridge horizontally creases the middle of his nose, defining the impact mark of a well-swung beer stein; it is an imprint bequeathed by the buddy of a man whom Luoma had just knocked on his butt. The man's buddy, according to Luoma, hit him from behind with a roundhouse swing that he started from "left field." Luoma is neither bent nor stooped, as are most of the tall men living here, nor is he one to beat about the bush. Hack is certain he was never of that disposition.

Hack, sitting up fully, lays aside the *Beacon* and feels with his feet for the slippers under his bed. When Luoma arrived, Hack was browsing the obituaries.

Before Helen died, he never read those brief, dispiriting memos. But he had to write Helen's. Their marriage was a good one, and writing her death notice was wretched down-time for Hack.

Marie Bates, a first-shift charge nurse, walks past the doorway to Hack's room, and Luoma, in a rough, grating tone, emits one of his loutish remarks, expresses his unambiguous opinion on her inability to correctly position a bedpan.

"Up yours, Luoma," Marie replies indifferently.

Marie did not cloak her voice, so Hack knows she is alone in the hall, in the corridor, as the aides and nurses call the almost double-wide, bed-accommodating halls at Cooper Greens. Marie's seriousness is a force that slants people toward her. An Italian, Sciere is her birth name, Bates her married name. Late-forties in age, ample breasts and wide across the butt, she is the mother of three: two boys, both married, and an unmarried daughter whose remark to any man after a second drink is approximately, "Your place or mine?" Lately she has been living with her mother, theoretically, under some kind of probationary house arrest.

If common sense were money, Marie would be a lineal descendent of John D. Rockefeller. A week after Hack moved in, before Luoma started his pestering, Hack set about convincing the home's residents in the wing where he was quartered, that Medicare had scheduled a physical therapy seminar for impotent seniors beginning promptly at seven p.m. in the dispensary on the following Wednesday. The swing-shift nurse on duty that night telephoned Security, and even with their help it was nearly ten o'clock before the st fired-up male resident was returned – was wheeled to his room. No way, of course, was Marie fooled, nd she gave Hack holy hell for that business. But Hack new she was secretly amused. Given that he was half rish, a "Murtaugh," BS-ing is one of Hack's inherent alents.

Hack pushes away from his bed and steps into his walker, a scratched-up, hand-me-down, Tinker Toy contraption of aluminum tubes that was left behind by a resident who passed on, a person who, as Kitty inevitably says of the dead, is no longer among the quick.

"Among the quick?" Hack always comes back, "Here?" Then he would kiddingly remind her that such disgraceful double meanings are unbecoming to a woman of her high social standing. Kitty and Hack are "good and great friends," and Kitty knows that Hack ascribing a lofty social status to her is off-the-chart absurd.

Hack's walker does not fold, not all the way, not to near flatness like it should, and instead of wheels on the rear legs, which it was designed for, the original owner had duct-taped immobilizing sponge pads in their place. When Hack moved into Cooper Greens, he brought along a forty-nine-dollar telescoping cane, an expensive gift to himself, but Marie, feeling overly maternal – after Hack had goosed Billie with it – confiscated the cane and stuck Hack with the beat old walker.

Hack makes it from his bed to the doorway of his room and stops to be sure no one is about to pass by: some wheelchair-bound residents hug the walls in transit, and he does not always hear one nearing. In fact, now and then two wheelchair-bound residents will collide at a corner where aisles intersect. Hack saw one head-to-head crash where the question of proprietary right-of-way would have been resolved physically had either man – men, naturally, were the antagonists – been able to spring from his wheelchair.

Hack moves slower than when he had his cane, and Luoma scowls impatiently from a few yards down the hall. Residents generally leave their room doors open, and, besides, the halls at Cooper Greens never give a person the feeling of narrow, suffocating passageways that crisscross cheap motels. Moreover, the walls and the ceilings are recoated with a light-colored paint every two years. Smoothly finished wood hand railings line both walls of every hall accessible to residents. Many of the residents who do not use walkers shuffle along with one steadying hand on a railing.

The halls at Cooper Greens are named after trees: Hickory Street, Plum Street, Maple Lane, etc. Hack's room opens onto Beechwood Drive – Hack's and his roommate's. All residents are quartered two persons to a room. Occasionally a disgruntled resident will mockingly refer to his or her hall as an *alley* hoping to unhinge a nurse or an aide.

Hack catches up to Luoma. "Feeling any better?" he asks.

Shrugging indifferently, Luoma continues looking straight ahead.

Luoma's hands are compacted into lumpy balls by arthritis. Virtually useless, the backs are scored as badly as old army brogans and are more rutted than a wood, hand-me-down kitchen cutting-board.

Both of Hack's knee joints are artificial – metal and plastic – and today the left one is paining him as it often does. If Hack had the utility of Luoma's legs, he would still be living at home. As far as that goes, if Luoma had Hack's hands, he would still be an oil-field roughneck working in Oklahoma. Luoma is sixty-five, five years younger than Hack.

Twice last year – hardly a month between – Hack back-ended cars making right-hand turns onto cross streets. For no reason that he could see, the drivers suddenly hit the brakes two-thirds of the way into their turns.

Luoma, when Hack described what had happened, offered: "Women drivers, right?"

"How'd you know," Hack replied. Then to himself, likely, "No, both were old men, but what the hell."

"I'm psychic," Luoma answers. "And tell me, how it was you thought you could manage a walker fitted with wheels? And no horn? Or turn signals?"

Ordinarily, Luoma is about as witty as a funeral director seeing to a viewing, but Hack gave him credit for that one.

When Hack was still living at his home, he did light work on his pick-up truck, kept the yard up, tended a small vegetable garden, and so forth. Monthly, he scythed a small field of scraggly, comingled, greensward areas and small clutches of wheat stalks growing on the other side of the road they lived on.

Helen loved fresh vegetables. She would whip up, and then consume, almost non-stop, sandwiches of sliced radishes smothered with mayonnaise or sandwiches thick with cucumber chips lathered with Italian salad dressing.

They did not have kids, though God knows they tried (yeah, yeah, being Catholic and all), so it was not a big garden. Helen gave away most of what they grew. Hack had to keep after her to eat meat. And fish too, for that matter.

Shortly after his second accident, Hack packed it in and moved into Cooper Greens – respecting the fact that he had intractable legs, that Helen had passed-on, and that they had no kids. Permanently moving into a nursing home seemed to Hack little different from motoring down a highway that suddenly becomes a bumpy dirt road. Or, perhaps, like driving down a road that dead-ends at a cemetery with a tombstone inscribed with the name Thomas "Hack" Murtaugh. Expecting to fire up this place, at least somewhat, Hack planned for that trip to be a long way off.

Hack caught up with Luoma. "You hear what your President Sleaze did yesterday?" Luoma says to Hack over his shoulder.

Luoma loathes President Clinton and regularly spits out the word Democrat. He knows Hack voted for Clinton, and he wants to bait him. When Hack does not rise to the come-on, he changes the subject: "Raymond eat breakfast?"

Hack answers that Raymond Snedeker, with whom Hack ate all meals, missed breakfast because he had the runs and was up all night. Luoma and Hack are both certain that Raymond's stomach is full of cancer. Hack never misses breakfast; Luoma, on the other hand, never eats breakfast.

"Ah, hell, Luoma mumbles glancing sidewise. "He's chronic."

"Yesterday I came across his sister here in the lobby," Hack says. "She did not know what ailed him. What a loser."

Luoma nods. "I've met her."

The two men pass Harley Agnew's room. Twice this week the air wafting from Agnew's doorway smelled like it was gusting from a dog kennel that had not been hosed down for a week. Harley turns in early – maybe too early. Evidently Cooper Greens' cooling system is efficient because odors do not linger.

Luoma coughs hard several times and loudly clears his throat. "Did the Pirates win last night?"

Luoma is a casual fan of the Pittsburgh Pirates major league baseball team, and Hack doubts if he frets over the outcome of *any* Pirates' games. The Pirates have been out of the pennant race for two months, their dismal showing authenticated a week ago by a four-game drubbing at the hands of the New York Mets.

Hack answer anyway. "Uh-huh, they won, six to two. They're only nineteen games out now. The Indians won."

"Like I give a shit," Luoma mumbles. Hack does not hear him pronounce the word "shit," but he knows Luoma well enough that he is sure Luoma did not use a polite synonym.

"C'mon, Murtaugh," he says, trying unsuccessfully to elevate his voice, "shake a leg."

"Gracious, Luoma," Hack says with mock sincerity. "You're a real Bob Hope this morning."

Luoma slightly grins, wants Hack to think he was being funny intentionally, but Hack knows better.

Miki ____, a tall, leggy nurse with naturally curly red hair, her snug-fitting uniform stretched tightly across her butt, hurries past. She works in another wing, and the two men seldom see her.

"Good morning, gentlemen," she says, glancing back

and favoring both men with her practiced professional smile. The aides and nurses always greet residents with a friendly hello, and usually by their name.

Hack and Luoma greet Miki ____ with lots of pep and then stare silently at her firm athletic calves and trim, not-quite-silhouetted thighs, until she rounds the corner at Chestnut Street.

"Hey, hey, hey, it's coming up!" Luoma says after Miki disappears from sight.

Actually, Hack knows Luoma has not had an erection since he moved here – has not boasted of one anyway, which is certain proof of that insufficiency.

"So is Christmas," Hack says, "only sooner. Slow down."

Luoma sighs and stops. His frown returns. "Damn, Murtaugh, we'll never get there. Where was Wilmer?"

Wilmer Higgins is Hack's roommate. He prefers to be called, Carl – his middle name – and he flatly will not answer to "Wilmer." Hack once asked him if he was named after Wilmer, Texas, a small city Hack had passed through riding alone to San Antonio in a bus while he was in the Air Force. Hack, Higgins said, didn't answer him.

Carl is lame on his left side, his face is lopsided, and it is obvious from the way he talks that his tongue does not flex adequately in pronouncing long words. Rehabilitating from a stroke, he is a good twenty years younger than most of the men living at Rolling Greens – probably in his mid fifties. He will not help himself, however, and Hack likens him to a self-indulgent pain-in-the-ass. Once, when Carl had only lived at Cooper Greens for one day, Hack had helped him make his way to the bathroom. By the time they arrived, Hack had wanted to launch Carl headfirst into the commode.

After Carl's first week of living at Cooper Greens, Hack was sympathetic but he no longer gave a damn. After forty-six years of marriage to a self-sufficient, uncomplaining woman, Hack had decided irrefutably that living with a whiner like Higgins was the pits. The staff will move a resident at least once to a different room – after several days of a roommate's wheedling – but Cooper Greens is fully booked: all sixty-six resident rooms are occupied, and there's no other place to put him.

Most of Cooper Greens' residents refer to the person with whom they share quarters as their "roomie." Evidently the diminution serves to trivialize a situation that Cooper Greens' citizenry would rather not own up to – not to mention glossing over the pain-in-the-neck nuisance of living 24/7 in the same room with a wholly obverse person. Yes, each roommate is provided his or her own TV, but roommates don't always like the same shows, and besides, in accessing a specific channel the TV slowly and noisily clunks through all preceding channels.

Hack stops to rest at Chestnut Street. Luoma loudly breaths another of his gratuitous sighs, backs against the handrail running the length of Beechwood, and crosses his arms. They are near a nurse's station, an all-white, eight-foot square, four-foot high enclosure. The front of the enclosure, topped by tough blue plastic, is dropped a foot or so to counter height.

Violet Swortwood, sitting on a desk chair inside the enclosure, aims a sullen stare at Luoma. Likely in her early thirties, Violet is a portly brunette. One of the home's few young aides who has not dyed her dun-colored hair yellow – canary as the women living here call that tint – she has a round face, tiny narrow eyes, and a neck that is proportional to the height and girth of a small round tuna-fish can. Hack tried unsuccessfully the week he moved into Cooper Greens to introduce civility to her.

"Well, well," she says in an annoyingly loud, graceless voice. "You boys on your way to Elm Street?"

"In your ear, Bushel Butt," Luoma snaps.

The telephone rings. Violet answers it and reaches for something, a pen perhaps. Luoma and Hack continue slogging along, and their few seconds of annoyance ebbs away.

Their plodding eventually carries Hack and Luoma to Cooper Greens' Alzheimer ward, to Elm Street, as it is delicately referred to by every coherent soul living or working at Cooper Greens. Hack has often wondered if he'll spend his final days in Elm Street – hoping that he will not, at least not until after he has rid Cooper Greens of its ever pervasive hang-dog disposition.

[2]

The corridors of Cooper Greens are laid out rectilinearly. Chestnut Street, the hall that Hack's and Wilmer's street opens onto, runs east and west, T-ing into the middle of Elm Street. Elm Street is the home's westernmost corridor. Its north leg provides access to specialty rooms, including an adjunct kitchenette, a custodian's make-do utensil closet, and a small lounge where visitors may privately grieve or relieve themselves. The south wing leads to the Alzheimer's Ward.

Hack and Luoma turn south onto Elm Street from Chestnut Street. Their path, after a few steps, is blocked by a double, metal-clad door with windows in the top half that are reinforced by a wire mesh. A numbered keypad on the wall operates the door latch that precludes entrance to persons ignorant of the four-digit code, 3 8 2 5, which corresponds to the letters D U C K. (And also to a similarly spelled four-letter profanity, as some aides like to furtively point out to certain visitors.)

Looking inside, a sense of isolation seeps into Hack's mind and his face seems to dim.

Beyond the door lies a large day-room comfortably furnished with posh, upholstered chairs and heavy oak tables, but, noticeably, no lamps – that might be easily knocked over. The posh aspect makes for a soft landing should a person purged of ordinary balance and cognition stumble and fall. At any rate, the Ward's day-room furnishings are the pinnacle of residential luxury at Cooper Greens. The peripheral, individual resident rooms, facsimiles of the ones where rooted residents are quartered, constitute the day-room's outer boundary. A lustrous white nurse's station, its approach unhindered from all directions, is situated in the center of the main room.

When a nurse or an aide mentions the words Elm Street, she is not referring to a street, per se, she is alluding to the ward for the home's severely demented residents, the ones nominally suffering from Alzheimer's disease. Once Hack asked, and Marie told him that a person's head must be opened and the brain studied to tell for certain if the sufferer had AD. "AD" is the expression she and the other staffers always refer to Alzheimer's disease. And in the next breath they assure their listener that every person living in Elm Street is so afflicted.

Most of the residents of Elm Street live in the past – are bodily current but spiritually live in the past. Hack is not sure that's a bad thing: once, walking across a street, he was hit by a car. Prostate in a hospital bed, he drifted in and out of consciousness for eleven days; fortunately he did not remember *anything* about the accident. Anyway, retrospective living is merely the main symptom of severe dementia, not the only one – at any rate that is Hack's judgment after a dozen visits to Elm Street.

The few residents of Elm Street who are too weak to aimlessly wander around, lie passively in bed where raised side rails prevent them from falling out. Some residents are loosely bound to their beds with lengths of cloth straps. They moan constantly, asynchronously, in a discordant pitch. Or they repeat the same sentence fragment over and over. They neither suffer physical pain – at least not that Hack could tell – nor struggle constantly to free themselves. Given the opportunity to choose a physical state when the shades are down and light dimmed, being somatically Alzheimer-oppressed would be Hack's last choice. But, then, his knees notwithstanding, he has never endured days of ongoing pain. So he isn't sure.

Hack visited Elm Street for the first time the day after the powers-that-be settled Toby Roofner into one of Elm Street's peripheral rooms. Before that day, Toby and Hack shared a room; once Toby was moved out Higgins was moved in.

Toby and Hack graduated from rival small-town high schools the same year, 1946. They played together on an all-star baseball team. Even totally healthy,

Higgins would assuredly suffer a hamstring pull just tapping a croquet ball toward a wicket.

Toby no longer remembers Hack, to put it mildly, nor did he immediately catch sight of Hack on Hack's first visit to Elm Street. Toby was sitting in a circle of Elm Streeters tossing a beach ball back and forth – when they were not fussing over who should retrieve the ball that had bounced a few yards away. Half the time one or more players is sitting stiffly, arms crossed, glaring at the other players who apparently have egregiously broken a sacred rule of indoor beach-ball etiquette. In high school, Toby was an all-star volleyball player. When he was young, volleyball was slowly catching on as a competitive high-school sport in northwestern Pennsylvania.

Toby is – *was* a good pinochle player, one of those persons who never lost count of how many trump cards, how many aces, or how many powerful off-suit cards had been played – and by whom. Now, however, the son-of-a-buck cannot add up the fingers on one of his hands. They had never played cards together, not until a spell after the two of them had settled into Cooper Greens. Few of the men raised in these agrarian acres of Pennsylvania ever played cards, except, maybe, to occasionally gamble in a blackjack game played at a volunteer fire department smoker.

Toby and Hack, up to when Toby became oblivious to all things, were close. Kitty, when she and Hack were alone together, referred to Toby and Hack as

Old Frick and Old Frack. Of course Hack asked, and of course Kitty knew that Frick and Frack were Swiss comedy ice skaters, who became Follies' stars.

Toby has new friends these days, only he doesn't know it. One is a woman who reminds Hack of comic-strip Popeye's girlfriend, Olive. Her arms are hardly bigger around than the cardboard tubes that center a roll of wax paper. Hack does not know who he reminds her of, but he knows positively that it is not one of her old flames.

Sharp-tongued, "Olive," Hack calls her, always harasses Hack if he nears Toby: "You, Mister!" she snaps, and a second later she is rushing at Hack like a mother goose chasing away a nosy cat. In the nick of time, she pulls up and lets loose again:

"Yes, you, Mister! You leave here at once! Right now, Mister!

"Get! Or I'll report you, Mister.

"Did you hear me? I ordered you to leave, Mister.

"I mean it! This *instant*, Mister!"

She catches sight of a fellow Elm Street resident plodding past a closed door and commands him to open it. "He's holding that door open for you, Mister," she snaps, her attention back on Hack. Indifferent to her command, the man pokes Zombie-like past the door. Eventually Toby's female protector burns out, takes up a position some ten feet from where Hack fruitlessly tried to reminisce with Toby, and glares daggers all the while Hack is sitting by Toby's side. A frail person, she is a retired school teacher, and obviously not the wife of a deceased farmer, as are most of the female residents living at Cooper Greens.

Among the dozen or so women quartered at Elm Street, only Olive seems to genuinely loathe Hack. Mostly, he is totally ignored. A few of the incarcerated, smile timidly when he walks past, and he always returns their smiles. Now and then a woman hauls at his arm and plaintively asks to be taken home. Or, as sad, she eventually makes Hack understand that he is to telephone her husband – who likely as not, has passed away. Hack seems to never know what to say. By and large, the men in the ward are oblivious to Hack's presence.

"Aw hell," Luoma says, staring through the mesh-screened window of the ward's left-hand door, his misshapen hands shielding his eyes. "Prunella is in the barrel." Asperity tinges his voice.

Hack inches forward to where he can see through the window in the paired right-hand door. For some reason Jan Prukowski, the Elm Street third-shift nurse, is working first shift – likely covering for someone. A big woman, she is never without a taut, serious look on her face. She sees Luoma from her place inside the nurse's station, and slowly shakes her head. Luoma shoots her his gnarly-hand version of a bird, but she does not move a muscle: it's as if he is the locked-on target of gun-sight radar. Suddenly distracted by something that Hack and Luoma can't see, she rushes off.

Hack turns away from the door. "Rained out," he says, sighing loudly so Luoma will think he is disappointed that the curtain has abruptly dropped on the sad but freakish side-show that Luoma had beseeched Hack to join him and watch. Only, Hack is not at all let-down. In fact, he wishes he had never shown Elm Street to Luoma. Hoping for a chance to catch sight of wrinkled, sagging, occasionally nude old women – lost souls who do not even know when they're naked – does not turn Hack on.

Luoma, however, is not so easily discouraged. Hack has barely spun his walker around when he frantically motions Hack back. Prukowski, heading toward the two men at a good clip, is maneuvering swiftly around Elm Street's mobile residents. Then Hack understands, that is, he sees where a female patient has set out from an unknown area to offer someone – whom only she can see – a pair of furry pink slippers supported on outstretched hands. Her hair looks like a Hollywood fright-wig. Except for a loop of orange and white beads dangling from her neck, and a white sock on one foot, she is alabaster naked. Prukowski with ardor but firmness guides her into the nearest resident room.

Angrily scolded by Prukowski, Hack and Luoma are back on Chestnut Street aimlessly working their way toward Hack's room.

"Cloud-cuckoo-land," Luoma says as they plod along. "They should live on Wal-*NUT* Street. Or, on Hickory-*NUT* street. If you catch my meaning."

"Or, on Coconut Street," Hack mumbles.

Something unpleasant fires Luoma's mind. "What the hell," he blurts out, "that's the way I want to go, demented and always out to lunch, de-ob'd. Put it in my will. Think you'll be around to see that band of angels coming after me?"

Hack snorts. "Band of *angels*? Maybe a throng of devils. Formed up like a detail of Army recruits . . . sent to police the area."

Luoma sighs. "You're probably right, Murtaugh. How's it feel to be right once in your life?"

They reach Hack's room, and Hack hesitantly invites Luoma in.

Luoma shrugs. "Why not."

Higgins is in the bathroom, so Luoma sits on his bed, which has been straightened up by Billie. Anyway, it is likely Billie did the smoothing because Higgins would not put out the effort. Billie, since being goosed by Hack, only fixes up the room when Hack is elsewhere.

"We playing this afternoon?" Hack says to Luoma, meaning, will they be playing pinochle?

Luoma thinks Hack's question over, taking a good 10 seconds to decide. "If Raymond plays," he says finally.

[3]

For the better part of a year, Hack, Joe Luoma, Toby and Ray Snedeker, played pinochle afternoons in Cooper Greens' dining room, often as not every day of the week. Their match was usually the only pinochle game being played. The card games of hearts and rummy strongly contend with watching the afternoon soaps, but usually about half the dining room's thirty tables come into play. Four women residents – always the same four – play dominoes together every afternoon. They constantly bicker.

But then, Toby Roofner began forgetting the location of his room, of the room he shared with Hack, among his other cursed memory defaults, and the powers-that-be moved him into Elm Street. The bosses, Marie told me, said they were afraid he would hurt himself. Now, Kitty is my partner.

Kitty has lived at Cooper Greens longer than any other resident. She will not say for how many years, but Marie told Hack that it has been more than ten, because Kitty was living here when she hired in. Usually residents live at Cooper Greens for one to a few years – and then die, to put it bluntly.

Kitty is near Hack's age – possibly a few years

older. She does not look it, however. Funny how the addictive guzzling of booze seems to do that to some people – gum-up their liver and kidneys, and God knows what else, but preserve the youth of their skin. Anyway, she keeps her age a secret.

Hack and Kitty are intimate. They coupled the second night Hack lived here. Nothing carnal intimidates Kitty. She voluntarily – and unhesitatingly – performed oral sex on Hack their first night together. It was Hack's first sex since Helen's passing, and he remembered thinking at the time that, considering his six-months of sexual inactivity, Helen would understand. Maybe, he later decided, after reminding himself that persistent sexual urge thoroughly disrespects a man's sense of goodness.

Kitty would not let Hack return the favor. She wasn't simply indifferent to reversing the act, she said it would be a waste of time. That was her attitude throughout some fifteen months of overtly bedding with Hack. Anyway, Hack let it go at that, quit worrying about returning the joy of orgasm. It did, however, fertilize the seed of doubt in his mind about whether women, after menopause, had the physical ability to orgasm. During his years of marriage he seldom pondered that possibility, though he was positive that on occasion Helen faked an orgasm.

All Cooper Greens' resident rooms have two-foot-by-three-foot cork tack boards attached to the wall either to the left or to the right of the room's two small dressers. The tack boards in the women's rooms are always, side-to-side and top-to-bottom, covered with pictures, with snapshots. Children, grandchildren, and great-grandchildren crowd out all other subjects. The prints of adults, usually far fewer in number, are always black and white and murky or frayed, or both. The cork boards of male residents' rooms are often mostly bare – and sometimes would be totally unadorned if it were not for a Xeroxed copy of the month's schedule of events and a thirty-day menu. The only other room trappings, at least the only ones that catch a person's attention, are chia pets – either growing unadorned in terra cotta planters or dressing up cartoon characters laying on crinkled aluminum throw-away pans.

Most of the photos on Kitty's cork board focus on herself, play up a short, busty woman with large dark eyes that are intentionally narrowed to support a come-hither smile and further buttressed by neatly plucked eyebrows and straight dark hair trimmed level across her forehead – banged, as that style is called. Maybe her face would not have launched a thousand ships, but it was still cute enough to step the mast of many a sailor.

In one picture, she is showing plenty of leg – for those days, anyway. In another, she is leaning back, supported by her elbows, against the grill of a shiny 1938 Dodge sedan, her breasts pushing out against a light-colored turtleneck pull over. Hack has said the car looks exactly like one owned by his folks during War II and for two years afterwards. Some rum-nosed goober wearing a fedora with a turned-up brim is pressed snug against the outside of the driver's door. The window is rolled down, and his right hand, as if to fortify his position, is possessively gripping the opening where the glass slides in and out of the door. Once Hack asked Kitty why he was not wearing a sling to support his honker, and it ticked her off.

Kitty is wider in the hips now and she is no longer

out-and-out busty, but otherwise she's hardly any different looking from the pictures – not when she's strapped up in her undergarments, anyway. Her resolutely tinted black hair is still cropped straight across her forehead.

Kitty is an alcoholic, a disease brought on by a recessive gene passed on by an American Indian forebear. At any rate, that's how she explains her addiction. It used to be that after a few drinks from a pint of hard-stuff Kitty would promote uninvited the idea of her bunking the rest of the day with the underwriter of the booze. She told me that herself. Doubtlessly, her alcoholism was instrumental in landing her at Cooper Greens. Nobody visits to look after her.

Kitty is pretentious over characterizing herself as a "Recovering Alcoholic," acts as if abstention entitles her to a good-citizenship medal. Maybe it does. Hack came near to quitting cigarettes, but it is doubtful that smoking addicts a person as strongly as alcohol. He still smokes a half-pack a day, always, come rain, snow, or high water – stepping outside when he does. It is not something he is proud of, but damned if he can quit.

Married three times, the last to a short-order cook, Kitty goes by the last name of her second husband, that is, by the name Proctor, by Catherine Proctor. Her third husband, she tells people, left her for a predatory young waitress, a "wanton trollop" who worked at the same diner as her husband. It's impossible to perpetuate BS in here where virtually every resident, aide, and nurse is native to the area, and Hack knows better. Her last husband split because she was serving up her fanny to any man who would buy her drinks, for the same reason her other – how many? –near-husbands bailed.

Kitty flies off the handle over incidentals, and Cooper Greens has adjusted to her as much as she has adjusted to Cooper Greens. She does not march to the beat of a different drummer, only to the cadence that beats inside her own head, which is always the same ponderous scat. Hack takes her at her word about almost everything, even silently swallows her insistence that she is part Indian.

Hack has exactly one picture pinned on his tack board, an enlargement of a slightly out-of-focus snapshot of Helen and him taken on their wedding day. It is the closest thing to a formally posed picture he and Helen ever owned. They're standing on the front-porch steps of her parent's home, splashily dressed. Helen is wearing heels and a two-color, two-piece dress, with padded shoulders. Hack is wearing black-and-white wingtips – his pants stop a good inch short of his shoes – and a light-colored suit with five-inch lapels. They are still wearing boutonnieres that were pinned on them by friends before the ceremony.

Helen's folks, the parents of ten kids, were poor, hard-working farmers. In age, Helen was near the middle of the brood – the sixth born, actually. Like her mother, she was a sturdy, good-looking peasant woman with light brown hair, a modest nose, blue eyes, and high Slavic cheek bones. Her sisters are not as pretty. They all married well, nevertheless. Only one of her brothers amounts to as much as a bent dipstick.

Helen was killed when she drove her car through an intersection in front of a car driven by a preacher – of all people – who had gunned the engine to beat a traffic light. After her death, Hack lived alone for almost five years, doing a lot of mourning the first year. The reverend who hit her was so tore up Hack felt sorry for the guy, not right away, but eventually.

[4]

Card games at Cooper Greens' begin in the dining room after lunch, after the tables have been cleared and the carpet vacuumed. A few games are already under way when Kitty begins dealing cards. A minute later Luoma and Raymond Snedeker arrive together. Luoma has brought along the slotted, one-inch-by-two-inch stick he uses to hold his hand of cards in a long, edge-to-edge row. Hack is close on their heels.

Raymond is short, maybe five seven, and-, just the opposite of Luoma. Somewhere, Hack once said to Kitty, hangs a picture of Raymond, age thirty or thereabouts, still with plenty of hair, wearing knickers, golf shoes (with a flap over the laces), a dress shirt with a bow tie, and a three- or four-color sleeveless sweater with diamond patterns. Raymond and two other similarly dolled-up golfers are standing together on steps leading into a golf course club house kissing the heads of their golf putters. Raymond never married. He doesn't talk about it.

Raymond's eyes crimp every now and then, grim confirmation that the pain of his stomach cancer comes in waves. He tries not to let us see. Raymond, like Hack, is totally bald, not counting the bands of white fuzz running in front and over of his ears and around the back of his head.

"Squaw!" Luoma bellows at Kitty as he and Raymond settle into their chairs. "Today. Are you a Seneca or an Onondaga?"

It riles Luoma no-end that Kitty insists she's part Indian; in his mind, being part Indian is a spartan, no-nonsense legacy he wishes to stake out exclusively for himself. His voice now sounds almost normal.

"Squaw, yourself, Wop," Kitty says half-heartedly, her mind on sorting her hand of cards.   Luoma's parents were Norwegian, and the only throw-back nickname that hacks him off is "Swede." Kitty does not know this, however, and if anything Luoma is amused by her inapt retort.

Kitty glances toward Hack. They make eye contact in a way that Hack can tell Kitty wants him to make a meld bid.

"You could have a speck of Indian blood," Luoma says. He compresses his lips as if mulling that possibility over in his mind. "All that gunky war paint you smear on your kisser."

Like most female residents of Cooper Greens, or Rolling Pills, as Luoma calls our home away from home, Kitty layers on the face paint. The excessive cosmetic foundation of our women residents, according to Kitty, is the consequence of the weakened eyesight of old age, of elders inability to discern subtle shading in colors.

"Bid, Luoma." Kitty snaps.

They study their cards while Luoma reviews his hand. "Fifty," he says finally; staring intently at Raymond, his gaze pleading for a meld bid.

Hack gives Kitty a meld bid, shrugging slightly as he does so she'll know that he can name trump if she can't. This is another thing that angers Luoma: Raymond will not signal the quality of his hand, as Kitty and Hack always do. Hack could read Toby's pinochle face as if he had messages printed on his forehead in high-lighted ink.

Raymond passes the bid.

"You don't have any meld at all?" Luoma pleads.

Raymond does nothing in haste, and while he's again painstakingly counting his meld, Hack says, "No talking."

"Damn," Luoma says. "That takes balls. *You* on *my* ass for talking."

Hack once told Kitty that he couldn't remember an afternoon when they did not argue over cheating. The game has hardly begun, however, and Luoma's complaint is too limpid to provoke serious bickering.

Raymond quits counting and shakes his head. Kitty wins the bid and she names clubs as the suit of trump.

Part way into the play, failing to notice that Luoma had played an ace on his own ace lead, Raymond leads the wrong card, not the suit that everyone at the table knew Luoma had a lock on, and Kitty and Hack easily win the hand.

"How bad?" Luoma asks Kitty, to whom we have permanently fobbed-off the job of keeping score.

"Seventy-five, zip," Kitty answers. "I feel your pain, Chief."

"We didn't save our meld," Raymond says quietly, almost to himself.

It is unclear if he's asking a question or making an observation.

"Damn, Raymond!" Luoma says sharply, "we didn't have any meld to save!"

A bond exists between Luoma and Raymond, a friendship that no Hollywood shrink could begin to explain. Luoma, an ex oil-field tool pusher, worked for Pennzoil, Exxon, and ARCO. His last gig (Luoma's noun), with ARCO, was near Enid, Oklahoma. Raymond taught public grade school and sold tomb stones part time; he never moved from the immediate area.

Luoma is so darned mechanically inclined that he can speedily adjust the leg rests on a wheelchair, a usually simple tune-up that even confuses Hack anymore. Raymond, on his best day, could not screw a nut on a bolt without carefully following written instructions. Oddly, at least to my way of thinking, Luoma has the better way with words: maybe it's because he uninhibitedly – and vulgarly, often as not – speaks his mind. It will hurt Luoma when Raymond cashes in at the multi-aisle check-out counter in the sky, an event that Hack and the others take for granted is not very far off. Again, in this place, death is a way of life.

Luoma clumsily shuffles, slowly deals the cards, and then resumes ripping on Kitty. "You're probably a Cornplanter Indian. If you have any Indian blood at all. Which all of us in Cooper Greens totally doubt."

"My great-grandfather was a Seneca," Kitty says indifferently. It is her stock answer to questions of her ancestry.

"Sure," Luoma replies, nodding. "And my great-grandfather was an Apache, a Mescalero Apache warrior chief. Probably scalped a hundred palefaces. And raped as many Seneca squaws."

Kitty, her attention having drifted to the table where Lon Fuller and Edith McGuire are arguing over their cribbage game, does not answer. It would be unusual if Fuller and McGuire were not arguing, so Hack and the others listen for only a second.

Hack is inclined to believe, as Raymond once told him, that his friend, Joe Luoma, truly is part Indian. According to Raymond, Luoma owns some Mohawk trinkets and other allegedly holy Indian charms. Of course those possessions hardly prove that Luoma is part Indian, but Luoma does not BS, Hack is positive of that aspect of his personality. We're on the fringe of Iroquois country here, where all four card players have roots, and the Mohawks were an Iroquoian tribe. So there is a fair chance Raymond is right.

"Damn it!" Luoma exclaims loudly. "Count. I'm short a card."

They count their cards, and Kitty has one too many. She slides a card face down toward Luoma, but he wants to select one from her hand.

"Tough grits, Geronimo," Kitty tells him, "that was the last card you dealt me."

Luoma starts to protest, but Kitty loudly interrupts him. "Too damn bad, Little Beaver! It's not my fault you can't count!" Luoma obviously has never heard of the cartoon character mentioned by Kitty, and he scowls. As mad at himself for mis-dealing as he is at Kitty, Luoma angrily paws the card that she does not want, to where he can lift it from the table and work it into his slotted stick. He lets on it fits perfectly in his hand of cards, but even Raymond knows that he's acting.

Kitty, when Hack stops evaluating his hand and

looks up, is again slanting her head toward the table where Lon Fuller and Edith McGuire are playing cribbage. Their argument has heated up. Luoma and Raymond also watch. Few of the other players have noticed. Of course, most of them do not hear well.

Hack does not like Lon Fuller. Husky, bull-necked, and coarse of features, he constantly boasts of his own ever minimal accomplishments: "Replaced my windshield wipers today. My God what a difference! I can see the road again!" Luoma cannot stand him either. If Fuller ever heard of Dale Carnegie he confused him with the other Carnegie, the steel-making guy from Pittsburgh. Edith McGuire is a still-trim, sixty-plus, attractive woman – if anything she is a tad skinny. She and Fuller are always together. It gripes Hack that some women go for goons like Fuller. Physicality matters, Hack tells himself. Kitty claims that with some women it's an Adonis thing. Of course she knows Adonis was only a kid, albeit handsome, and when she made that observation she probably hoped editor Hack would fault her for the age mismatch so she could quarrel about it with Hack. Kitty is an aggressive woman, much more so than Helen ever was, and she tests men every chance she gets.

"Kick him where it hurts, Edith!" Luoma yells from the side of his mouth, pretending his attention is on the cards in his stick. His throat is obviously at afternoon healthfulness.

Fuller, who had risen to his feet – presumably too angry to continue playing – turns and glares at Luoma. Luoma casually looks around, pretends he's unaware of what's happening. Fuller, however, is not fooled. Slamming his cards on the table, he heads our way, poling himself every other step with his cane. Fuller is too stupid to have been an alpha male, but he *is* a husky man.

Luoma jumps to his feet, closes his hands into the best make-do fists he can devise, and heads toward Fuller. "C'mon moron," he yells, tucking his chin into his left shoulder and setting his fists in a boxer's defensive stance.

Hack hears a scattering of shrieks and is aware of a male player gingerly approach the two combatants.

Fuller grips his cane with both hands, briefly steadies himself, and swings it at Luoma's head. It lands, on Luoma's upper arm, apparently misdirected by the momentum of the swing. Luoma, who seems not to have felt the blow at all, seizes the cane, and the two men, glaring furiously at each other, begin to struggle over its possession. Though Luoma appears to be the stronger man, Fuller has the better hands and he soon jerks the cane to himself.

Fuller swings the cane again. This time he hits nothing but air, and his unchecked momentum lands him on the floor. He turns the cane loose and starts to rise but then sinks slowly to one knee and begins gasping for air.

Luoma kicks the cane away and orders Fuller to get up.

Struck dumb by what's happening, Hack is suddenly aware that Raymond is nose-to-nose in front of Luoma. "They'll throw you out!" Raymond cries, his manner at once both imploring and threatening. He pushes Luoma back.

Raymond, in his own quiet way, is a determined person. Maybe he could have held Luoma off, but not likely. It doesn't matter, however, because Luoma only feebly resists before knocking Raymond's hands away and marching out of the room.

Fuller refuses Raymond's offer of help, and Raymond, giving Hack a what-more-can-I-do shrug, returns to our table.

Shortly, Buster Mook arrives and helps Fuller into a nearby vacant chair. A tall, slack man in his early forties, Mook is Cooper Greens' superintendent of maintenance – and informally – the head of security. His first name is Sylvester, but he goes by Buster (that's an improvement?). He offers to walk Fuller to his room, but Fuller shakes his head, his jaw no longer the tightly clamped bench-vise of minutes earlier.

Edith hands her boyfriend his cane. Fuller gathers himself and they leave together. His limp is decidedly worse than it was the last time that Hack had noticed. He watches him immoderately drag a foot and decide he's largely faking it.

Buster strides determinedly toward the table where the three of us are sitting. He pushes Luoma's chair back into place. Standing and gripping the top of its back, he looks to Kitty for an explanation.

"They got into an argument, is about all," Hack offers.

"Oh? Buster exclaims skeptically, focusing on Hack. "That's how Mister Fuller ended up on the floor?"

"He stumbled. On his own. Really." Hack latter admitted that he hoped Buster, whom everyone likes, did not think he was being a wise guy.

"Who're '*They*'?" Buster asks Raymond. "Who was Mr. Fuller arguing with?"

The question seems to confuse Raymond, and Buster

turns back to Kitty, who is squaring our playing cards for boxing.

Kitty flashes Hack a conniving look and then in a soothing voice says to Buster, "Go back to work, Dear."

While Buster waits for a better answer from Kitty, Hack repeats one of the L. A. Lakers' game announcers frequent characterizations of a minor game illegality. "No blood, no foul."

"It was nothing," Kitty throws in. "Two boys squabbling, calling each other bad names."

Hack presumes she mentioned the name-calling in case Buster heard Luoma's loud swearing.

"Okay," Buster says, drawing out the letter O. "I'll talk to Mister Fuller."

"Let us know," Kitty says, looking away as if she couldn't care less.

Whether Buster actually questioned Fuller, Hack never heard nor did he much care: Hack would testify, if it came to a disciplinary hearing, that Fuller charged at Luoma and that Luoma was defending himself. The thought cooled down Hack.

This Hack did know, however, that Lon Fuller and Edith McGuire, for a good month after the fight, did not play cards in the dining room – if they played cards anywhere. The whole first week afterward, Kitty, when she arrived to play, would not take a chair, but would instead look carefully around the room and then say, faking a bemused thought, "I wonder where Ken and Barbie are today."

"It is *here*, Cooper Greens," Hack back in his room is thinking to himself, "that I am going to perk up the behavior of the residents? The likes of Luoma and Fuller? Right?

Quit masturbating, Thomas Murtaugh," Hack scolds himself.

Still, if there is anything Hack has learned in his seventy plus years of living on this planet, it's that . . . a man has to have a goal, has to keep his eyes on the prize, as the song has it. Or he vegetates.

[5]

"It's too bad Fuller missed his head," Kitty says to Hack as they are leaving the dining room. Most residents have resumed playing cards; some are still prattling about the scrub fight between Luoma and Lon Fuller. "It couldn't have hurt his looks," Kitty adds unsmilingly, "maybe would have improved his disposition."

"And bust Fuller's cane!" Raymond interrupts giggling, "if he had connected with Joe's head?"

"A-men," Hack says.

Kitty's room is at the end of Beechwood Drive, the hall on which Hack's room opens. Her room is opposite a heavy outside door with a full-width horizontal bar that works the door latch. Kitty, the room's only occupant, had vexed former roommates to the point where they demanded to be moved to another room, and she may have hurried the death of one. Hack's room, that is, his and Higgins, is two doors from the nurse's station – maybe sixty yards from Kitty's. Since Raymond lives in another wing of the building, directly across the hall from Joe, he silently veers away a few steps from the dining room door. No one mentions the possibility of the four of us playing cards together the next day.

Kitty writes a column for the *Cooper Thymes,* Cooper Greens' monthly newsletter, and she knows virtually all of the home's residents, aides, nurses, maintenance men, and cooks – not to mention a variable number of repeat visitors. And between Hack's hobbled gait and Kitty's chats with all comers, it is a half hour before she and Hack reach Hack's room.

The word "Thymes," a word near to the pronunciation of "Times," struck Hack as a perfect name for Cooper Greens' news letter. With a compliment in mind, he asked Kitty if the name was her choice. And he knew from her long wordy answer that it was not, so he saved his praise.

Carl, when they reach the room where he and Hack live, is lying on his bed in what Kitty calls his "fetal curl." His back is to the door, and our TV is tuned to a soap. He watches those afternoon saucers of eye-candy religiously. He is not stupid, so Hack cannot help but wonder if he just eyeballs the attractive female characters.

Hack refers to the TV in his room as *our* TV. It is not "our" TV, it is Hack's TV. Only, Carl, his chintzy fink roommate, won't pay his share of the cable fee, which gobbles up half of Hack's State-administered monthly allowance. Hack resists the urge to march up to the TV and turn it off. Luoma, when Hack moans about Carl's unconcern about the TV's rental cost, tells Hack to either get off the pot, shit, or quit his damn whining.

Hack is frustrated by Carl, thinks he is more able than he lets on. Hack had an uncle who suffered a stroke, and like Carl he would not lift a finger to help himself. A couple years later his sister, Hack's aunt, of course, suffered a more severe stroke and she would get sulky as a wet chicken if you even offered to help her.

Strokes run in Hack's family, as he is reminded daily by Carl's mopey, shuffling presence. His father had a stroke when he was sixty-four. He recovered totally, except for lightly dragging one leg, and he lived another nine years. He died suddenly of heart failure while playing golf. The circumstances attending someone's death is a popular topic at Cooper Greens, and those who knew of Hack's father's quick and pleasantly surrounded death were quietly envious.

Kitty nods at a pocket book lying on Hack's dresser. "What are you reading?"

Visitors bring Cooper Greens grocery bags of used pocket books. The book on Hack's dresser looks and smells as if it had been stored in a dank cellar. Carl seems not to have heard Kitty's voice. Likely, he is pretending indifference.

"*I, the Jury,*" Hack answers Kitty. She knows better, of course.

Hack truly read that Mickey Spillane potboiler in 1951 – he thought that was the year anyway. A fellow airman recommended it, said he couldn't put it down. Hack also read the beginning of Spillane's *My Gun is Quick*, but it was hardly different from *I, the Jury,* and he passed it on after reading a couple chapters.

The next novel Hack read was Herman Wouk's, *The Caine Mutiny*. He came across it in 1953 in a shelter serving as a library that was put up by Army engineers at Kimpo Air Force base in Korea. Wouk's book was brand new. If it wasn't for service duty, Hack would have read it straight through, it was that good. Hack was a machinist by trade, but he enjoyed reading action fiction.

Hack involuntarily recalled reading *Silas Marner* in high school. He even proudly remembered the author's name, George Elliot. Elliot, he knew, was a woman. Anymore it takes Hack several seconds just to recall his internal Cooper Greens' address. Sometimes he just quits trying to recall a word.

After Hack's hitch in the Service, he resumed learning the tool-and-die-making trade at Talon, Inc., in Meadville, Pennsylvania. Back then, in the early fifties, Talon made zippers, gadzillions, Army quality, civilian quality, metal, plastic, short, long, all colors. Anyway, as one of the early companies to mass produce zippers – slide fasteners as they were first called – Talon employees had to design and build, for Talon's production lines, special tools and machinery;

consequently the company needed a first-rate, well-provisioned machine shop. Today, Talon survives in name only – if that. Hack irrefutably thinks that cheap, far-east labor foundered sales. "Come to think of it," Hack thought to himself, "I am not much better off than Talon. Nor is anyone else living at Cooper Greens. Hell, we are alive in name only, living on our past glory – real or imagined."

Hack never quit reading, however. And he looks up the meaning of words. Not many machinists are so inclined. Do not, he often reminded others, think tool-and-die-makers, or car mechanics, or cabinet makers, for that matter – are short of brain power just because, say, they do not know that Medusa was an ugly, wrinkled old gal with reptilian hair who slayed people that looked at her. Like most of the craftsmen that he knew, they were men indifferently ignorant about anything that was not machine-made or machine-driven, but they are not stupid; written explanations bore them, and they seldom bother reading about a topic that they could easily distillate in their mind to its vital essence. If advertisers, it was Hack's opinion, could ever get that into their rag-filled heads and stop thinking that mere word manipulation was a paramount human faculty, TV and paper commercials would not be so relentlessly vacuous. Moreover, it was Hack's immense conviction, that politicians would stop thinking they could fool constituents at will, that if political administrations did not always fall back on the game of musical chairs, played to music that never stopped, the country would be far better off – would be run smarter and more honestly. Elected officials and some Washington pundits – to Hack's thinking "so called pundits" – claim it takes years to learn the ropes, to make important people-connections and learn how to negotiate solutions to political problems. Compared to what? To learning in one school semester the science of rocketry? Of understanding the interactions of particle physics in two semesters? Of learning how to think through to the solution of solving partial-differential equations? Of two years of of sowing, nourishing, and harvesting the edibles of human consumption.? Utter nonsense.

Hack recalled how a Washington bureaucrat once described TV as a "Vast wasteland." Hell, today, that description, Hack was certain, would be a compliment. TV, he knew, has become a vast, un-drained septic tank that was stirred by TV "executives" and bled by "insider investors" who made millions sending that crap into homes. They tell themselves, Hack was sure, that "garbage is what the public wants," that Americans would tune-in to elephants vigorously making little elephants rather than watch a circus parade. Baloney! Was Hack's nice one-word summary, the synoptic description that he used in mixed company. Vacuous filth he knew very well is cheap to produce and therefore infinitely profitable.

Kitty, of course, knows that Hack is not reading *I the Jury,* that he is trying to be cute. She steps past him and flips over the pocket book lying on top of the dresser.

"I should've got a shot of penicillin," she says, sniffing and fanning her face with her free hand.

The book is John Updike's *Rabbit, Run*. Left at Cooper Greens by a Good Samaritan, the book cost sixty cents, according to the price on the cover. Hack is at page twenty-four and long past conceding that Updike and his dull, endless sentences are his, Hack's, or anybody's cup of tea.

"Any good?" Kitty asks as if she is barely interested in Hack's opinion.

The question, Hack knows, will be her way of slipping into a stuffy lecture, probably another of her self-serving rebukes on symbolism, metaphoric allusions, or some other literary abstractions. Kitty is convinced – and she's mostly right – that Hack is clueless about those subjects. In the same vein, Hack thinks that the profound inferences of book reviewers are more the product of the reviewer's unconstrained imagination and exceptional word-skills than of an author's cleverness. Hack also believes, just as massively, that most song reviewers are no less fraudulently fanciful.

Kitty is smarter than Hack. She's also smarter than Joe and Raymond but not Toby. At least she was no smarter than Toby before AD decomposed his mind.

Hack had watched as Kitty worked a big Sunday newspaper crossword puzzle almost as fast as she could print the letters. One time, after he had boasted on her, someone reminded Hack that the Pittsburgh Post-Gazette is not exactly the New York Times; he inferred that the Times' puzzle must be harder. Kitty likes to tell people she cannot remember the last time she forgot something.

"In a word, boring," Hack answers Kitty, giving her his assessment of *Rabbit, Run*. "At least it's not a dumb self-serving autobiography like you're always reading. Who in the hell is Ida Tarbell anyway?"

Hack has become even more of a reader himself. In Cooper Greens only the brainless and the soporifically infirm do not read. Kitty and Hack often bicker over their choice of reading matter. Biographies, Kitty argues, are both great reading and educational. Hack tells her he'd rather waste the time watching a candle burn than spend five minutes reading about some long-dead president's long-dead wife. "Updike," Hack finishes, "finds wallpaper fascinating."

"No," Kitty says, "he's over your head." It's her stock reply whenever Hack slanders an author she likes.

"Oh hell, here it comes," Hack says. He points at Updike's book. "Hand me that thing a minute."

Kitty offers Hack *Rabbit Run*, and he thumbs through a few pages. "Listen to this," Hack says, stopping and reading aloud:

"With loving deftness, deftness as complimentary to the articulation of his own body as to the objects he touches, he inserts the corners of the hanger into the armholes of the coat and with his long reach hangs it on the printed pipe with his other clothes."

"My God," Hack says, "he couldn't simply write that the guy hung up his damn coat?"

"Oh hell, Thomas, *anybody* could write it that simply, even . . . ."

"Even me?"

"Updike's a gifted writer. A poet. A . . . ." Kitty does not finish her thought, leaning back in a way to suggest that elaborating for Hank's benefit would be a waste of time.

"He's a phony," Hack says. "All words and no plot; a ten-gallon hat and a three-foot lasso. If it wasn't for adjectives, he'd—"

"Bull!" Kitty snaps. "You just don't hear the rhythm. He's our best living writer. Among the top four or five, anyway."

"I was a top-five machinist," Hack replies, his restorative pride explicit.

Kitty looks past Carl toward the bedroom window and shakes her head. "Murtaugh," she says, "thy name should be Mel Larkey." She reflexively glances at Carl, who seems not to have heard her.

"Really, Kitty?" Hack asks. " How in the *hell* do you rank authors? Or any kind of artists? Or even rank scientists? That's self-serving crap. The only people who even try to gin up a hierarchy of smart people are either newspaper columnists or magazine writers – occasionally a journalist inflating a column."

Hack thought he'd gone too far since Kitty thinks all writers are inherently brainy. She only shrugs, however, and he is relieved.

Kitty takes a step toward the door, and Hack moves his walker out of her way. "You feeling okay?" he pleads hopefully. "Up to a game of double-solitaire?"

Kitty knows that Hack is neither much interested in her rarely deficient health nor at all interested in playing a game of cards.

"Today's Friday," Kity says, glancing at Carl, who is still lying curled up on his side and has yet to make a sound.

"So?" Hack says.

"So. You're a Catholic, aren't you?"

Hack sees her point, understands that as a Catholic he is supposed to avoid meat on Friday.

"Not a candle-lighting Catholic," Hack answers grinning. "Besides, we don't have–"

Kitty dryly interrupts. "You're as bad as Luoma."

Reading too much into her answer, Hack swallows a grin.

"Don't be an ass, Hack," Kitty says. "You know where I'm coming from – not from there."

Hack is not instantly relieved, and he nods mechanically.

"Give me a half hour," Kitty says, after again glancing at Carl. "Goodbye, Carl," she adds, raising her voice.

Carl doesn't answer, and Kitty, giving Hack a quick half-wave leaves the room.

Kitty, when Hack reaches her room, is wearing her blue terry-cloth bathrobe, white socks, and red-sequined, pink slippers. The cuffs of her bathrobe are becoming threadbare; Hack has been saving to buy her a new one for Christmas. She would like that. Hack doubts Kitty will receive any other gifts, except for one of the small individual baskets of fruit given to each resident by the employees of Cooper Greens.

Hack undresses, and they embrace. He unbuttons her bathrobe, and pulls her to himself. If Kitty is part Indian, she is certainly the whitest old Redskin Hack had ever expected to romp with. Women in their forties have more folds and creases, and they aren't as white as Kitty, not as white as the finish of a kitchen refrigerator.

Kitty has placed a Kleenex box and a tube of KY jelly on her bed stand. Her TV is turned off, and her little a.m. radio is playing music at a barely audible volume.

With Kitty's help, Hack attempts penetration. His erection does not fully enlarge, as usual, and he is reminded of the saying about the futility of trying to push a rope. Anymore, his penis seldom fully swells, even when rallied by Kitty. Viagra, Marie tells Hack – he prompted her to opine on that matter at Kitty's suggestion – was never on Medicare's list of approved medications. Marie also ordered Hack to quit pestering her about finding a contraband source, even threatened to lace Hack's food with saltpeter if he did not quit beating that dead horse. As usual, if it was not for Kitty's unselfishness – or whatever it is – Hack likely would be just another dirty old man.

Hack completes his toilet, dresses, and while Kitty is still in her bathroom, relaxes in her recliner, an ageless, leather, overstuffed chair that was left at Cooper Greens by the kin of a resident now buried in a nearby Linville cemetery. Kitty finally emerges neatly dressed in a skirt, blouse, white socks, and pink Keds. Kissing Hack on the forehead, she says she wants to read. They are good friends, not unfledged lovers, and Hack directly leaves.

Marie, as Hack approaches the nurse's station, is measuring out medicines. Her indifferent glance Hank's way – he is heading to his room from Kitty's – is, Hack decides, intentionally meaningless. Since it is Marie, he frankly does not much care what Marie hopes her expression means.

[6]

Likely as not, Hack thinks of Marie Bates as Marie Sciere, which is her family name. Marie and Hack are both from Snow Lake, one of a half-dozen boroughs of several hundred to a thousand mostly blue-collar families situated within a twenty-minute drive of Meadville, Pennsylvania.

Meadville is the seat of Crawford County, which lies immediately south of Erie County, the Pennsylvania County that sticks a tab into Lake Erie. Although not a rust-belt city – in the sense that its industrial base was never oil or raw steel – Meadville's population has slowly declined from some nineteen thousand citizens – its census reaching that zenith during the booming war years of the 1940s – to some fourteen thousand residents. Titusville, famous as the site of the world's first commercially productive oil well, is situated in the south-east corner of Crawford County.

The borough of Snow Lake forms around the south end of Snow Lake itself, which is seven or so miles directly west of Meadville. Its population falls to under one thousand residents in the winter but becomes clogged with people and traffic by mid-June when all cottages around the three-mile-long lake are occupied. Swimming the half-mile width of the lake around midnight in June is a rite-of-passage for the borough's youngsters. The boys swim it naked and always have. It is rumored – among the boys anyway – that a few adventuresome girls have also taken to swimming it naked.

Marie is a plain, matronly woman. Wispy black hair unkindly tints her cheeks, and her nose is a Lebanese hook passed on by her Italian father. Still, Hack does not recall knowing of an evening when she left Ombrey's Bar in Snow Lake unescorted: her allure enhanced by the power of whiskey to concentrate a man's thinking on his crotch. Of course the next day her date would brag that he was gratuitously provided oral sex, which boasting likely was male bull-shit: men are assholes that way.

Until recently, Marie worked the swing shift, reported to Cooper Greens at three p.m. and left at eleven thirty. Most of the residents of Cooper Greens turn in by nine o'clock, so a nurse on swing shift is seldom harried her last couple hours of work.

The first time Hack came across Marie sitting alone at the desk in the nurse's cubical she caught him appraising her breasts and demanded that he explain the reason for such unseemly prurient interest. Hack answered that it was her hefty fanny not her so-so boobs that he could not wrest his stare from, and Hack and Marie have been insult-trading pals ever since.

Marie knows about every happening at Cooper Greens: Bernice Goodson, our activities director, apparently directed one too many evening activities because she's pregnant by Tom Hazlett, Buster Mook's right-hand man; Florence Wilkie was caught and sacked for rifling a resident's purse; Judy Johnson, another aide, was busted when a female resident stumbled on her energetically bathing Ben Spencer's private parts (Cooper Greens' bathing accommodations are unisex), and so on. Marie, Hack is sure, knows about his romancing Kitty – or whatever their participatory evening activity becomes.

Marie's other virtue, over and above her first- and second-hand knowledge of all that goes on at Cooper Greens, is her steel-trap memory for jokes. Before switching to the first shift, she told Hack several raunchy jokes every week. Hack, as he has admitted, can't remember a joke long enough to repeat it the next day. "When I was a kid," Hack would say, "even bad, cheesy jokes stuck in my mind – sometimes into adulthood."

A section of the Cooper Greens' rear parking lot is visible from the window in Hack's room, and over the last three weeks he has three times seen Marie leave work on the arm of a short, chunky, bald-headed man wearing a quilted, sleeveless jacket, the kind that advertises a man's rugged, outdoor-loving nature. Hack thinks he knows the man by his walk but cannot tell for certain from his room's window. Marie no longer hangs out at Ombre's.

Nurses rarely have slack time at work on first shift, and Hack seldom chats with Marie anymore. She not only never chats with Luoma, but she also becomes unsettled if he is nearby – certainly not because he doesn't hit on her, an avoidance she would naturally take to be the ultimate insult since he crudely affronts every nurse and aide working here.

Hack likes jelly beans, and he usually carries a few in his shirt pocket; of course, Luoma often reminds Hack that jelly beans were President Reagan's favorite candy. One evening, a month or so ago, while Marie was sitting at her desk updating paperwork, Luoma, like an idiot school boy, snatched a couple jelly beans from Hack's pocket and dropped one into Marie's cleavage.

Infuriated, Marie called him a brainless ass, threw down her pen, and began openly fishing around for the jelly bean. Luoma, discounting the extent of her anger, said to let him retrieve it. Marie stopped Luoma at the entrance to the nurse's station and threatened to paste him in the chops if he even so much as set a toe inside the station.

Hack figured that damn few men, let alone a woman, had ever told Joe Luoma to his face to clear his rear-end out of anywhere, and he pulled up as if she'd hit him between the eyes with a crowbar. For a moment

Hack thought Luoma might apologize. He knows Luoma better now, and he would be surprised to hear that Luoma had ever apologized to anyone. Luoma said to Marie that she should not flatter herself as he never intended to enter her little goddamn playpen anyway. He flicked his screwed-up right hand in her face and called her a fuckin' birdbrain. She no more flinched than would a face on Mt. Rushmore. Luoma finally backed away, and Marie lit into Hack for being Luoma's his friend. He's the biggest horse's ass in here, she insisted, raising her voice to be sure he heard. Luoma has avoided her ever since.

Marie has finished taking Higgins' vitals and is about to leave Hack's and Higgins' room. Normally, at this hour in the morning Hack is thumping his way around Cooper Greens' large back parking lot, his only exercise anymore. For the second consecutive day, however, it is raining steadily.

Hack looks up from pretending to read *Rabbit, Run*, which he is now a third of the way into and still unable to endure Updike's endlessly rambling sentences. "You know, Nurse Marie," Hack says, scowling as if annoyed, "I can't keep track of who is banging who around here since you turned uppity on me. Apprise me. Which of the aides give it a go on grave yard?"

"None," Marie says. "None that I know of. They don't have the time."

Hack rolls his eyes. Don't take the time, you say? You know how long it has been since I heard a good salty joke?"

Backing toward the door, Marie minimally shakes her head.

"I don't know either," Hack says. "That's how long it's been."

"I really haven't heard any lately," Marie says, shrugging. "Besides . . . I don't want to excite you."

"I can handle it," Hack says.

Pausing for a moment in the doorway to give Hack a little gotcha grin, she says, "Maybe alone in your bathroom. After I leave."

A woman wearing hard leather heels clacks by and greets Marie by name. Marie meekly returns her greeting and stares silently at the woman as she walks down the hall.

Lowering her voice she says, "I'd send Judy Johnson by, only Gina put her out of business."

Hack concludes that the woman who had just walked by was Gina Babcock, Cooper Greens' head of human resources.

"Gina?" Hack asks. Marie nods and leaves.

"That's all you ever think of," Higgins says, only he muffs the t's and the v and it sounds as if he said, "Aas all you ar hink of."

He has been quietly sitting on the edge of his bed, where Marie had left him; Hack had forgotten he was there.

For a moment Hack is confused, and then he says, "And just what in hell do *you* think of all the time?" Hack resists the urge to address him by his given first name, "Wilmer."

"Not that," Higgins says.

Part of Hack's dislike of Higgins stems from the slight, permanent, upward curl of Higgins upper lip, although Hack is sure the tiny sneer existed before his stroke. Anyway, Hack cannot help himself. It's the shanty Irishman in me, he tells himself.

"Not that *what*?" Hack asks sharply.

Instead of answering, Higgins struggles to swing his legs up and onto his bed. Hack makes his way to Higgins' his side and helps him. Higgins groans, breathes a whiney sound, and then curls up on his side, his usual position for watching TV. His eyes, Hack saw, were moist.

Feeling like a jerk, Hack says, "I'm going for coffee. You?"

Higgins shakes his head.

Immobile residents get meals delivered to their rooms, and Hack has read maybe another ten pages of Updike's endlessly tedious prose, as he judges it, when he gets a whiff of the aroma of hot food. Not often – but too often, all the same – it is a smell mixed with the stink of shit-dirtied bedding, and on those days Hack skips lunch. It is 11:05 by his dresser-top clock, one of those jobbies with huge, high-lighted, neon digital numbers that Helen bought Hack years ago. Though

Hack is determined to finish *Rabbit, Run* – to prove to Kitty that he, too, can enjoy the splendor (her word) of Updike's writing – he sorely welcomes the chance to break for lunch.

While Hack is in their bathroom, a lunch tray is delivered to Higgins, and when Hack leaves the bathroom Higgins is sitting on the side of his bed gnawing on a chicken wing. Chicken, in every form, is a food staple at Cooper Greens. Higgins' affliction has not lessened his appetite, Hack has noticed.

The cable company's group-rate TV fee is sixteen dollars a month, and Hack spends most of what remains of his "swag," as Kitty calls the monthly State honorarium, on vending-machine snacks. And on Scope mouthwash. There is enough bad breath at Cooper Greens, it is Hack's sense, that the act of striking a match in some resident rooms could ignite an explosion.

Hack showers and washes himself, including the near hairless top of his head, with the Ivory soap provided by the home, and he brushes his teeth – his own teeth – with Ipana toothpaste, another of the free residency perquisites. Hack is sure the gratis toothpaste is made explicitly available to encourage residents to use it often. He has little need for postage stamps, stationery, cosmetics, or the other items indigent women residents blow most of their monthly thirty-dollar allowance on.

Besides his clothes, a TV set, and pocket change, all Hack owns anymore is some forty dollars, cash, which he has been squirreling away a buck or so at a time for Kitty's Christmas present. He hides the wad in the toe of one of his oxfords – which have hard-leather heels that clatter loudly when he walks on a hard surface. He hates those noisy, damn shoes, and is delighted that he will never have to wear them again.

Hack sometimes wonders how much anonymous money the Cooper Greens aides find stuffed under handkerchiefs in coat pockets, in shoes, and in bottom dresser drawers after a resident dies. A story that circled at a month back has it that one aide came across a thousand dollars inside a rolled up stocking and used it to buy a used car. Hack heard it from an old bitty living in another wing of the home. When he pressed her for details, their discussion warmed, and she has snubbed Hack ever since. "Hell," Hack muses, "maybe it is a true story, and maybe I should have kept my mouth shut. I should have more patience with the morons who believe everything they hear."

Raymond, when Hack arrives at the dining room, is sitting at the table waiting to be served. He has unrolled his silverware and spread his napkin over his lap. That has become Hack's habit too, which he presumes is proper dining-room manners.

"No Luoma, yet?" Hack asks.

"He stopped to water his horse," Raymond answers, his wit, as usual, on the cutting-edge.

The three men eat lunch together every day. They humor Luoma, who never eats breakfast, by dining at eleven with the luncheon early birds. Toby, before they walked him to Elm Street, always joined them. Actually, Toby lived here before any of his fellow diners. So, more accurately, "they met *him* for lunch." Kitty dines with two women at another table.

The entree today is chicken a la king, and it's not bad. Generally, the food at Cooper Greens is reasonably tasty, usually not cooked until all the flavor is wafted away in gaseous steam. The table linen is always freshly laundered and the silverware is always clean – which is more, Hack knew, than he could say about the silverware of some restaurants hereabout. Today, a visiting pianist is working her way through songs of the musical *Oklahoma*. She stops after every song and waits for the diner's applause. No one, it seems to Hack, is listening, and the clapping is unenthusiastic and spotty.

Luoma walks into the dining room and falls heavily into the chair across from Raymond. "What's this shit," he asks, stirring his food.

No matter what is served, Luoma sneeringly puts it down. In this respect, he's little different from many other residents – meaning there's a load of daily, petty complaining that goes on at Cooper Greens. Hack is reminded of his Air Force hitch: young men, used to home-cooking, always whined about mess-hall food.

"You're unzipped," Hack tells Luoma softly.

"Damn!" Luoma replies loudly. Pushing back from the table he showily pretends to zip up his fly. "Advertising," he says, glancing about to see if anybody sees him wrench up his zipper. "Same as a TV spot."

Hack snorts. "You should stick to radio broadcasts."

Luoma has not yet seen Lon Fuller, who is sitting with Edith McGuire and two other women four tables away. Hack has not seen Fuller since the day he and Luoma putatively squared off. When Hack came in, Raymond, for Hack's benefit, chucked his head in Fuller's direction.

While Hack is considering whether to point out Fuller to Luoma, Raymond says quietly, "Your buddy's here today, Joe."

Luoma frowns confusedly. "Do what now?" he asks of Hack as if Raymond's utterance did not make sense.

The question, "Do what now?" Hack has learned, is indigenous southern-speak for Huh? What? What do you mean? And so on.

Hack cuts his eyes toward the table where Fuller is eating. Luoma turns that way and glares. Fuller does not notice.

"Screw him," Luoma says loudly after finally turning back to their food.

The three men resume eating in silence. Hack does not like white cake, or variations thereof, which is served often, so Luoma eats his piece. Raymond eats his small square of cake but little else.

Raymond suddenly stiffens: Lon Fuller is quietly approaching the table. Luoma sees him and starts to rise, but Fuller squints and gives his head a don't-be-concerned shake.

"I was wrong," Fuller says walking past Luoma. He neither breaks stride nor glances back.

Luoma stares after him. "You're goddamn right you were," he says a few decibels below a shout. "I still ought to kick your ass," he adds. His remark, Nack thinks, is meant to impress the two of them more than threaten Fuller.

Raymond says to Luoma, "You ought to shut your big trap's what you ought to do."

Several times Hack has heard Raymond sharply warn Luoma about his verbal nastiness, and Hack is again surprised when Joe does not grab Raymond by the throat and throttle him, as he likely would another man.

When Fuller reaches the dining room entrance, Luoma turns back toward our table. "I ought a kick *your* ass," he says to Raymond indifferently.

The men finish their coffee and rise together. "We playing this afternoon?" Hack says.

They have not played pinochle since the aborted fight between Luoma and Fuller.

"I don't think so," Raymond answers weakly. "I'm going to take a nap."

Luoma and Hack nod sympathetically, their concern for Raymond's ailment too obvious, it seems to Hack, and the three men head back to their rooms.

[7]

Sometimes, for no sensible reason, Hack's prostate gland flares up, becomes a boil the size of an overripe, rust-spotted beefsteak tomato – or so he imagines. It swelled over the weekend. Unfortunately for Hack, a digital massage of that gland, a kneading of nearly unbearable pain, is the only treatment that settles it down.

Once, while he was visiting Luoma, Hack mentioned his problem and Luoma said it was the consequence of his not getting his oil changed regularly. Hack, from Luoma's remark, gathered that Luoma did not know he was rendezvousing regularly with Kitty – which then reminded Hack that Luoma was not on speaking terms with Marie, the one person abreast of everything that goes on at Cooper Greens.

Luoma, before Hack left his room, offered Hack a full bottle of Tylenol pills that he uprooted stirring through a mangled heap of clothing in his bottom dresser drawer. Tylenol, Luoma said, did not work for him. When Hack said it did not work for him either, Luoma chucked the bottle into his wastebasket.

Dr. Bonifanti, her medical practice newly listed in the telephone book Yellow Pages under the heading

Physicians and Surgeons, DO, will visit Hack today. She has visited Cooper Greens professionally before. Always in a hurry, younger even than Dr. Voth, whom she replaced, in Hack's eyes she is still a kid. Hack, however, concedes to himself that she is a looker, body and face.

Dr. Voth treated Hack three times before he quit calling on patients at Cooper Greens. The first time he medicated Hack for a cold, the second time for a throbbing prostate gland, and the third time for what Hack knew positively was genital herpes. Hack was also certain he had picked up the infection from Kitty, since a week before he had slept with her for the first time.

Hack's herpes, it turned out, was a yeast infection, a docile rash that his wife suffered every now and then. He had thought that only women came down with yeast infections. No, Dr. Voth explained, yeast infections are occasionally the bane of uncircumcised men. Marie stored a salve in her desk that practically cured Hack overnight. (It took Hack about as long to describe his problem to Marie.)

Dr. Voth called on Cooper Greens for one year – probably a contract stipulation – and Hack doubts that Dr. Bonifanti will stay longer. Medicare sets under-market limits on what doctors may charge for treatments, and then pays a percent of that amount. Not long after Hank's Medicare kicked in, the Murtaugh's long-time family doctor retired, and four doctors turned Hack down as a Medicare patient before he found one who would see him – a rookie doctor, naturally.

Hack is not an especially modest person, nor is he easily embarrassed, not at seventy. Yet, he was uneasy over the idea of facing (facing?) young Dr. Bonifanti about his tender prostate gland. So, he tracked down Marie for advice.

Marie is amused: "Don't be silly. Doctor Bonifanti is a Doctor, a professional. She likely has seen more male plumbing than you have."

"Yeah, well . . . she could get rich doing lap dances. Suppose she does something provocative and I become aroused?"

Of course, Hack is kidding, as Marie well knows.

"Have a can of varnish handy," Marie says, crimping a smile. "Take a snap shot of yourself. Call the *Beacon*."

"And afterwards," Hack says, squinting as if confused, "where do we meet, you and me?"

"In your dreams," Marie answers. Her focus returns to the form that she was working on when Hack interrupted her.

"I'm serious, *Nurse* Marie," Hack pleads, "how . . . should I act?"

Marie does not look up. "So am I, *Mister* Murtaugh. Doctor Bonifanti is a doctor, and you might as well be the back leg of a pig." As an afterthought, she adds, "Provided it's withered."

"Up your bucket," Hack says. "Seriously, how do you handle that sort of thing? When you visit a doctor?" Hack, as do most men and women of his generation, thinks the word doctor is a masculine noun.

"It depends on the doctor," Marie answers. Her grin is slight, just enough to let Hack know his question is open to interpretation.

"Depends on the doctor. How, exactly?"

"Oh, if he's handsome, I tell him I'm suffering a bad

rash in a private place that needs his healing touch."

"Screw you," Hack says, turning to leave.

"Come back anytime, Thomas," Marie replies sweetly.

Hack is but two yards away when Marie says authoritatively, "And don't forget, Dr. Bonifanti wants you fasting."

Hack almost trips spinning in his walker to face her. "Fasting! For a damn prostate exam!"

"Yes, for a prostate examination," Marie answers, her attention again back on her work. "It turns out, that if–"

"For how long?"

"Three days," Marie answers, concentrating hard on her work.

Higgins protests when Hack unfurls the privacy curtain that divides their room.

"What the hell do you care," Hack says to Higgins. "You're always watching TV anyway."

"I get claustrophobia in here, as it is," Higgins replies in a whiney voice. Still, his articulation has improved to where he no longer hisses every other word.

"Suck it up for an hour," Hack tells him. "It won't kill you."

Higgins mumbles something, and a moment later a different program excretes more waste from the television.

At nine o'clock Marie sticks her head in the doorway and says that Dr. Bonifanti is running a little behind. Hack reminds her that Dr. Bonifanti is, after all, a small woman. Marie answers that Dr. Bonifanti is usually punctual, and Hack does not bother to make it clear that he is joking, that he is alluding to Dr. Bonifanti's nifty – as he judges that part of her anatomy – little butt.

Bonifanti, accompanied by Marie, arrives at ten forty-five. After rapping lightly on the door, which Hack had meticulously positioned to be one-third open, she marches into the room and stops near Hack's bed. "Good morning," she says, barely glancing at Hack before taking a three-ring binder handed to her by Marie. "Your prostate's bothering you?"

Dr. Bonifanti is absorbed in thumbing through Hack's chart, so he makes up his mind not to answer until she looks up.

"How'd Doctor Voth treat you?" she asks, stopping at a page of his chart.

Dr. Bonifanti's bedside manner is so damn business-like that it reminds Hack of his being tersely questioned by a police officer that has stopped him for speeding.

"He prescribed an antibiotic," Hack answers finally.

"Uh-huh," Dr. Bonifanti says, for the first time looking Hack in the face. "Naprosyn. An anti-inflammatory. Did it help?"

"I guess. Along with a massage." Hack rolls his eyes to expend the word "massage."

Dr. Bonifanti ignores his try for sympathy. "Okay, Mister Murtaugh," she says, "I'll write you a prescription." She scribbles herself a note and then says, "Let's do it."

Hack hems and haws, and Dr. Bonifanti snaps, "Turn around and lay your chest on the bed. Show me your bottom."

Hack orders Marie to leave, to wait out in the hall.

"I can't," Marie says, grinning. "House policy."

Hack says, "That's . . . yogurt."

To Dr. Bonifanti, who has begun working her hand into a latex glove, Hack says, "Nurse Marie hates men. It's a genetic thing." Dr. Bonifanti does not respond.

"At least close the damn door," Hack says to Marie.

Marie gives the door a little shove, and it swings a few inches. Hack shakes his head disgustedly, lower his pants and shorts together, and bends over on a side of the bed until his chest is lying flat on the top.

Dr. Bonifanti, Hack soon finds out, is a more thorough prostate examiner than either Dr. Voth or his last family doctor, and in five seconds Hack is all but begging for mercy.

"I think that'll do it," Hack says, straining not to whimper. "Holy . . . I've about had it," he adds, his eyes beginning to water.

Dr. Bonifanti at last withdraws her finger; it will be a half-hour before the pain subsides, however. Hack stands, pulls up his pants and shorts, turns his back to the women and zips his fly.

"One side's firmer than I'd like," Dr. Bonifanti says, removing the medical glove from her hand.

Hack shrugs and nods somberly.

"What was your last PSA?" Dr. Bonifanti asks, inquiring of the results of Hack's last prostate-specific antigen test.

"It was good. Under three."

Dr. Bonifanti finds the test in his chart. "Uh-huh, two point six one."

She continues to study Hack's chart. "Still," she says, allowing her face a discontented look, "to be on the safe side, let's get a biopsy."

Biopsy is a less popular word in a nursing home than most other places. Hack accedes by nodding once suddenly, and mouthing the word "shit" through clenched teeth at Marie.

Dr. Bonifanti measures her next words. "Likely, nothing is seriously wrong, Mister Murtaugh. But, why chance it?"

"Makes sense," Hack says, hoping he sounds more earnestly committed to that proposition than he feels.

"I'll set it up," Dr. Bonifanti says, "at Meadville City Hospital." She tells Marie that her office will call with specifics.

Marie nods. "I'll see that he gets there."

Higgins, as soon as the women leave, asks Hack to re-bundle their privacy curtain. Hack tells Higgins he does not feel like it, but when he hears sounds of movement coming from Higgins' side of the room, he steps rapidly to the curtain's edge and jerks it back until it's bunched at the head-ends of the beds.

Still feeling the pain of Dr. Bonifanti's digital examination, Hack skips lunch. At eleven forty-five, Luoma and Raymond walk into the room. Luoma knows of Hack's prostate problem. "Guess what," he says to Raymond, "Ol' Thomas here got his oil checked this morning."

"Oil, water, and transmission fluid," Hack mumbles.

"And?" Raymond says between coughs, which he tries to stifle but cannot.

"And," Hack says, "Dr. Bonifanti wants a biopsy."

Raymond nods once slightly. "Been there, done that."

For no good reason, Hack is surprised. He says to Raymond, "You've . . . been there?"

Raymond slowly nods his head again. Hack waits, hoping Raymond will elaborate but he does not.

"Bonifanti said mine was too firm. Whatever in hell that means."

"What good is it doing you anyway," Luoma asks with a knowing smirk.

Hack shakes his head. "Speak for yourself, Little Beaver."

Luoma seems suddenly aware of the double-edged implication of his remark. Scowling, he ineptly tries to explain it away.

"Let's not jump to conclusions," Raymond says interrupting Luoma. "Biopsies are usually negative. Mine was."

"Is that so?" Hack says.

Hack knows Raymond's intentions are good, and he would like to believe him, but he doesn't. To Hack, the glass is always half empty. Hack likes to kid people and he likes to horse around, but he is not a naturally optimistic person.

Hack again reminds himself of that steadfast personal quality, and he again questions his hope of blustering away Cooper Greens' steadfast fog of gloom. He imagines himself serenely jogging in a marathon only to start clip-clopping awkwardly near the finish line.

[8]

It is sunny outside, and from Hack's bed inside his Cooper Greens' room it looks to be a warm morning. The temperature, however, is in the low twenties, which is a normal reading for mid-January in northwestern Pennsylvania.

Hack arrives at the hospital "physicked as a woodpecker," as his wife would have put it. He never did understand why that saying meant a person's bowels were cleared of any food residue, but he never remembered to ask her for an explanation.

Buddy, one of Cooper Greens' part-time drivers, helps Hack out of the van and offers to see him into the hospital to register for his surgery. Hack is using his cane – returned to him for the occasion by Marie – and Hack tells Buddy that he can make it on his own. Buddy says he will wait in the lobby.

Hack is admitted as an out-patient and wheeled to an examination room by a chatterbox of a young candy-striper. A long, plastic-topped table sits in the middle of the room. Enameled white metal cabinets with glass doors line most of one wall, and electronic instruments supported on wheeled stands sit around here and there. The odor of disinfectant is strong.

A sandy-haired orderly wearing two-piece, loose-fitting scrubs brings Hack a neatly folded hospital gown – opening full length in the back, of course – and tells him to undress and slip into it. The orderly leaves but shortly returns and politely orders Hack to climb onto the examination table.

"Turn on your right side, Mister Murtaugh," he says in a soft but commanding voice.

Hack rolls onto his side and the orderly slips a rolled-up towel under his head. "Are you cold?" he asks. The question answers itself, as both men know, and Hack says, "Hell yes, I'm cold. I'm freezing my . . . tail off."

"I'll fetch a blanket," the orderly says smiling. Clearly, the mere act of pleasing Hack will make his day.

The orderly returns with a heavy, loose-knit blanket and tucks it over and around Hack as best he can. Embroidered on the pocket of his pullover is the name Walter. He is not wearing a wedding band, and Hack can't help but wonder if Bare-Ring-Finger is an authentic male. The last time Hack was hospitalized, maybe three dozen years ago, all the nurses were females.

"Doctor Egli will be here shortly," Walter says, making a box of prophylactic gloves handy. "Anything I can get you?"

"Who is Doctor Egli?" Hack asks, though he does not particularly care to know.

"A surgical urologist. He'll do your procedure."

"Is he any good?"

Hack knows it is a wasted question, that no matter what, Walter will tell him that Egli is tops. But Hack is nervous.

"I'd ask for him," Walter replies reassuringly.

Hack feels better, but later decides it was most likely Walter's stock, becalming answer to that kind of question.

Hack answers Walter's casual question about fetching him something: "Yes, a martini."

Other than being nervous, Hack has no idea why the name of that drink popped into his mind. Gin, the main ingredient of a martini, Hack thinks tastes like thinned crank case oil. And vermouth, the subsidiary ingredient, he thinks is only good for weatherizing deck lumber. Worse, Hack knows that martinis are a favorite *woman's* drink. He secretly emptied the first, and last, martini he ever tasted into a toilet bowl.

Walter titters politely at Hack ordering a martini and leaves the room. Ten minutes later a female nurse walks in. Greeting Hack cheerily by his first name, she comments on the weather and then steps behind him. Hack hears a cabinet door click, equipment being moved, and other foreboding noises. The sounds stop, and the nurse informs Hack that Dr. Egli will arrive shortly. At the doorway she experiments with the ceiling light switches until the space surrounding Hack's table is illuminated to what presumably will be to the doctor's liking. A cantilevered TV monitor is swung into place behind Hack, where he can't watch the screen.

Some ten minutes later the female nurse returns and says that Dr. Egli is caught up in surgery support but will arrive soon. She leaves, and Hack rolls onto his back. Scanning the instrumentation that will be at Dr. Egli's disposal, he recognizes only the TV monitor. The rest of the instruments, all kin more or less, are decorated with switches, knobs, meters, and red, green, and amber lights.

Hack is near to dozing off when Dr. Egli greets him by name. Sporting a Van Dyke beard, kinky-haired, and young, he is wearing a loose-fitting two-piece smock and granny eye glasses. The female nurse moves to a place behind Hack.

"How do you feel, Tom?" Dr. Egli asks.

"Okay. All considered."

Dr. Egli tells Hack to roll onto his side. The nurse tells him to press his knees together and fold his legs. "A little more," she orders. "More."

"Christ," Hack says harshly, "I could launch a mortar round."

"Uh-huh," she says.

Hack, from her perfunctory answer figures that she has no idea of what a mortar is.

Dr. Egli, who is busy behind Hack fidgeting with an instrument, moves to where Hack can see him. "I'll want three specimens," he says to Hack. "You'll feel a little pinch each time, but it won't hurt. There are almost no nerve endings where I'll be doing the snipping. Later you may see a tint of blood in your urine, but it'll clear up in a day or two. If it doesn't, be sure to have it reported."

Hack judges from the slant of Dr. Egli's last remark – "have it reported" – that Dr. Egli knows he is living in a nursing home.

"Okay," Hack answers.

Dr. Egli moves out of Hack's field of view. He says a few words to the nurse that Hack cannot make out and then Hack feels a probe enter his anus and move inward. The sensation is weird but painless.

"Right there," Dr. Egli says abruptly. Hack hears a sound that reminds him of a pistol being cocked, and Dr. Egli says, "I'm going to snip off a tiny piece of tissue, Tom. You'll hardly feel a thing."

Hack hears a clunk and a muffled tap. Only, he does not "hardly feel a thing," the "snipping" damn well hurts.

"Actually, I felt that pretty good," Hack says, his manly pride shading his true sentiment about the pain.

The probe slightly moves and stops, and Hack steels himself for another "snip," which occurs and hurts as much as the first one. Hack feels sweat beading on his forehead.

"The last one," Dr. Egli says with a Buddhistic exuberant acceptance of pain. And the wasp stings again.

"Good," Hack says bravely. He feels, diametrically opposite, like a bummed-out tot unaware that he was about to be vaccinated.

"Now that wasn't bad, was it," Dr. Egli says. He helps Hack sit up and braces Hack's back with his palm.

"I guess not," Hack mumbles.

"Remember," Dr. Egli says, giving ground to the nurse, "if bleeding persists, have someone call my office."

Hack nods. "What did you find out?"

"I'll have to see the lab report."

"You can't tell me anything now?"

"Can't chance it, not until after I study the report."

"Whatever," Hack says dispiritedly. Dr. Egli nods and leaves.

"You can dress, Mister Murtaugh," the female nurse says, all bubbly again. "I'll call for a blue-coat."

It is a long fifteen minutes before a volunteer arrives with an empty wheelchair. He swings by the cashier's window on their way back to the lobby. Hack dutifully signs a form, and they continue.

Hack is Buddy's only passenger, and he tells Buddy to take the scenic road back to Cooper Greens.

Buddy laughs good-naturedly and asks Hack if prefers the roar of ocean waves or the spectacular boldness of the mountains

[9]

Buddy eases the van to a stop in front of Cooper Greens' front entrance. Buddy, Hack learns on the return trip, is a very considerate man, the kind of driver whose politeness creates trailing queues of automobiles operated by men teetering on the edge of road-rage. Luoma has said that Buddy drives like a dumb broad.

Hack slows in the lobby to admire the extravagantly festooned Christmas tree. Asymmetrical and locally harvested by a Cooper Greens' maintenance employee, it takes up most of a large, front-facing alcove.

Molly Seidel, Cooper Greens' receptionist, is talking on the telephone. She is plainly too young to have worked here very long. Her hair, a straight, weathered-beige color reaches to her shoulders. She is not wearing a wedding band, and, being of the old school, Hack pretends not to notice that she is very pregnant.

"Any calls for me?" Hack says smiling amicably.

Molly knows Hack is kidding: since last Christmas, he has received exactly one telephone call, a Happy-Birthday wish from his brother who lives in Dallas – in Big-D Dallas. Dan, three years younger than Hack, is his only sibling. He has three children, two boys and a girl. Hack guesses that they're all still alive because, God knows, they never write to him or call on the telephone. Mother died soon after Dan was born – from "complications," is all Hack was told. He doubts if his father ever knew exactly what caused her death. Hack's and Dan's father dated a woman for several years, but he never remarried.

Molly, being a saucy young lady, says, "Um, let me check." She pretends to shuffle through a stack of notes on her desk. "I think . . . if I haven't lost it. Oh, here it is! From . . . wait. Oh yes, one from President Clinton! He said to just sign his note Bill C. I confused it with your other message from Bill G."

"Bill G?" Hack asks.

"Mr. Gates."

"Oh, Gigabyte Bill."

Grinning, Molly says, "Exactly, Mister Murtaugh."

Sometimes Hack gets a message from either talk-show-host Jay Leno or his competitor Dave Letterman. Other times it is a message from Mike Hargrove, the manager of the Cleveland Indians. According to Molly, Hargrove always wants Hack to suggest a starting pitcher for the Indian's next game. Yesterday, Santa Claus wanted to know if "Mr. Murtaugh,"could fix

Rudolph's nose so that it pulsed on and off instead of glowing steadily.

"If you can break a hundred dollar bill," Hack says to Molly, "I will right away return the President's call. He *needs* bucking up."

Last Saturday, or thereabouts, the U.S. House of Representatives voted to impeach President Clinton for lying to a federal grand jury over his oval-office shenanigans with a White House intern. The buildup had been headline news for days.

"He didn't do anything wrong," Molly says, shaking her head, "The darn Republicans are just out to get him."

"Sure looks like it," Hack says.

Hack is a Democrat. He voted for Clinton, but he is troubled that Clinton does not seem to have a speck of moral integrity. Luoma calls Clinton President Sleaze. Hack doubts Luoma ever voted in his life – possibly for George Wallace the year he ran for president between his terms as the governor of Alabama. A middle-aged couple, likely the children of a resident, enter the lobby. Molly greets them graciously, and Hack plods away.

Hack finds Luoma sitting on his bed reading the *Morning Beacon*. Since the bathroom door is closed, Hack knows that Higgins is inside on the pot loosening the wall paint. Regularity, Hank has learned, befriends Higgins and it's his time of day. Once, as Higgins was exiting the can, Hack said, "I hope you flushed the dead canary down the commode!" Higgins didn't get it.

The *Beacon* is Luomas' kind of newspaper. Its publisher, T. Lisitor Morgan – popularly Tin Lizzie Morgan – once wrote in an editorial that welfare is the handmaiden of sloth, that food kitchens only nourish the lazy, and that good will is wasted on the poor. His editorials meandered endlessly and were steeped in euphemisms, but that was basically his message – was what he meant.

"They should print this rag on toilet paper," Luoma says, folding the *Beacon*. "How'd it go?"

"All right," Hack answers, shrugging. "Ever been there, done that?"

Luoma stands, ambles past Hack, and pulls up at the foot of Higgin's bed. "Nope," he says, shaking his head. "My joy gland has never misbehaved."

"Lucky, you," Hack says, as if envious. "The damn doctors . . . why do they always say it won't hurt? They know damn well it hurts."

Striving to emulate a female contralto, Luoma says, "*This may hurt a little.*" Then, in his normal voice he continues: "And in six weeks you'll be up and about and frisky as ever. Damn sawbones always tell you that. It's a motto they learn in school."

"It wasn't Bonifanti," Hack says. "It was some kid named Egli. A urologist, with one of those stupid pointy chin beards. I'm supposed to watch for blood in my urine is all."

"It's always six weeks," Luoma says, reinforcing his point. "They're full of shit. Six months is more like it." He glances at Hack's knees. "You should know."

"Yeah, all of six months," Hack says.

Hack hangs up his jacket and squeaky-clean John Deer gimme cap, which he unwillingly paid ten bucks for because he couldn't persuade the store clerk to respect the fact that he once owned a John Deer riding lawn mower. When he turns back, Luoma is squinting hard at the *Morning Beacon*, which he has spread on the top of Hack's dresser. He wants Hack to discuss his prostate examination, but being Joe Luoma he won't admit it.

After a minute Hack says, "You ever notice" – he pauses as if he is about to say something noteworthy – "how women have longer fingers than men?"

Luoma waits, hoping that Hack will go on.

Knowing, however, that Luoma is too egotistical to ask him to explain the significance of the extra length of women's fingers, Hack lets on that his remark is clearly self-explanatory.

"Is that so," Luoma finally mutters, pretending to obsess over something he's reading.

"Marilyn," Hack says, making up a name, "had exceptionally long fingers. Longer than mine."

Hack lays it on, claims that "Marilyn" held back his nuts while Egli probed his butt.

"Right," Joe says uncertainly. "Not much of a procedure."

"Naw," Hack agrees.

The knob on the bathroom door rattles, haltingly the door opens, and Higgins steps out. Luoma says loudly and with explicit earnestness to Higgins, "Good afternoon, *Wilmer!*"

Higgins answers back timidly, and Luoma giving Hack a gross-out look, sloppily folds the newspaper, and leaves.

As usual, Higgins turned the exhaust fan off when he left the bathroom; he does not fully close the door. Hack noisily thumps his way around his bed, turns the fan back on, and slams the door shut with as much force as he can muster – not that much, as he is hampered from being caged inside his walker. The bathroom is small and seamless, Hack's legs are more balsa than oak, and the soft "whump" that results, does not adequately convey his feeling of chagrin. Higgins does not seem to notice.

The throbbing pain deep in Hack's butt has let up and has become infrequent minutes of mild discomfort, so Hack decides to visit Kitty. Her door is open, but he knocks anyway. Propped against the headboard of her bed, her left foot pulled back and her right leg stretched out flat on the bed, Kitty lays aside the book she is reading and sets her face in a concerned look.

"It hurt like a son of a . . . buck," Hack says, stopping short of her bed.

Kitty motions toward her recliner, but Hack frowns and skews his mouth in a way to suggest that sitting would be painful.

"Kind of what you expected?" Kitty asks. Her initial motherly concern has faded.

"I guess so," Hack answers. "He cut off tissue in three places. Whatever."

"Bonifanti?"

"No. Some . . . boy doctor."

"How do you feel?"

"Okay. Good. Better, now." Kitty nods approvingly, and Hack adds, "So don't be looking for an excuse to cut me off."

"You're already cut off, Dear," Kitty says, her face a smirky gotcha grin.

Hack grins too, before realizing that Kitty is not alluding to him going without sex but is remarking on a personal dimension.

"Think big," Hack mutters.

"About small things?" Kitty says, her grin returning. But she reads the discontent in Hack's face and changes the subject. "Did you finish *Rabbit, Run*?"

"Almost."

In fact, Hack pitched Updike's novel, before cracking the last half, on the day Dr. Bonifanti found his prostate gland less than fully pliable.

Hack admits the truth: "Christ no, I didn't finish it. The man's got an unbending hard-on for adjectives."

Kitty shakes her head disgustedly. Hack's remark, she says, is stupid, unoriginal, and unfunny.

"What," Hack says, "are you reading? America's long-simmering debt to weasels?" He stares hard at the book that she had set aside when he arrived.

Kitty reads fiction that would bore Hack to death. Books – some anyway – that are advertised as making the New York Times' best-seller list. She will not admit to enjoying them, however, and calls them kitty lit, meaning that their text is mild, superficial porn that is written for women – and often written *by* women.

Clearly reluctant to leave Updike's literary talent undefended, after several seconds Kitty answers. "Them," she says finally.

Hack is not sure that he heard correctly: "Let me see."

Kitty shows Hack the book's cover. It's an old volume. The cover is soiled and not a picture of a buxomly woman and a man with an unbuttoned collar – the depictions on the covers of her usual kitty-lit novels.

"Them?" Hack says. "Like in, them on first, they on second . . . those on third?"

Kitty settles further back against the headboard, and Hack says, "What's it about?"

It's another long second before Kitty answers. While Hack waits, it dawns on him that likely he has narrowly escaped being ordered from her room.

"I suppose you've never heard of Joyce Carol Oates," Kitty says, scowling and shaking her head as if Hack's presumed ignorance is beyond belief.

"Joyce who?"

"Joyce Carol Oates is one of America's great writers. Many . . . serious readers believe she's our finest."

Hack is skeptical: "What about Upjohn, or whatever his name."

"Updike," Kitty snaps.

"May I look?" Hack says, extending his hand.

Warning him not to lose her place, Kitty gives Hack the book.

"By God," Hack says, honestly surprised, "'them' is really the title. Oat, or whatever her name, must be a hell of a writer. To get away with naming a story 'them'."

Kitty sighs and looks away hopelessly. "She explains the title in a Forward, *Dear*."

"I'll bet she does. "'Them', I suppose, are all horses' asses of the male persuasion."

"No," Kitty says. "But that would work, too."

Hack sets aside his walker and hobbles to the side of Kitty's recliner. After slowly sinking onto its seat, excessively favoring his duff, he skims a couple of the book's promotional quotes and reads the first page.

"So," Hack shrugs, returning the book. "She can write a little. Does she actually *say* anything?"

Kitty, Hack knows, enjoys fictional prose word by word, sentence by sentence independent of the context, and indubitably so. Hack does not. He needs context, sentences that frame a topic. But not paragraphs plumping the charm of aged wallpaper.

"She talks to me," Kitty says, nodding.

Hack scoffs. "Think she'd know a plot if it bit her in the rear?"

"You can be so stinking boorish, Murtaugh. It's no wonder Mickey Spillane's your favorite author."

That is not true, of course. Hack likes George Orwell, however, whom he knows Kitty champions, and he decides on the spot that Orwell is his favorite author.

He tells Kitty that fact, and she slightly raises her chin. "What's his real name?"

Hack has forgotten. "Samuel Clemens. Samuel Longhorn Clemens."

Kitty ignores him. "Blair. Eric Author Blair. Name two of his books, two you've *actually* read."

"Of course," Hack agrees coolly. "Uh, 'Animal Farm' . . . 'Down and Out in London and Paris' . . ."

"Paris and London," Kitty interrupts sarcastically.

"Whatever. Keep the Aspidistras Flying."

Kitty, focusing on where in the book she was reading *Them,* when Hack came in, she says, "So, you're not totally incorrigible."

"Moreover," Hack says, "I'm lovable."

"Don't push it, Thomas."

Her mind obviously back on Oates' novel, Hack sighs loudly and stands up. He makes like he is trying hard not to show pain.

She glances up. "Go to your room, Dear."

"Bad night, huh?"

Kitty does not answer.

"Bad hair day?"

Still no answer.

Hack stops in front of her tack board of snapshots and points to a picture of her cozying up to a man wearing a dark, pin-striped business suit and a shade-lighter fedora with the brim turned up in front. "Who's the palooka?"

"Come here," Kitty orders, tilting her book away and pushing her glasses up.

When Hack reaches her side, she pulls him to her and firmly kisses his forehead.

"Now, damn it. *Go home, Dear.*"

Kitty takes up Oates' book again, and Hack tells her she gives new meaning to the word, pussy-whipped. Kitty lets on she does not understand, and Hack leaves.

A week later, to the day, Marie visits Hack's room to tell him that Dr. Bonifanti's office called and said his prostate biopsies were negative.

[10]

It is early March, and the wind is gusty. Broiling, the sky seems to bear down everywhere like a heavy gray quilt. To the west, however, along the horizon, the cloudscape is a swath of bold, unbroken azure.

Two-foot-high mounds of brown-tinted snow line the sides of Cooper Greens' main entry road, and six- to eight-foot-high off-putting mounds bulwark both ends of the big rear parking lot.

The front of Cooper Greens looks out on a lawn that stretches left and right a little to either side of the complex, and runs frontward seventy yards before ending at State Road 204. Ten feet beyond SR 204, a wall of high, straight-up maple trees begins abruptly. Every tree is virtually limbless for the first twenty or thirty feet above the ground. Near the front-middle of the heavily wooded stand, a huge dead sycamore tree seems to jump out at passing vehicles. Its white, helter-skelter limbs resemble the animated trees that come from nowhere to grab at people in kids' movies. Kitty says sycamore trees bring good fortune, and she named the one in the stand of trees in front of Cooper Greens Methuselah. Did she remind Hack that Methuselah was the oldest man mentioned in the Bible? Does a jackass bray?

It is snowing lightly, but enough flakes have fallen to thinly dust parked cars and barely overlay Cooper Greens' front yard. A couple inches of glint-less old snow lies underneath the new snow. Hack cannot see Cooper Greens' large American flag flapping in the wind, but he can hear the sharp, irregular clanging of its lanyard whipping noisily against the two-story high, hollow metal flag pole.

Hack makes these observations from Kitty's room, where, for the better part of an hour, since a little before eight a.m., he has been watching for the ambulance that will carry away Raymond Richard's body.

Suddenly Hack hears sounds of another person in the room, and when he looks around, expecting to see Kitty, he finds Joe Luoma instead. Arms crossed as if settled in shielded self-containment, Luoma is standing near the foot of Kitty's bed.

"I wondered where you were," Luoma says softly. He does not move, and Hack assumes he has just arrived. His comment is so calm and uncharacteristic of Luoma that Hack unintentionally stares hard into his face. Luoma's gaze, however, remains fixed on the wintery scene outside.

Anticipating his unspoken question, Hack says, "Not yet." He turns back toward the window. "How long you been standing there?"

It's a little bit before Luoma answers. "Five minutes," he says.

Neither man speaks for several moments. A dozen vehicles – mostly pickup trucks – scoot by on the road in front, and then a Snow Lake Volunteer Fire Department ambulance rolls slowly into view and turns onto Cooper Greens' front driveway. Apparently Dickey's Funeral Home could not free up a hearse: unlike Snow Lake, some nearby boroughs do not have funeral homes, so their volunteer fire departments' emergency vans serve as ambulances.

"A meat wagon," Luoma complains.

Hack is sitting hunched forward on the edge of Kitty's recliner, which, after several hard tries he had moved it to a position facing the window. As the ambulance slowly turns onto the street crossing in front of the Cooper Greens building, Hack says, "That's Boyd Smalley driving. Hell, he's a *good* five years older than I am!"

Hack watches the ambulance's slow progress until it turns to the right and disappears behind the east wing of the building. Suddenly he feels very tired, and he falls back. Luoma, when he turns away from the window, has left the room.

Kitty is sitting with Maude (whose last name I, fortuitously, have forgotten), and Hack is sitting alone in the seat behind Milton Freuhoff, Raymond's recent roommate. Freuhoff will soon have another roommate; probably tomorrow. Enfeebled and virtually deaf, Buddy had to have excessively helped him into the van.

Buddy revs the van's engine. Hack asks him to wait a bit, hoping Luoma will show up. Buddy locates Hack in his rear-view mirror and nods. A minute later he looks up, and Hack shakes his head.

The visitor's register is spread open on a lectern that is standing near the entrance to the gathering room, and Hack and the others take turns signing it. There is one other name, in a shriveled, feminine hand. It is on the top line. It seems to read, Rebecca Snedeker. Raymond's elegy consists of a mute relative, three negligible friends, and a small clay pot of flowers, a Cooper Greens' proxy.

At first Hack does not see Rebecca Snedeker, Raymond's sister, who is standing off to the side of the casket in a two-piece, navy blue suit and black, high-heeled patent leather shoes. Her skirt is deeply wrinkled; her eyes wander up and down Raymond's body.

Raymond's face is slightly puffy, but in death his cheeks bloom as if he were alive. He appears to Hack to be healthier than he had seemed in months. Hack vulgarly says to himself, "maybe I should ask for his embalmer." Then he has a second thought: who besides Kitty would give a thimble of spit about his immortality.

Hack and Kitty had decided beforehand not to attend the burial service. Hack's bladder, while returning from Dickey's Funeral Home, fills to capacity, thanks to Buddy's excessive consideration of every other driver's intentions, and Hack dribbles a sprinkle of urine every time the bus hits a pothole – every time Buddy unavoidably drives a wheel over one of the craters that inexhaustibly pockmark Pennsylvania's secondary roads in the winter.

Kitty mocks Hack, offers to sponsor his membership in what she calls Cooper Greens Toilet-Seat-Down Social Club. In other words, she wants Hack to sit down to pee. He will not, saying that he is old but not yet completely shameless.

[11]

Hack pulls on clean undershorts before changing back into his blue jeans, dons a short-sleeved shirt, and slips into his black, thick-soled, corduroy slippers. At Cooper Greens, clothes, except for skivvies, last longer than the residents and outer-wear apparel often end up on the hangers and shelves of a Salvation Army store.

For a reason that baffles medical doctors, not to mention a cause that utterly puzzles Hack, neither of his knees is aching today. Leaving his walker behind, he heads for Kitty's room.

"Hey, hey!" he spouts at Marie who is studying something lying on the desk inside the nurse's station.

Hack strolls past her – rather soberly, he thinks – when two steps farther his left knee buckles, and he tumbles hard to the floor.

Marie rushes to help him onto his feet, and he learns how very strong she is. It crosses Hack's mind that she actually might have decked Luoma the time he dropped one of his jelly beans down the front of her uniform blouse.

Settled on his feet, Marie circles her arm around Hack's waist and holds him tight against her side.

"I'm okay," Hack says weakly.

Marie gives a that-is-what-you-say bob of her head and squints in a way to mean that she severely disagrees.

"I wouldn't have stumbled if I had my cane," Hack says breathing heavily.

He apparently utter those words less for Marie's benefit than for the ears of the half-dozen residents lounging in wheelchairs by the nurse's station, the usual gathering of chins-on-chests or nodding heads.

"Where's your walker?" Marie demands – not too kindly it seems to Hack considering that he had just tumbled hard on the thinly under-padded floor carpet.

"It's busted," Hack answers, flexing his leg, the one that buckled.

"Let's get to your room," Marie says firmly.

Hack tells her that he can make it on his own, but his words vanish unheeded.

Marie, Hack's walker under one arm, escorts Hack to where he can sit on his bed. She eyes him sullenly for several seconds and then steps away to examine his walker. Roughly tilting it to and fro, she demands to know, "Where, exactly, is it broken?"

"The front legs. Both of 'em."

Marie fiddles with the left leg and then the right leg. "Where?" she demands crossly.

"The wheels came off! Buster stole them for a TV stand. I'll never—"

"Murtaugh, *you* are a pain in the ass."

In deference to Higgins' presence, apparently, Marie mouths the words, "in the ass."

"Return my cane," Hack says sharply, pretending he is angry.

Marie marches from the room, her skirt crackling. "You heard me," she says over her shoulder.

Hack's left knee, the one that gave out, has begun throbbing, as it often does, but usually for no apparent reason. So he decides not to visit Kitty, and he scoots further back on the bed.

Higgins, whom all the time Marie was in the room never took his eyes off the TV, rolls over just far enough during a commercial to ask Hack how he feels. Expecting another of his frequent requests for a favor, Hack tells him that he feels crummy, that he fell flat on his face. "I'm going to take it easy for a while," he finishes.

Higgins nods skeptically, and when the commercial ends he resumes watching TV.

For a while Hack watches the soap opera program that Higgins has on the TV before realizing that he had seen viewings of a deceased where there was more action. He would bitch about Higgins choice of shows, only there's nothing on TV in the afternoon that he believes is worth watching. Hack cannot afford the TV company's extended TV program package, which includes ESPN.

Hack awakes slouched against the headboard of his bed. It is almost five o'clock. When he last looked, it was five minutes to four, and credits for the *Raging Tumor* – or whatever the program's name – were rolling. He flexes his neck, which has stiffened.

Most of Cooper Greens' residents nap during the day, including Hack. This time, however, Hack has stupidly slept for an hour, which means he probably will not fall asleep tonight until two or three a.m. Carl is eating his supper, and Hack assumes that the smell of food woke him up; he did not hear the aide deliver Carl's tray. He is suddenly aware that his knee has stopped aching. He visits the bathroom, relieves himself, runs water over his hands, and, supported by his walker, disorderly ambles to the dining room.

Kitty and Emma Pankhurst are eating alone at their usual table. Kitty's other close friend, Yvon Chafee, has apparently skipped supper; some residents often do because it is always a light repast, a cup of soup and a half sandwich. Kitty looks up and waves Hack to their table. He asks her if she has seen Luoma, and she shakes her head.

Emma Pankhurst is a short, stout, pop-eyed woman – due to a thyroid condition, Kitty says, – with thinning hair that is milk white the first quarter-inch from her scalp but reddish-orange everywhere else. She prefers being addressed as "Panky." Kitty claims that she is very intelligent. Sometimes the air around her smells as if she needs to change her underwear. Soon after Hank met her he advised Kitty that her friend should only be approached from upwind. Kitty was not amused.

Panky did not see Kitty's invitation to Hack. He therefore, in Panky's mind, has intruded on the privacy of their supper meal, and for a few seconds Hack's arrival causes her displeasure.

"Am I interrupting something?" Hack says pointedly to Kitty.

Panky preempts Kitty's reply. "No, no, Tom," she assures him. "Not at all." Mincingly wiping a corner of her mouth, she adds, "I'm sorry about Raymond. He was such a nice man."

"Yes," Hack says, settling into the chair opposite her. "He certainly was."

"I thought that multiple myeloma was curable," Panky says, staring at Hack for an answer.

Hack shrugs and turns to Kitty, who says to Panky that Lina Dekker, Cooper Greens' director of nursing said that multiple myeloma was curable but only in the sense of effecting a long remission.

"Wait a minute," Hack says firmly. "Exactly what is multiple . . . whatever? I never did hear what it was that killed Raymond."

Kitty repeats the words "multiple myeloma" syllable by syllable, adding, "It's bone marrow cancer. They couldn't . . . cure it."

"Had they caught it sooner Raymond might still be alive?"

"Lina said the symptoms aren't obvious, that early detection matters . . . and so on. You know the program."

"When did they find out?" Hack asks.

"His last hospitalization. Dr. Bonifanti ordered a bone scan."

"She suspected . . . something, huh?"

Kitty shrugs. "I guess so."

"And when they decided his cancer was incurable they just delivered him back here? Just carted his withered ass back to this . . . big boarding house of peace and quiet for old folks? To let him just shrivel away and die?"

Kitty, after spearing several string beans with her fork says simply, "He was readmitted the day after his first chemo treatment."

"Hell," Hack says softly, "then he was only back here, what? Two . . . three days?"

"They brought him back Sunday, and Milton found him Tuesday morning."

"*Milton* found him!"

"Uh-huh."

"Christ, Milton Freuhoff's deaf as an adder."

Kitty, following Hack's thinking, shakes her head. "I knew the moment I woke up that Jen had died. That's just . . . the way it is."

"That *who* had died?"

"My last roommate. Before you moved in, Thomas. There was something . . . different that morning. I knew the minute I woke up."

"Hell yes there was something different," Hack says antagonistically. "She'd stopped breathing."

Panky throws in her two-cents worth. "It's truly inexplicable, Tom. Almost supernatural. When Mary–"

"What'd this Jen die of?" Hack asks Kitty, interrupting Pankhurst.

"A heart attack."

"So I guess that's how come they didn't move you out of the room the day before?"

(Cooper Greens' usual procedure is to temporarily relocate a roommate who is teetering on the edge of death. It's a tough call. Some overtly dying residents hang on for days.)

Kitty nods slowly. Hack can tell she's beginning to get the drift of his questions."Yes," she answers, "Jen died unexpectedly."

"Yes," Hack says, "but Raymond had a strong heart."

"It's possible," Kitty says thoughtfully, "that he died of a brain aneurysm. That would be instantaneous. How did you know about his heart?"

"He told me," Hack says. "He had bypass surgery some years back. I distinctly recall him saying that his Hamot cardiologist told him his heart itself was healthy."

An aide brings Hack the usual Cooper Greens' light supper. She leaves, and Kitty says, "Yes, but you don't know how badly that chemo affected his . . . other bodily parts."

Hack digs away at a bite of the salmon patty with his fork. "Not bad," Hack says, his mind on Kitty's question.

Panky asks, "When did Raymond undergo heart surgery?"

"I don't know," Hack answers bluntly, but after a moment of disgust at his own bad manners ne adds, "Before he moved here."

Hack concentrates on eating, and Kitty finally says to Panky, "You ready?"

Panky nods and wipes her hands on her napkin.

"Enjoy your supper, Tom," Kitty says, pushing back from the table.

"What's on the tube tonight?" Hank asks, not specifically addressing either woman.

Kitty gives him a disbelieving look and says, "Check the *Beacon*."

She knows, however, that *Law and Order*, one of the few programs that both she and Hack enjoy, comes on at ten o'clock and that a few minutes before ten Hack will make his way into her room where they will watch it together, as they have since the start of the Fall TV season.

[12]

By himself, now that Kitty and Panky have left the dining room, Hack's thoughts turn to Joe Luoma. He has not seen him for two days, not since the morning the ambulance came for Raymond's body. They are not close, Luoma and Hack, nor were they ever, nothing like the friendship Luoma and Raymond enjoyed, and Hack no longer has any intention of asking Luoma to join him in rousing the residents of Cooper Greens from their collective hang-dog paralysis. Still, Hack decides, two days is a long time not to run across a familiar face somewhere inside Cooper Greens. He finishes eating and heads for Arch Street.

Luoma, when Hack reaches his room, is sitting on the side of his bed. His pillow is lying on his lap. Tough, crusty old Joe Luoma with a pillow lying across his thighs? Hack stops in the doorway. Luoma welcomes him with a wordless nod and tosses the pillow aside.

Luoma believes that any show of civility by a man is attributable to a flawed manliness, to misplaced genes, so Hack blows off his skimpy greeting. The TV is tuned to an NBA game that Norman Vorhis, Luoma's roommate, is watching. Vorhis played first-base for the long-defunct Boston Braves during World War II, and he's still remembered around these parts as a local boy who made it to the Bigs. Vorhis has become withdrawn and lives in the glory days of his past. He and Luoma get along in a way not uncommon for roommates at Cooper Greens: they never speak to one another; they haven't exchanged a word since Vorhis returned from two days in the hospital to find the letter N, in the word NORM printed on his three wooden coat hangers, transformed into the letter W, changing NORM to WORM. Hack greets Vorhis, but he is sound asleep.

"How's it going?" Hack says to Luoma, who has begun to rub a misshapen hand against his thigh.

Luoma takes his time answering. He does not say that he is still ambulatory and still horny, his usual reply to that question.

"How's it supposed to go?" he asks irritably.

"We'll miss him," Hack says after a few seconds. "Raymond, I mean."

Luoma uncharacteristically mumbles a reply that Hack cannot make out.

"Have you stopped eating?" Hack asks.

"Nope."

"I guess we've missed each other at lunch time."

Luoma does not answer, so after a little while Hack says, "You know Yvon Chafee, don't you? Kitty's friend?"

Luoma's eyes narrow. "The one with orange hair?"

"No–"

"What about E-von? Balls, I'd rather French kiss a groundhog's ass. If that's–"

"No, not . . . her," Hack interrupts. "You're thinking of Panky Pankhurst. Yvon is the one with the pushed-up tits and – and wears light-sensitive glasses."

Luoma, for the first time, looks right at Hack. "She's not bad."

"Do you want to play pinochle? Against her and Kitty?"

"Damn right. Think I wouldn't like to trump her goddamn ace a couple times?"

Hack gives a little unlikely-that-will-happen snort.

Luoma's patented smirk leaves his face, and his habitual sour look returns. He stares at the basketball game playing on the TV. "Those goddamn spades *can* play basketball," he says after a few seconds.

Luoma is an inveterate user of ethnic slurs: Negroes are spades, Italians are dagos, Jews are sheenies, Slavs are grinders, Hispanics of any nativity are wetbacks, and so on. Luoma never mentions either the word Mick or the word Mack, never disparages the Irish, and Hack wonders if he simply does not know the pejorative association of either word.

Hack dislikes Luoma's habit of putting down ethnic types. On the other hand, Hack knows every adult , whether admitting it or not, is innately proud of his or her own heritage, of his or her ethnicity, and sometimes without real malice they defame the legacy of person's of ethnicities different from their own, so Hack does not chasten Luoma for his vileness. Besides, Luoma would accuse him of lip service if he did – qualifying "lip service" with a demeaning adjective or two.

"Which ones are the spades?" Hack asks innocently.

"The ones," Luoma snaps, "with wangs hanging to their knees! Goddamn it Murtaugh, don't start in."

"No," Hack replies, "I'm serious. Which ones?"

"You're all fucked up," Luoma says turning away from the TV.

Hack sides with Kitty in thinking that the differences between blacks, browns and whites are superficial. Luoma vehemently disagrees, says their anatomical dissimilarities are many. It's not just skin color, he argues. He tells Hack that if it wasn't for his head, he wouldn't have a point at all. And so it goes.

When the coach of the Atlanta Hawks, who are losing, calls a time out, Hack asks, "Where's this month's bumper sticker?"

Luoma saves car bumper stickers, and he brought a small stack with him when he moved into Cooper Greens. Each one is open to interpretation: Do Unto

Others, Politicians Happen, Up Uranus, and so on. He stores them on the shelf in his clothes closet and pins a different one to his bulletin board every few weeks. Today, however, the only parchment affixed to his bulletin board is the Cooper Greens monthly calendar of events, which was attached by an aide making her rounds.

Hack's question springs Luoma from where he's sitting. He pulls the sticker "Olympic Broad Jumper" from the stack on his closet shelf and pins it across the top of his bulletin board.

Luoma thumbs through the stack of bumper stickers, and while he is studying one Hack tries to come up with a short remark apropos of his plan to invigorate Cooper Greens. He doesn't, however, but saves the thought of one-day composing an appropriate bumper-sticker.

Luoma, back sitting on his bed, focuses on his Olympic Broad Jumper, plaque. "Happy now?" he asks.

Hack gestures at his closet. "Where'd you get all those?"

"I have friends in high places," he says.

"In low places, you mean," Hack counters.

Ignoring Hack, Luoma twice picks up his pillow and each time throws it roughly back on his bed. The second time it lands at the head of the bed. Luoma smoothes it with swipes of his arthritic right hand and then lays down on his back.

Hack sighs. "How long has it been since we visited Elm Street? Two weeks, anyway."

Luoma shrugs. "At least."

"Come by in the morning and we'll catch an early show."

"Maybe," Luoma replies apathetically.

Hack's knees reminds him that he has been standing for too long. He points his walker at the door. "Then I'll see you tomorrow morning?"

Luoma slightly nods. "Okay."

It's a long haul to Hack's room, and his bed, though disheveled from his earlier nap, is a welcome sight. Higgins is watching a magazine-format TV program, either *Dateline* or *48 Hours*. Hack smoothes his bed, crawls onto it, props his head up, and also begins watching the TV.

For a while, every Sunday evening, Hack religiously watched the program *60 Minutes*. Then he came to realize that, appearances to the contrary, Mike Wallace and his pals always took the liberal, politically correct angle of an issue. Hack presumes that is the nature of those shows. Anyway, he before long quit watching them, and anymore he mostly watches sports programs, straight news, and *Law and Order*. And *Cheers*, which is in re-runs. Even Kitty likes *Cheers*. Hack conjures Kitty's name only because she goes for a tear-jerker over a comedy every time. Hack had to stop reminding her that attitude was a gender predisposition because it ticked her off.

[13]

At nine forty-five, Hack brushes his teeth and heads for Kitty's room. He pretends not to hear when Higgins asks him where he is going. Like many moderately deaf persons, sometimes Hack only hears what he wants. The halls are empty, as they usually are at that time of night. Though he is certain she saw him approaching, Lorrie does not greet Hack until he is well past her seat at the desk in our nurse's station.

Lorrie Hoover took Marie's place when Marie transferred to first shift. She is young, for a nurse working here evenings, and pretty. She is also a strong-willed Florence Nightingale control freak who will not give an inch on any issue. Hack was ready to strangle her the first time she insisted that he drink every drop of a full glass of water to wash down his night-time medicine. "Christ," he told her, "I'll have to pee every half hour."

"We're not sleeping tonight, Tom?" Lorrie Hoover calls out sweetly.

"What, you and me together?" Hack's reply is as sugary. He does not stop or look back.

"Can I get you anything?" Hoover asks after several seconds of complete silence. Of course she means for Hack to address the question, "Where are you headed and why, Murtaugh?"

"Nope," Hack answers bluntly, again without turning. He is certain her gaze is lasing his back, but she has no more questions.

Eleven rooms separate Hack's from Kitty's, six that open on one side of Beechwood and five that open on the opposite side. Only one of the rooms' doors is fully closed, the one to Dirt Jamison's quarters.

Jamison snores loudly, generates a sound like the uneven growling of a chain saw ripping through a rotting tree limb. Whether inhaling or exhaling, the sound of air rushing through his nose competes with the roar of a jet taking off. Naturally, a mere closed door does not entirely muffle his snoring, but at least the level of noise that gets through does not stop visitors in their tracks – as sometimes happens when he's napping in the daytime. Even insisting that his appeal was in earnest, Hack could not prevail upon Marie to move Higgins, his ever woebegone roommate, into Jamison's room.

Kitty's door is open. Hack enters her room, and with a front leg of his walker works the door to within an inch of it being closed. *Law and Order* is an NBC network program, and Kitty has her TV tuned to the

NBC affiliate located in Erie, Pa. Hack knocks lightly on her bathroom door.

"In a minute!" Kitty yells.

The bathroom door opens an inch, closes for several seconds, and then swings wide open. Kitty emerges wearing a white blouse, plaid blue and green stirrup slacks, and white socks with faux-leather soles. A dark blue scarf is loosely tucked inside the collar of her blouse. She has put on a face, so her cheeks are a shade too rosy. Of course Hack does not say anything. Kitty greets Hack and he returns her "Hello," beaming in a way meant to compliment her appearance. They embrace and kiss lightly.

"You're late," Kitty says, making her way to the other twin bed in her room, which has been unoccupied for over a year that Hack is sure of.

Hack fibs: "I dozed off."

He sets aside his walker and climbs onto Kitty's bed. She hands him the pillow from the other bed. He props it against the headboard next to Kitty's pillow, and they stretch out together under the thin, light, checked comforter that is one of the home's standard issue bedspreads. Their legs intertwine, Hack's hand finds Kitty's and their eyes conscript *Law and Order*. It is a re-run, as they both knew it would be. Regardless, they will still enjoy the warmth and solitude of being alone together, their bodies, though fully dressed, tactilely side by side. Kitty would indulge him, Hack is sure, but he knows it would be like her agreeing out of some unspoken duty, and he does not even hint at that possibility.

The show has hardly begun when suddenly Kitty pulls her hand from Hack's and gently nudges him in the ribs with her elbow. For a few seconds Hack does not understand, and then, following the line of her vision, he sees that the door to her room is slowly opening.

"Yes!" Kitty yells loudly, propping herself up enough to look past Hack at the door.

The door swings open, and the ceiling light comes on. Lorrie Hoover strides rapidly into the room and stops near the foot of the unoccupied bed that is situated between Kitty's bed and the room's door. She levels a hard look at Kitty. "You know we're not supposed to close our doors at night, Kitty."

"It *wasn't* closed," Kitty snaps.

"That's bullshit, Lorrie!" Hack blurts blurt out angrily. "Get your ass out of here." Hack all but loses it: "We're screwing ourselves blind, so just butt the hell out! That's all you're here for, to see what we're doing. And it's none of your goddamn business."

"Now, Mister Murtaugh," Lorrie says soothingly. "There are rules that we *all* must obey."

"Lorrie," Hack says, swinging his feet onto the floor. "If you don't leave this room right this damn second, I will shove a leg of this walker right up your ass."

"Another word," Lorrie says sternly, "and I *will* call Security."

"You can call the Chinese Army!" Hack says, "For all I care."

Hack is not sure of her reply, because the next thing he remembers is seeing Kitty padding rapidly past the foot of the bed that he and Kitty had settled in, with Lorrie fast in her cross hairs.

"You cheeky little snot!" Kitty barks. "Just who in hell do you think you are?"

In Kitty's right hand is a foot-and-a-half length of broom handle. Hack had seen that dowel in her room before, and he had assumed it was for propping her window open.

Kitty, quicker than Hack thought her possible of moving, reaches Lorrie and jabs her hard in the stomach with the cut-off end of the broom handle. Lorrie gasps, latches onto the handle, and begins yanking. Kitty, however, will not give it up. When she does finally let go, she and Lorrie are face to face, drawn together by young Lorrie's superior strength.

Kitty Proctor has been a resilient toughie since her early teens, something Lorrie apparently did not know. And while Lorrie considers her next move, Kitty, as if wrapping her fingers around cow teats, grabs Lorrie's hair left and right with both hands and begins ramming her knee toward Lorrie's crotch.

What happened next is almost funny. Lorrie, dropping the broom stick, grabs Kitty's wrists and begins jerking this way and that, which only adds to her misery as Kitty will not let go of her hair. This continues until Hack manages to close in and separate Kitty from Lorrie, whose face is now almost as red as Kitty's make-up. Kitty and Hack fall backwards, and while Hack is holding Kitty at bay, she aims a kick at Lorrie that falls short.

"Now get out of here," Hack says to Lorrie, who is distractedly smoothing her hair. Hack continues to restrain Kitty from near the foot of the unused bed where Kitty and Hack had tumbled earlier. Hack tries, but he cannot read the slightly pensive expression on Lorrie's face. He is also confused over the fact that Lorrie did not once, during the scuffle, utter a word of fear or anger.

"Whore!" Kitty blurts out.

Lorrie favors Hack and Kitty with several tiny, pursed-lip nods of the "to-be-continued" sort and leaves the room.

"She's an ass," Hack says, releasing Kitty from his arms, a restraint that he is slow to realize is unnecessary.

Kitty nods without answering and retrieves the section of a broom stick that Hack has just learned is Kitty's version of a billy club. Pushing away from the bed, Hack steps into his walker.

Kitty lays the club on her dresser and looks back at Hack uncertainly.

"I guess you better go," she says shrugging.

"Are you sure?" Hack asks. "She's a strange girl."

"She's . . . something," Kitty replies.

Hack says, "I better hang around a while."

Kitty shrugs indifferently.

Five minutes pass, and for the next half-hour Hack lies awake on top of the spread covering the room's unoccupied bed, listening enviously to Kitty's deep, steady breathing.

[14]

Hack is impatiently fidgeting outside the smaller of Cooper Greens' two conference rooms. It is the day after Kitty tangled with Lorrie Hoover, Cooper Greens' voyeuristic, self-important second-shift nurse. Inside the conference room, the powers that be, led by Stephen Harris, are grilling Kitty. It is fifteen minutes after ten a.m. Kitty's appointment was for nine thirty and Hack's was for ten o'clock. Kitty has convinced Hack that they will easily prevail, and they do.

At twenty minutes after ten, Hack hears a muffled clunk, the sound of a chair being pushed against a table, and shortly Kitty casually leaves the room.

"Not exactly a high-noon moment," she says to Hack softly. Smiling irreverently, she adds, "Break a leg."

Substantially supported by his walker – hoping that a play for sympathy will help his cause – Hack hobbles slowly into the conference room. The room is windowless, and a ceiling vent weakly stirs the air. The maroonish-colored carpet needs a good steam-cleaning.

The lower third of all four walls are wood paneled, giving the room a feeling of stature – notwithstanding the fact that the paneling has the look of oil-cloth fabric. A gender-neutral demonstration manikin, naked except for a baseball cap turned backward on its head, stands immodestly in a corner where it cannot be easily seen from the doorway.

Stephen Harris is sitting at the far end of a dark wood rectangular table that seats two people along each side. Probably not yet fifty years old, clean-shaven, and dark-haired, Harris is wearing a charcoal-colored, two-piece business suit, a light-gray shirt, and a perfectly knotted, dark-red necktie, a color that Helen would have called vermillion – a word she liked. Lying on the table before Harris is an open notebook.

Lina Dekker, Cooper Greens' director of nursing, is sitting to his left. Kitty cannot stomach her and Hack soon learns why. Birdie Yoder is sitting to Harris' right. Hack isn't sure of her title or of her function.

Hack enters the room and Harris says pleasantly, "G-G-Good morning, T-T-Tom."

Hack had forgotten that he stutters, and for an instant showed his surprise. Hack nods, and Harris waves him to the empty chair turned out at the other end of the table. The two women, Dekker and Yoder, exchange quick, knowing looks. Hack guesses that Lina Dekker is 45 years old, 50 at most, and Birdie Yoder is 30, possibly younger. Both women are wearing slightly accessorized, one-piece dresses, and both have short, stylish, combed-back hairdos. Dekker is Amazonian; Yoder is an everywoman.

Harris gives Hack a few seconds to set aside his walker and settle into the chair. "I believe you know Lina and Birdie ," Harris says. He struggles to begin the sentence and pronouncing the women's names, and Hack understands why Kitty's interview exceeded her allotted half hour. Both women slightly nod. Dekker slides her glasses down her nose and scorches Hack with her eyes: clearly, she wants his head on a pike.

Harris taps his notebook. "Yesterday I received a report from Lorrie Hoover stating that Wednesday night she caught you and Mrs. Proctor in a compromising position. And–"

Hack cannot restrain himself, and after Harris finally pieces the words "compromising position" together, he interrupts: "Darn, Stephen, I don't know what you mean by compromising position." He feigns dismay.

Dekker begins to speak but Harris holds up a hand.

"My god," Hack says meditatively, while Harris' mouth apparently tweaks the words of his next utterance, "I've traveled all over the world, Canada, Mexico . . . even Korea. I've heard that there's, what? Five starting positions in ballet? I understand that airplanes in the sky and the ships at sea constantly give positional reports. Uh . . . some jobs are referred to as positions, though not one I ever held. Exactly what do you mean by compromising position, Steve?" Hack sets the words compromising position in quotes with his fingers.

Dekker, glowering as if her bowels were impacted, says, "What Mister Harris obviously meant was that Lorrie said you and Kitty were being intimate."

Hack thinks over her explanation. "Well . . . hell, I guess we were. Depending on what you mean by . . . ." Thunderstruck, he blurts out, "You think we were . . . copulating!"

After a long moment, during which the tiniest of grins bends up the corners of Harris' lips, Dekker says, "Call it whatever you want. But–"

Hack shrugs bewilderedly. "We were holding hands."

Harris, after tussling to articulating the th sound of "that," gives up and says, "I-I-It's a-a-all you w-w-were doing?"

"Exactly, Stephen," Hack answers, "that's *all* we were doing."

Harris looks at Dekker and then briefly at Yoder. "W-w-well then . . . I g-g-guess w-w-we're s-s-satisfied . Lina? he says, fixing his eyes on Dekker.

Dekker gestures at Harris' notebook. "Lorrie said that Kitty assaulted her. Physically."

Hack tilts back puzzled. "Did *what*?"

"Poked her with . . . a weapon," Dekker snaps.

"Lorrie," Hack says impassively to Harris, "is full of beans. Lorrie attacked Kitty. She's a disagreeable little snot. I've got to tell you, Sir, she may be a first-rate nurse. I wouldn't know, but she is weird. Can her butt. You don't, and mark my word Stephen, someday she'll give you one hell of a migraine."

"Lorrie," Dekker says harshly to me, "is a fine person and a highly qualified nurse." While Harris considers Dekker's portrayal of Lorrie, Dekker says to Hack, "You didn't hear my question Mr. Murtaugh?"

"What question?" Hack answers. "You didn't ask me a question."

Dekker pushes back from the table, rises, and begins pacing slowly back and forth behind her chair. Hack is reminded of a rooster maneuvering to alight on an unsuspecting hen. Stopping behind her chair, then leaning around it and poking the table hard with her index finger, Dekker says, "Are you claiming that Kitty did *not* physically attack Lorrie?"

"Yes!" Hack exclaims. "Exactly that's what I'm saying. Kit is *eighty* some years old." He leans back and crosses his arms.

Dekker, returning to her chair, gestures again at Harris' notebook. "So. Lorrie made this up?"

Hack shrugs. "I'm telling you *Miss* Dekker" – he intentionally stresses the word "Miss" – "that Lorrie Hoover is in need of an attitude overhaul. At the very least."

"You don't deny," Dekker replies sharply, slightly shaking her head, "that she and Kitty had a physical . . . encounter?"

"I don't deny," Hack says, "that Lorrie shoved Kitty. And after that I'm not sure what happened."

Dekker glares at Hack. "Mister Murtaugh," she says after a second, "I believe that you are intentionally misleading this panel."

Hack glares back. "Frankly, Miss Dekker, I don't give a damn *what* you believe."

BirdieYoder , after a long moments of quiet, says, "I have carefully reviewed Lorrie Hoover's personnel file and I must tell you, Mister Murtaugh that her referrals and her work record here at Cooper Greens, are absolutely beyond reproach."

Yoder says this to Hack, but she is plainly kissing up to Harris.

Hack throws up his hands. "What," he asks, "has that got to do with the weather in Zanzibar?"

Yoder seems not to understand that Hack judged her remark to be irrelevant, so he tells her that it was. She sputters and Harris interrupts: "You just don't like Lorrie Hoover, do you Tom?"

His remark, uneven and herky-jerky, is more of an observation than an accusation.

While Hack is considering a reply, Dekker begins to say something. Harris, however, stops her, and Hack says, "Lorrie Hoover cannot get it in her pea brain that we residents are *adults*, are grown-up men and grown-up women. Yeah, we stumble around in walkers and wheelchairs, and some of us drag a leg when we walk. And yes, we are slow on the uptake and we are sometimes incontinent and . . . occasionally burp out loud, and pass noisy gas.

"We do a lot of disgraceful things, Steve, but goddamn it we are not *children*! So what if Kitty and I were intimate" – Hack glances at Dekker – "to use her nice-nellyism word. Which we *weren't*. It was none of Lorrie Hoover's goddamn business. In fact, Stephen, it's none of *your* business – as long as Kitty and I couple agreeably. And we're not bothering anyone else." Hack feels the warmth of anger in his cheeks.

Harris nods slightly several times. "We're not morality police," he says, mangling the word morality so badly that Hack can barely catch what he means. "But . . . Cooper Greens obviously can't have residents accosting staff members, either." Each of the words "obviously," "residents," and "accosting" is lopped unapologetically into parts.

"Stephen," Hack says, fixing his face with what he intends to be a rapt expression, "if I ever accost one of your nurses have me arrested."

Dekker, not about to give in, shakes her head bitterly, leans back, and folds her arms: "And, if another resident attacks a nurse?"

Hack pretends not to catch her sarcasm. "In self-defense?"

"You're not cute, Mister Murtaugh."

"Your dumb question answers itself," Hack says dismissively.

Harris, after giving his notebook another quick glance, returns it to the table. "I don't have any more questions'" He turns to Dekker.

Dekker shows Hack a final hostile face, one that would loosen the treads of an Army tank, and then disgustedly pushes her chair under the table.

Harris looks at Yoder, who shakes her head.

"Thank you, Tom," he says.

[15]

It is noon when Hack reaches the dining room. He makes his way to the table where Joe Luoma is eating by himself, the same table where he, Luoma, Toby and Raymond ate lunch together every day for a year.

Luoma is dismissively stirring his beans. "Where the hell you been?" he asks gruffly, the manner he assumes when other residents are within earshot.

Hack drops into the chair on his left. "Talking to Harris."

Luoma's brow slightly furrows. "Steve Harris?"

"Uh-huh."

"You and he tight now?"

"Always have been."

Luoma shrugs. "Well?"

Positive as Hack is that Joe Luoma would be the last person on earth to pass along conversations that he wanted kept private, he is reluctant, nonetheless, to tell Luoma why he had just been in a meeting about Kitty's and his alleged misbehavior, which was presided over by Cooper Greens' top executive officer. While Hack ponders replying, an aide sets his lunch on the table.

Hack unrolls the paper napkin that is wrapped around his silverware and begins buttering his roll. "I had a disagreement with Lorrie Hoover," he says finally. "And she reported it."

Luoma scoffs. "That's all?"

Figuring he is sure to eventually learn that Kitty and he were both involved, Hack elaborates: "Kitty was there . . . at our inquisition . . . today. Last night I kept her from busting Lorrie's ass."

"Hell, I'd liked to have seen that," Luoma says, chuckling. "I thought you couldn't stand that damn Lorrie Hoover?"

"Nobody can," Hack says. "I told Harris to sack her ass."

Luoma snorts, finds it amusing that Hack would advise Harris on the staffing of Cooper Greens. "What'd he say?"

"Nothing," Hack answers. "Hell, he was just going through the motions. I could tell."

"You met in his office?"

"In the little conference room next to his office."

"Besides Harris, who all was there?"

Hack shakes his head, and Luoma understands that Hack will not answer any more questions regarding his meeting with Harris, Lina Dekker, and Birdie Yoder.

"What happened to you yesterday morning?" Hack says, "I thought we were going to visit Elm Street?"

"I didn't make it," Luoma says, pushing aside his dinner plate.

"No shit," Hack replies.

Not that Luoma would ever apologize, but he seems uncertain of how exactly to answer. Luoma was anything but indecisive before Raymond died. Young people sometimes seem to reframe their mind overnight, but not oldsters. Hack, after reminding himself of that unseasoned manner of youth, remembers that Raymond had died just five days ago. "Give it time," he tells himself.

"Well . . . hell," Luoma says, rising. He leaves without finishing his thought. Hack is not sure that he knows he is in the dining room let alone what is his next destination. Hack considers approaching his first-shift nurse, with the idea of a doctor prescribing Luoma an anti-depressant. "Hell," Hack tells himself. "Sooner or later, all of us living here end up daily quaffing a Prozac or two."

Hack glances at Kitty's table. Alone now, she was eating with Panky when he arrived. She signals Hack to join her and he does, bringing along his coffee, which is tricky going using a walker to get around.

"Luoma can't seem to snap out of it," Hack says, settling into the chair vacated by Pankhurst.

Kitty indifferently shrugs. "I talked to Yvon. She absolutely will not play if Luoma is your partner."

"Oh balls!" Hack blurts out, "tell her to grow up."

"Tell him to grow up," Kitty fires back. "He's a consummate ass, Tom. He'd make one of his gutter comments and . . . it's no wonder the damn fool was never married."

"Luoma never married? I had figured him to be divorced . . . at least separated."

Kitty's put-down frown is meant to tell Hack that Luoma's marital status is something she's known all along. Being aware of every resident's social situation at Cooper Greens, whether past, present, or a coming attraction, is important to Kitty.

"Anyway," Hack says halfheartedly, "I don't think it matters . . . won't until he regains his sense."

"What sense?" Kitty mutters.

Hack nods and addresses the subject that is really on their minds. "How'd it go?" he asks softly.

Kitty swiftly scans the room and then pushes herself away from the table. "Come by in a half hour . . . and I'll wax your butt in a game of double-solitaire."

Of course she means for Hack to visit her room where they will discuss their inquisitions.

Hack's glance circles the room. "Synchronize your watch."

At half past three, Hack leaves his room and hikes he way to Kitty's room. When he arrives, the TV gameshow *Jeopardy* is over. Kitty would skip a Thanksgiving meal before she'd miss a game of *Jeopardy*. Anymore, even for sex, Hack knows he wouldn't skip a celebratory meal.

Hack is a step from leaving their room when Higgins asks him where he is headed. Higgins has propped himself up and is leaning back on his elbows.

Bowling, Hack tells him. Higgins forces a laugh – tries to – and asks Hack if he'll be passing a vending machine. Hack sighs loudly and stops.

Higgins says, "On your way back, mind bringing me one of those little bags of peanuts?"

"I'll be a while," Hack says sharply.

Higgins says to never mind and falls back heavily.

Hack fetches him a bag of peanuts and from just inside the doorway of their room tosses the bag on Higgin's bed. "You owe me four bits," Hack says. He does not wait for an answer.

Hack passes Lorrie on his way to Kitty's room, and she greets him as if they were old friends. Hack has his faults, but he is not an out-and-out hypocrite. He gives her a long dirty look, managing, as he does, to drift close enough to the wall with his walker to scrape two middle knuckles of his right hand.

Before entering Kitty's room, Hack checks, out of habit, to be sure no one is behind him. He is alone, and since Kitty's door is open, he goes in without knocking. They embrace at the foot of Kitty's bed. She slips free, and after surveying the hall herself, gently closes the door.

"I let on that you and Lorrie never really tangled," Hack says from Kitty's recliner where he has settled and was removing his loafers. "It's what we decided on."

"You're a good man, Thomas Finbar Murtaugh."

"I know that. What'd you tell them?"

"Same thing," Kitty says, unbuttoning her bathrobe. "I was highly indignant."

"That . . . damn Dekker!" Hack spits out the name. "And who's that moron Birdie Yoder? What was she doing there?"

"Moron is right," Kitty says. "Birdie Yoder couldn't find her ass with a mirror in one hand and a flashlight in the other. Don't get on the wrong side of Dekker, though," Kitty adds with narrowed eyes and a tiny warning tilt of her head.

"It's too late now," Hack says, as Kitty follows him onto the bed.

Kitty is both vigorously willing and reasonably tireless, but she cannot manually stimulate Hack to a full erection.

"You're too tense," she says in a tired monotone.

"No Ma'am," Hank says. "It's nothing Viagra wouldn't cure."

"No. You're too stressed out."

Hack works his eyebrows up and down in the same way that Groucho Marx used to flex his heavy black caterpillar-size brows. He says, "Think I could hustle Lorrie out of a couple of Demerol pills?"

"Try conning her out of her panties," Kitty mutters. "You'd get further."

"Like, I would want to," Hack grumbles.

Kitty's hand finds his penis again, and her eyes tunnel into Hack's. "Full Monte?" she says.

"If you . . . please," Hack answers.

[16]

It is mid-Spring, and for two consecutive days now it has been unseasonably warm and muggy. The daffodils growing in the sectional gardens lining the front of Cooper Greens are in full bloom. Tulips shoots are waiting anxiously. A strong breeze suddenly comes up, and in Hack's mind's eye he sees broken and shredded maple-tree branches scattered all over the lawn that used to encircle his home. Hack says to himself, "No longer my problem."

Luoma is still wandering aimlessly about in a grey funk. Often as not he skips lunch, and Hack eats alone. When Luoma does show up, he barely opens his mouth, but if he says anything, his every sentence is laced with curses and epithets. When Hack eats alone, he reflects sadly: Toby and Raymond are long and forever gone, and the mind of Joe Luoma is aboard a jet airplane flying, to where, Hack hasn't a clue.

Toby no longer knows Hack, never shows a glimmer of recognition. Topy had crapped himself Hack's last visit to Elm Street, and Hack had to wait for an aide to clean him before she led him to where Hack was waiting. Cooper Greens' young female caregivers fight over whose turn it is to help bathe Pete Mando. Pete is probably eighty years old. Tall and rawboned, he is still ruggedly handsome. Hack has never seen him naked, but he presumes, from the way the aides form around him, that he is hung like a horse.

Hack asked two male residents to be his pinochle partner. Both turned him down. Hack was neither surprised nor disappointed, knowing that few of the men living at Cooper Greens have played a dozen games of cards in their lives. For recreation, they hunt, fish, and trap – muskrats, mostly. Between seasons, they build garages, sheds, pole barns, deer stands, and gazebos; they landscape and garden when they are not building something.

Kitty has begun playing the card game Five Hundred with Yvon Chafee, Emma Pankhurst, and an eighty-something woman with snow-white hair who moved in a month ago. Yvon, Kitty tells Hack, is clueless when it comes to playing cards, something she did not know before they started playing regularly.

The sun is out, and while he is tightening the laces on his sneakers, Hack decides he will ask Luoma to accompany him on his daily hike around the back lot at Cooper Greens. If Luoma refuses, as Hack expects, he will not seek his fellowship again, not for any purpose, recreational or otherwise. And that is Hack's disposition, weary hard-headedness, when he reaches

Luoma's room. He waits in the doorway while Luoma puts away his freshly washed underwear.

"Christ, are you still ambulatory?" Luoma says, when he spots Hack.

Not only does he greet Hack before Hack greets him, contrary to his usual reaction when they cross paths, but he falls back on his standard salutation – he even has the hint of a smile on his lips.

"Gracious," Hack says, looking about as if confused. "You get laid by Miki last night, or did you just have a good BM? Not that you could tell the difference."

Luoma's manner fools Hack again: he slightly guffaws at Hack's crude attempt at wit.

"Neither," he says. "And an erection is a terrible thing to waste."

"As if you'd know," Hack says, smiling wryly.

"What the hell do you want?" Luoma says. His words are intentionally surly, but his face belies his manner.

"C'mon, walk with me," Hack says, chucking his head toward the window, which is a rectangle of blinding sunlight. "Get the stink blowed off."

"Jesus Christ, Murtaugh. You want me to miss lunch?" Luoma, contrary to the gist of his reply, means that Hack moves slowly and that he accepts my invitation.

"You're *really* eating lunch today?" Hack asks.

"Hell yes," Luoma answers snappishly, Hack's question striking him as boringly redundant.

Luoma walks past Hack and opens the door to his closet. Holding up a faded, orange and black nylon windbreaker, he asks Hack if he thinks it will keep him warm. Luoma is not one to ask for advice of any kind from anyone, and Hack is again surprised by Luoma's Hyde-back-to-Jekyll personality transformation.

"It's windy, but not cold," Hack answers.

They leave through an entrance at the end of Acorn Street. Like the exit near Kitty's room, it is a heavy, well-braced door with a latch bar running its width. The outside air smells like moist, new-turned earth.

The path that Hack walks every day, which he guides them onto, includes stretches of the home's front sidewalk, its east and west driveways, and its rear parking lot. The sidewalk, four-foot-squares of brushed concrete, parallels the whole front of the complex, serving most of its length as an outer boundary for thickly mulched gardens that feature rhododendron shrubs.

The area immediately in back of Cooper Greens is taken up by a frequently patched, Macadam-surfaced parking lot. Twenty or so yards beyond, a brook, too small for fishing but glutted with minnows that bass cannot resist, meanders east to west. If it gurgles loud enough to hear, as Hack suspect it does, he cannot tell.

Beyond the stream lies a hilly span of mixed, once arable land belonging to the once mighty Strickland family. For the last twenty years, maybe longer, the land has been worked cost-free by local "squatters." In the distance – perhaps a tenth of a mile away – an oil pump jack rhythmically pecks at the ground. Farther on, a dark bulwark of trees walls in the arable land.

Other than two young, guyed, red-maple saplings growing mid-lawn out front, there are no trees anywhere on the grounds of Cooper Greens – no cover to inadvertently hide a demented, bewildered resident from a panicked nurse.

Hack and Luoma have been trudging along for several minutes, and Luoma has yet to bitch about the slowness of their progress. Hack remarks on what he proposes is one of God's common follies, but Luoma ignores him. Hack clams up and decides to wait Luoma out.

"He was a tough little bastard," Luoma says at last. "In a lot of goddamn pain. Constantly . . . ."

Uncertain of where his reply will lead, Hack cautiously tells Luoma that his characterization was also his own assessment of Raymond Snedeker's toughness.

"Damn right he was," Luoma says, his manner intent.

Neither man speaks for a minute. Suddenly Luoma mumbles something and briskly sets off for the field lying beyond the parking lot. He turns sharply when he reaches the little stream that Hack knows is brimming with minnows and chubs. As if hypnotized by the scene at his feet, Luoma slowly follows its twists and turns. Hack slogs along in the same general direction by himself. They are some thirty yards apart but almost directly opposite each other when Luoma turns and heads toward Hack.

[17]

Hack and Luoma enter a sheltered area near one of Cooper Greens' back doors, which has been furnished with a metal patio table and three folding metal chairs. All four pieces are chained together.

"Let's rest a minute," Hack says, making his way to a chair sitting off by itself.

Luoma shuffles close to where Hack is sitting but remains standing. His mind is obviously elsewhere.

"See any minnows?"

"No," Luoma answers distractedly. "I mean, yeah, a lot."

"When does trout season open?" Hack asks in a detached tone. "Do you know?"

"April fourteenth. Why? Are you going this year?"

Hack shrugs. "Probably. Of course, it depends—"

They hear voices and shortly four kitchen workers, each wearing an apron with the bib folded down, and gauzy, all-white hair nets, burst noisily through the doorway nearest their temporary refuge. Obviously surprised at their presence, the women nevertheless greet Hack and Luoma warmly. Gathering in a tight circle, they help each other light cigarettes. Many, half anyway of the home's nurses and caregivers, habitually smoke as Hack reminds himself.

Luoma ambles a few steps in their direction. "One of you pretty young ladies by any chance have an extra smoke?"

As if pleased to have been asked – none of the women are young or very pretty – two rush to offer him a cigarette. Luoma struggles, but eventually pulls one from the pack offered by the woman who reached him first. She offers Hack a cigarette, and he thanks her but refuses to take one; somehow Hack has it in his head, wrongly he's sure, that few people at Cooper Greens knows he smokes. Luoma begs a light, mutters a word of thanks, and draws in a full chest of smoke. After a second he begins coughing, and his eyes tear up.

"Out of practice," Luoma says weakly, hacking hard between words.

Luoma, when the women begin chattering among themselves, motions toward the exit path with his head. "Ready?"

"I suppose," Hack says, rising and stepping into his walker.

They're a half dozen yards along when Luoma, in his customary way, stops and remarks loudly on what he perceives as the shortcomings of Cooper Greens' cuisine. The four women are still within earshot, and Hack flashes him a warning look – which disturbs

Luoma's conscience like the impact of a snow flake landing on a hot plate.

They resume walking. "Like to hear my philosophy of life?" Luoma asks, flipping away his cigarette butt.

Hack sniggers. "Hell, you can't even spell philosophy."

"It ain't worth the never-fucking-ending pain."

Hack shrugs. "You're born, you suffer, and you die. So what else is new?"

Luoma knows that Hack is not clever enough to have composed that terse adage on his own: "Where'd you hear that?"

"I only now just thought it up," Hack answers.

"Whoever the son-of-a-bitch was," Luoma replies, matter-of-factly, "he got it right."

Hack asks, "So. You're thinking of pulling the plug?"

"I don't have the balls."

Hack is not what one would call a good Catholic, but he is a Catholic. "Bullshit," he says earnestly. "It takes more guts to live than to cash out."

Luoma impatiently shakes his head. "You're all screwed up, Murtaugh."

They slowly walk another couple yards without talking.

"Raymond wanted to die," Luoma finally says, looking about helplessly.

"You know that for a fact?"

"He told me he did. Every damn day of his last month on this shitin' planet."

Intent on absolving Raymond, Hack says grimly, "He was in a lot of pain, Joe."

Luoma's expression darkens. "He begged me . . . ."

"Begged you?"

"To . . . help him."

Hack stops dead. "Help him! Help him do *what*?"

Luoma slows and looks away.

"Help him!" Hack repeats loudly. "How?"

"You know . . . help him," Luoma answers, his expression thoughtful.

"Christ, how'd you handle that?"

Luoma takes his time answering. "I didn't. What the hell could I do?"

They reach the parking lot's east end, where arriving vehicles enter. A dirty, beat-up, compact car rounds the corner of the building and chugs by. The driver, a housekeeper who sometimes works the street on which Hack lives, waves and he waves back.

"Tune it!" Luoma yells harshly at the back of the passing car.

They leave the rear parking lot and follow a driveway leading to the front of the complex. The building now shelters them from the wind, and for several steps they silently enjoy the sun's steady rays of heat.

"Did you take geography in grade school?" Luoma asks, breaking the spell.

"Did I do what? Where'd that come from?"

"Remember that . . . odd-looking, orange-peel map in geography class, the one with the countries of the world in different colors?"

"Yeah," Hack says, "Sure. Canada, Australia, New Zealand, India, South Africa – hell, I can't begin to name them all. All the countries in pink were part of the British Empire."

"Yeah, they were," Luoma nods. "On which the sun never set. It was a hell of a lot better world, then . . . the thirties."

Hack is sorely tempted to reply, to conditionally disagree, but there's no arguing with Luoma over anything bearing on the human condition, past or present, so Hack doesn't bother.

Luoma resumes: "In the seventies I worked two years for Shell in Saudia Arabia. Good money, but I ain't no damn teetotalin' celibate. Anyway, I didn't used to be."

"Did you see the sights while you were over there?"

"Athens, Cairo, Rome . . . Jerusalem . . . Amman. Sure. You know the city that was the rottenest?"

Luoma looks at Hack, and Hack shakes head.

"That goddamn Rome. Rome, Italy. We had an expression, 'When in Rome, do as the Romans do. But be goddamn sure to always count your change."

"The Eternal City?" Hack mumbles skeptically.

"No, the Eternal Shitty," Luoma counters harshly.

Hack is both amazed and saddened to hear Luoma's censorious criticism of the generic dishonesty of Rome's citizens, which deportment is at odds with his measure of friends who are Americans of Italian descent. Afraid that it might induce a mean reply, Hack does not tell Luoma that he and an Italian neighborhood kid, a close friend, enlisted in the service together.

"How'd you become an oil-field roughneck?" Hack asks, remembering that Luoma liked being referred to as a roughneck.

Having drifted ahead, Luoma stops and turns around. "Did you know old man Huffington? Hedrick Huffington? Huffy?"

Hack shakes his head. "I knew of him."

"He was from Trundel Mills. Died in . . . fifty-three." Luoma stops walking. "I think. Somehow, Huffington acquired eighteen oil leases in and around Bradford, and I caught on with his drilling crew. All you needed was a strong back. It didn't hurt, neither, if you had a weak mind."

They reach a point where the driveway passes a front corner of Cooper Greens. The wind is in their face now, and Hack tells Luoma that he needs to stop and rest. Luoma shrugs, and they pull up.

Two dark, mud-splattered cars drive by on their way to the back parking lot. Hack does not recognize the driver of either vehicle nor does either driver wave.

"Where'd you work last?" Hack asks, uninterested in hearing any more about Hedrick Huffington's business.

"Texas. Ten miles south of Odessa. You know what crude was selling for when I hung 'em up?"

"When was that?"

"Nineteen eighty-eight."

"Thirty, thirty-two bucks a barrel?" Hack answers tentatively.

Luoma disgustedly shakes his head. "Fourteen something a barrel . . . on a good day."

They resume walking, and Luoma says, "But then, what the hell do I care?"

"You got grandchildren?" Hack asks.

Luoma is pretty sure that Hack knows better, and he doesn't answer.

In addition to the back parking lot, which is mainly for employee parking, there is also a span of parking stalls that run the full width of the front of Cooper Greens. As Hack and Luoma mear those stalls, Hack spots a faded blue-and-white "Clinton for President" sticker on the rear bumper of an old four-door Dodge that is parked in the third stall from the end. Hack calls it to Luoma's attention, suggests that he add it to his collection. Hack is joking, of course: Luoma would sooner do hard-time in a Tijuana jail than favorably associate himself with Clinton's presidency. It sets him off, however, as Hack had hoped it would.

Luoma stops. "You happy that damn sleaze is still our president?" On his face is a look of pure anger, one Hack had seen twice before: on the day of his fight with Fuller and the time they were leaving the dining room and a woman behind them loudly said something to the effect that Clinton was the best president we ever had.

"So he fooled around," Hack says mildly, having second thoughts over bringing up the subject at all. "So, throw him out of office for that?"

Luoma shakes his head; his teeth, Hack suspects, could not be pried apart with a crow bar. "When you say, 'for *that*?'" Luoma asks, his voice sharp and demanding, "exactly what do you mean by the word 'that'?"

"What he did," Hack answers.

Luoma more fervently shakes his head. "For chrissakes, Murtaugh! Spell it out! What exactly is it he *did*?"

"I just told you," Hack says, starting to feel a little hot himself. "They were consenting adults. If Hillary can live with it, why do you give a rat's ass?"

"Bullshit, Murtaugh! Clinton was tried for perjury! And obstruction of justice! Read the damn Articles of Impeachment! You're no better than the rest of that claque of suck-ups that defend him. There's the trial that took place in the Senate and then there's the imaginary, cover-your-ass trial that went on in the heads of those goddam freaks! Not one chicken-shit Democrat had the guts to vote his conscience!"

Hack stops plodding along. "Bullshit yourself, Luoma! Cut through the Republican Party's phony reverence for morality and their pretense about political . . . uprightness and what you really have is a private, consensual sexual affair! Ever see birds eating shit on a road? That's Republicans gnawing on the petty troubles of Democrats."

"Petty my ass," Luoma says. "I must have overlooked reading about the Clintons purchasing the White House."

Hack cannot check his anger. "You just don't get it, do you Luoma?" He pronounces each word separately, as if he is addressing a backward kid.

Luoma whirls, plants himself in front of Hack's walker, and leans forward until his face nearly touches Hack's. "No, Screwhead!" he screams. "*You* don't get it!"

They glare at each other, and for a moment Hack is close as he has been for years to pasting another man in the teeth. He is honestly not sure why he didn't. Luoma could handle Hack, no doubt, and fear probably played a part. Still, Hack was Irish, and he had tangled before with men bigger than he was – and always endured getting the crap kicked out of him.

Luoma breaks eye contact. Shaking his head disgustedly, he turns and begins walking away at the same slow pace as they were moving before. He has gained a dozen steps before Hack has cooled enough to follow.

Luoma stops and looks at his watch. "They start serving in twenty minutes," he says over his shoulder.

Luoma is offering Hack an olive branch, and Hack grabs it. "I'm coming," He says loudly.

Luoma waits for Hack at Cooper Greens' westernmost front entrance, one that most nearly closes the shortened circle of their path. He holds the door open until Hack is inside and well clear of the doorway.

"Straight to lunch?" Hack says.

"I'll meet you there," Luoma says, rapidly walking away.

Hack watches until Luoma turns a corner. "And at one time," he says scornfully to himself, "I considered recruiting Luoma to help me spread cheer around here?"

[18]

Hack and Luoma arrive at the dining room at the same time. Luoma has changed into a blue polyester shirt with buttons down the front. One third of a plain white envelope is sticking out of the shirt's breast pocket.

They say little while they are eating. Luoma, as usual, finishes well ahead of Hack who continues eating until he finishes dessert, which is vanilla pudding topped with a dab of whipped cream serving as a pouch for a Maraschino cherry. Luoma drains a second cup of coffee. He studies Hack – pretending not to – his intense interest stemming from their near fistfight, Hack assumes, and Hack lets on that he doesn't notice.

Hack finishes his dessert, and they leave the dining room together. Hack is surprised when Luoma follows him, which is in a direction different from the way to his room.

"I've got something for you," Luoma says once they are alone in the hall.

Luoma removes the envelope from his pocket,

looks it over, and then shoves it roughly into Hack's shirt pocket. Hack instinctively reaches for his breast. "Don't open it until I say," Luoma warns.

Hack stops and crimps his eyes. "What? You're moving out?"

Two women leave a resident room together and head our way, and Luoma does not answer Hack until they are well past. "No, but . . . I've made arrangements."

"Humor me. About what?"

"It's all in there," Luoma says, gesturing at the envelope in Hack's pocket. "I might want it back, so don't fuck with it. Besides. It's no big deal."

Hack resurrects the timeworn cliché about Indians' grave reluctance to permanently give away anything: "You really are part Indian," he says.

Luoma is not riled, and Hack decides that Luoma missed his point.

"Whatever," Hack adds, sighing to make it clear that he will respect Luoma's wish regarding the disposition of the envelope.

They split at the intersection of Beechwood and Oak streets, and Hack heads for his room, where he finds a note on his bed from Marie. "See me," it says simply.

Hack lays the note aside and removes Joe's envelope from his shirt pocket. Printed thickly on the front is Hack's full name. Beneath, underlined three times, are two all-caps words: PERSONAL and

PRIVATE. The flap is sealed. Hack holds the envelope up to the rooms outside window, but he cannot determine its contents let alone read the message. He stows the envelope in the bottom drawer of his dresser under a stack of pocket books that he has co-opted from one place or another for his personal reading.

Marie, when she returns to the Nurse's Station serving Beechwood Drive, where Hack has been waiting, tells him that, as of today, Lorrie Hoover is out scuffing shoe bottoms looking for work. Other residents are lingering nearby, and she conveys this message as a soft aside. Hack sneaks her a thumbs-up and asks if Kitty knows. Marie nods, tells Hack to come back later, and attends to the needs of another resident.

An hour later Hack comes across Marie, alone, in the laundry room tracking down a resident's missing brassiere.

"I was surprised," Hack says to her, "Cooper Greens sacking Lorrie over the . . . incident with Kitty. Don't get me wrong, I approve, only it didn't seem to me to be that big a deal."

Marie stops pawing through the clothes inside a huge round dryer, steps into the hall, and looks both ways. Returning, she says, "There's something that I don't think even Kitty knows."

Hack looks at her quizzically.

"Lorrie Hoover is a lesbian."

Hack is out-and-out surprised. "No shit. I never . . . thought . . . ."

"She hit on an aide that I'm certain of."

"I guarantee you," Hack says, "that Kitty doesn't know or she'd have told me. When?"

"I'm not sure. Last month."

"Which aide?"

"A pretty one."

Hack waits a moment, but Marie will not elaborate.

"What, ah, what happened?"

"Another aide reported her friend's . . . unwanted attention. But that's all I know for sure."

"Do you think–"

"That's all I know for sure, Tom. I'd just as well you didn't say anything about this to *anybody*. Including Kitty. Especially Kitty."

"I won't, then," Hack promises staunchly.

They hear steps coming from the direction of another hall. A door closes and the sounds stop.

"So," Hack begins slowly, "Lorrie Hoover had it in for boy-girl sex."

Marie slightly grins, and Hack realizes that he may have inadvertently implied that he and Kitty were having sex together. "I mean," Hack says, "that Lorrie had it in for heterosexual sleep-over's."

"Of course you did," Marie says her smile fuller than before.

Marie leans to see past me. "I thought so. Somebody's coming."

"Thanks for your help," Hack says loudly, and he leaves the laundry room.

The room is shadowy when Hack first awakes, and he checks the time. It is twenty minutes after six, about the time when he usually wakes up, provided he slept through the night. He can just make out that Carl Higgin's bed is empty. A thread of light outlines the closed door of the bathroom, so Hack lays back and waits. Hack finally hears Higgins climb back into bed, which he does with the help of a little stool provided him by Buster Mook.

Hack finishes his toiletry, and he is sitting on the edge of his bed struggling to pull on one of his socks when Marie busts into the room.

"Well, c'mon in," he says, hurrying his struggle.

Marie orders Hack to sit back down and then pops him right between the eyes: "They found Luoma dead in bed this morning." Several times she nods as if expecting that Hack would doubt her message.

It is a long second before Hack can remark sensibly. "Yesterday we walked around the building together."

Marie gives a little shrug. "Well, you won't today."

It's a stupid question, Hack knows, but he is unable to keep from asking Marie if she's certain of her facts.

She ignores his question. "You feel all right?"

Hack nods mechanically several times. "I'm just–"

"I can bring you something."

"No. I'm okay. It's not like Joe and I were close."

"Tom, if you're sure, I've other people . . . ."

"Is the body still here?"

"I don't think so." Her voice tails off. "Not likely."

"What, ah, how'd he die?"

"They don't know yet. Heart attack, I suppose. Dulcie found him. He was lying on top of his bed, fully dressed, shoes and all."

"Is the word out?"

Marie reacts to my question like I'd asked her if the planet Earth was spherical. "Of course. I have to go."

She leaves, and Higgins, whom Hack had forgotten about, says suddenly, "I'm sorry, Tom."

"Me, too," Hack says, without turning his way.

Hack knows, however, that in his heart of hearts he truly will not miss Joe Luoma. He doubts, moreover, that there is another man, woman, or child alive anywhere on earth who will miss Luoma's passing. Raymond Snedeker, Hack presumes, is biding his time in Heaven.

[19]

Kitty sometimes skips breakfast, but this morning she is sitting by herself at the dining-room table where she and her girlfriends eat lunch together. Kitty tries to hide it, but she hears poorly from her left side. Hack caught on after realizing that she always finagled a seat putting her right side nearer to him.

Hack eases into the chair on her right. "I guess you heard."

She looks away. "Only, that he died."

"Yeah," Hack says, "that's as much as I know."

"He was your buddy, not mine."

" Not like Toby was my buddy, he wasn't. Wait. I just remembered. Joe gave me an envelope yesterday. And . . . you don't suppose . . . ."

"I don't suppose what, Thomas?"

"Nothing. I just . . . it's sealed, and Luoma told me not to open it. I'm going back to my room."

Kitty's look is leery. "Let me know."

Higgins has finished his breakfast and is watching a TV talk show. He would not have heard Hack enter the room, but a kitchen aide retrieving Higgins' breakfast tray greets Hack. Answering her question, Hack says that he has nothing more to add about Luoma's sudden death. Higgins turns back to his program.

Hack expected to find a handwritten last will and perhaps a sketchy, personal obituary in the envelope foisted on him by Luoma. It contains neither, however. Inside are two sheets of plain white typewriter paper folded together. The outer sheet is blank, apparently meant only as a shield against prying eyes. The text written on the inner sheet is undated and unsigned. The first sentence, firmly underlined, orders Hack to destroy the note after he reads it. The next – and last sentence – smudgy from redactions, states, without any illuminating support, that Raymond Snedeker died of "oxygen deprivation."

Hack is still sitting on the side of his bed, his mind on Luoma's confidential note, when Marie, after knocking lightly, pushes a medicine cart into the room. Her attention is on a medical chart, and she does not see Hack slip Luoma's note into the top drawer of his dresser. Marie, waiting until after Higgins downs his pills, given to him in a tiny paper cup by her, matter-of-factly, asks Hack if he'd heard any more about Luoma's demise.

Unpleasant thoughts had settled in Hack's head when he read the words "oxygen deprivation" and it is a second before he answers. "No. Only what you told me earlier. I was hoping you knew something."

Marie offers Hack his paper cup of medicine pills. "Like what?"

Hack is again slow to answer. "I don't know. Like, what the hell happened? He was all right yesterday."

"Joe Luoma was never, *all right*," Marie says almost soundlessly. Glancing at Higgins, she tries masking her loathing of Luoma with a quick, tiny smile. Higgins attention is on the TV, and he does not notice.

"I meant," Hack says, "that he was healthy." Hack swallows his medicine.

"So did I."

Hack turns his head as if flustered at what he heard. "Saint Peter will stick out a leg and trip you as you go by," he says.

Hack's mind drifts back to Luoma's deposition, and he does not know what Marie said, if anything.

Marie has left, and Hack has not moved from where he was sitting on his bed when she brought the medicines. Kitty walks past the room. She looks in but continues without stopping. It is another ten minutes before Hack makes up his mind and decides that, contrary to Luoma's written orders, Kitty should also read Luoma's last will – or whatever it was. Hack is bothered by his decision: Luoma, for all his faults, would never have violated Hack's trust.

When Hack reaches Kitty's room, she is standing stiffly in front of her window looking at the scenery outside. Hearing Hack enter, she turns and tips her head toward her recliner. After lightly bussing Hack's cheek, she continues on and closes the door.

"Is it what we thought?" Kitty says, backing onto her bed.

Hack, from her recliner, says, "It's not what *I* thought it would be."

Hack hands her the envelope containing Luoma's handwritten note. She glances at Hack's name and the warning on the front, removes the double-folded papers from the envelope, and begins reading the inside sheet. Her hand flies to her mouth. "My God, Tom!" she cries, "he killed Raymond!"

Hack nods. "That's what I make of it. And then . . . himself."

Kitty slowly, absent-mindedly shakes her head. "You better destroy this," she says, handing Hack the sheet on which Luoma's confession – as both Hack and Kitty instantly interpreted the meaning of his words – is printed. Folding the sheet, Hack slips it into his shirt pocket.

"How?" Kitty asks skeptically.

"How what?"

Kitty is annoyed because Hack does not instantly catch the drift of her question. "Damn, Tommy, how did he . . . how did Luoma, pull it off?"

Shaking his head, Hack pushes himself up from her recliner."You sit here, Hon."

"What are you going to do?"

"Get your other chair. My knee hurts."

Kitty keeps a "borrowed" Cooper Greens' wooden folding chair hidden in her closet behind a handful of hanging dresses, all of which are straight-cut numbers. They scarcely provide the shield she wants.

Hack fetches the chair and positions it in front of Kitty's recliner, which Kitty has dropped into.

"I've thought about that," Hack says, folding his arms, "about how he did it. Assuming he did . . . what we think happened"

"And?"

Hack falls back into the folding chair, inhales a full breath of air, and allows it to escape his lungs. "He smothered Raymond with his pillow."

Hack tells Kitty about Luoma's recent odd behavior, of how, in the days before and after Raymond died that Luoma could not turn loose his bed pillow. Hack repeats the essence of Luoma's remark, that Raymond badly wanted to die.

Wary, Kitty looks away.

"I'd bet on it," Hack says.

"I don't know," Kitty says. "There'd be a commotion. The noise of a struggle."

"Maybe, Hack says. "How long has it been since you saw Raymond? I mean, how long has it been since you last saw him *up close*?"

Kitty, after thinking about it, says, "That's a good question. Several weeks, a month. Sometime before his last hospital stay."

Hack says, "I'll bet he'd lost twenty pounds since then. For two weeks he never left his room, had his meals brought in . . . and didn't eat half of the food. I stopped at least four times. I wasn't certain, not then, that he had cancer."

Kitty resumes answering Hack's question. "He was still plodding around when I last saw him . . . talking to Birdie Yoder in a hall."

Hack nods agreeably. "Yes, but the day he died, he *couldn't* have fought Joe off. I don't care how hard he tried."

"He was that weak?"

"That, and Joe was a damn powerful man." Thinking back to his near fistfight over the issue of President Clinton's impeachment, Hack says, "I'm glad that Joe and I never tangled."

"He put Fuller in his place," Kitty muses.

"Uh-huh. He almost certainly knew Raymond had cancer. He never told me, though."

Kitty nods slowly, as if mentally elaborating on the diningroom fight between Luoma and Fuller. "Yes," she says finally, "but he couldn't have known until sometime after Bonifanti ordered that bone scan."

"Right," Hack says. "Raymond probably told Joe as soon as he knew himself. And you can damn well bet that that was when he told Joe he wanted to . . . pack it in."

Kitty, reaching for Hack's hand, gives him a long vacant look. "Maybe you're right." She pulls the back of Hack's hand to her lips and lightly kisses it.

For a while neither Hack or Kitty speaks.

"I'm not sure what to do," Hack says finally, slowly shaking his head

"You do *absolutely* nothing, Thomas. What would it possibly matter to anyone?"

"Christ, Kit, we're talking about a murder and a suicide."

"You don't know that, Tom, not for a fact. You said yourself that Raymond was deathly sick. How do you know it wasn't his heart? You don't know."

"It wasn't his heart," Hack replies dully.

"It could have been. It was probably Joe's heart, too. We just don't know."

Hack shakes his head decisively. "Joe killed Raymond. And himself."

Kitty slightly nods. "Possibly. But, how?"

"He smothered Raymond," Hack says, "and then overdosed on Demerol – or whatever. I'd bet on it."

"It'd take a whole bottle," Kitty says. "Where would he get that much?"

"Save it up. One pill at a time." Hack shrugs. "Steal it. Hell, I don't know."

Kitty fixes Hack with a long unwavering look. "You've figured it all out, haven't you?"

"Maybe. Who the hell knows . . . Joe, I suppose."

"A judge could order an autopsy," Kitty says, looking sideways as if to provide Hack a moment to form an answer. "Doctor Bonifanti," she adds, "would have to write an opinion on the cause of death."

Hack snorts at hearing this. "Hell, Kit, Bonifanti has *never* examined Joe. Never even spoke to him is my guess. I'll guarantee you that Joe never once saw a doctor while he was living in this place. I doubt he ever had his vitals taken."

Kitty nods. "She'd still have to sign the death certificate. What'll she put down for the cause of death?"

"Heart failure," Hack answers quickly. "What else? It'll be bull, but it *will* be heart failure. You can take it to the bank."

"I'm not so sure," Kitty says. "She's a young doctor, barely out of residency. Sometimes they get carried away with propriety."

"I suppose you're right," Hack says. "But no one on this planet gives a damn that Joe died. Or for that matter cares to know how he died."

Kitty after another long intense, solemn pause mildly agrees. "Probably. Still, you know what'll happen if you stick your nose in. Raymond's sister will want his body exhumed, a coroner will find out he was smothered, and Sis will sue Cooper Greens for negligence and win the court fight. To the tune of a million bucks."

Hack grins, but not at the events described by Kitty. "She does, and Joe climbs out of his grave and smothers her, too."

Hack had often seen Luoma go ballistic every time he read where a jury rewarded an alleged victim millions on a charge with no more legs than God gave a garter snake. It was Luoma's opinion that the collective stupidity of any particular jury was rivaled only by the collective stupidity of womankind and that the inherently greedy were attracted to lawyering like hogs drawn to slop.

Hack informs Kitty that Joe Luoma was not kindly disposed to the American way of justice.

"As far as I could tell," she replies, "Joe Luoma wasn't kindly disposed to anything or anyone."

Hack shrugs. "He liked Raymond."

"That's true . . . I guess. Well, it's your call. But if I were you . . . ."

"Yeah, but you *ain't* me." Hack rises, folds Kitty's chair and uses it for support when he stands up.

"Let it go, Tommy," Kitty says softly as Hack works his way to her closet, manipulating the chair like a cane.

"I can't," Hack says. "The plain fact is Joe Luoma killed Raymond Snedeker. We both know that's what hap–"

"I don't know that," Kitty snaps. "And neither do you."

"Then how do you explain this," Hack says, touching his shirt pocket, where he had tucked away Joe's note.

Kitty shakes her head. "Why did he leave any message at all?"

"He had to, Hack says. "Joe absolutely had to let someone know. You didn't know Luoma, not like I did. In his own mind he was doing the right thing. He was on a trip, Kit, on a high."

"And in this . . . instance," Kitty says, "he *was* doing the right thing. Raymond was miserable with pain. Both men knew it was only a matter of time. If you're still around, don't let me suffer that way. Promise me, Tom."

"Miracles do happen," Hack mumbles.

"Promise me," Kitty repeats.

For a long moment, Hack does not answer. "I'm not God, Kitty."

Kitty shakes her head unhappily. "Really, Thomas. All I can say is that your God is a hell of a lot less compassionate than mine."

"I don't think so," Hack says unconvincingly.

"Well I do," Kitty says.

Kitty leaves the bed for a place in front of her window.

"I'll think about it," Hack says to her back.

She does not reply, and Hack tells her that she's never able to see things from his point of view. Again Kitty does not reply, and Hack leaves.

A week has passed since the morning when Cooper Greens' aide found Joe Luoma's body lying on his bed. Dickey's, the funeral home that saw to the burial of Raymond, also tends to Joe's remains. Hack was the only person who showed up at the viewing, unless someone visited after he left, which he doubted. Buddy, who drove Hack to the funeral home, stayed in the van.

As it turned out, Luoma died of a heart attack, of myocardial infarction – according to Lina Dekker's secretary, who passed the word on to Kitty. Of course Hack did not believe this, but he took Kitty's advice and did not show anyone the note left to him by Joe. It was Luoma's plan, his hand, his crime, Hack told myself, and reporting it was more an obligation of citizenship than a moral responsibility. Deep down, however, Hack knew that he was just kidding myself. Neither Kitty nor Hack ever again mentioned Luoma's name since the day Hack showed her Luoma's hand-penciled note, which Hack kept. Hack wasn't exactly happy about Joe's demise, but he sure in hell never shed any tears.

[20]

For two weeks, beginning the day after Luoma's funeral, Higgins and Hack played chess every afternoon. Raymond and Joe are in heaven or hell or somewhere else – if there is a somewhere else. The residents of Cooper Greens are still a dour and bleak gathering of depressed souls hardly different in spirit from the day Hack moved in.

Playing chess was Higgins' idea, and they play with his set of men. In fact, when Hack loses – so far, every game – he blames his usual "scorched earth" defeat, on using Higgin's pieces, implying that Higgins has somehow "marked" them. Hack thinks this is a mildly funny appraisal of the situation, equating Higgins' chess pieces to a deck of marked cards, but Higgins doesn't seem to get it. Higgins is not stupid. Subtle humor, however, crosses his mental radar screen like a stealth fighter jet zipping intermittently across a radar CRT.

Lately Higgins has been quicker to accomplish routine personal grooming on his own. He's stopped asking Hack to run his candy-fetching errands, speaks clearer, and he is less of a whiny jerk than when he was first moved into Cooper Greens. The one game he nearly lost to Hack, he blamed on his sickness, on the remnants of his stroke, which Hack knew for certain was a phony excuse: Higgins lost interest and almost blew it.

Higgins can reason better than Hack, faster anyway. Hack is still able to think his way through a problem fairly well, provided, as in a chess game, all pieces of the puzzle are on the table. Given enough time, Hack can recall the capital of the State of Utah, the name of the Republican dandy that Harry Truman defeated for the presidency of the United States in 1947, the year the New York Yankees' Joe DiMaggio hit safely in fifty-six consecutive baseball games, and so on. But anymore his memory gives new meaning to the expression "short-term" – a meaning closer, in Hack's case, to the saying "long-gone."

Anxious to begin a game, Higgins, when Hack returns to their room after eating lunch, has the chess board set up. Hack opens by moving the king's pawn ahead two squares. That move, Higgins once offered, is a good opening; "Deploy first," he added, with, as usual, a slightly superior lift of his head.

Higgins counters aggressively with his queen's knight. And eight moves later Hack's king is "threatened," as the "dumb shit" – Hack's private nickname for Higgins – unfailingly puts it when he gets Hack's king in the crosshairs of one of his attacking chess pieces. Another two defensive moves by Hack and Higgins checkmates his king.

It is not yet two thirty, so they play another game. So far, they have played some twenty-odd games, and Hack has won exactly none.

Rachel, Higgins' wife, looks in on him every two or three mornings. If she has visited Higgins on consecutive days, Hack missed seeing her. She jumps up and dashes away if his physical therapist or any other visitor arrives. Rachel is easily ten years younger than Carl. She wears buckskins, usually a fringy, napped jacket, an above-the-knee skirt of the same yellowish-gray fake leather as the coat, and knee-high cowboy boots. Annie Oakley may be her hero, but Hack infers that she's closer in personality to Calamity Jane – whom, Kitty once told him, charitably succored many a lonely cow-puncher. In fact, Hack would involuntarily smirk if someone told him Rachel was *not* philandering her way around the neck of the woods where she and Higgins live. She even vamps Hack. Maybe it's only because she thinks Hack is too crippled to respond – or whatever.

Higgins is a mechanical engineer, a graduate of Case Western Reserve University. Not many Cooper Greens' residents have college degrees, not counting the half-dozen or so retired women school teachers residing at Cooper Greens. Agriculture is Crawford County's biggest industry, tool-and-die-making is the second largest, and healthcare is third. Meadville calls itself Tool City USA, because of its plethora of tool shops manned by squads of machinists. Most of the tool shops were founded by ex-employees of the Talon Corporation's one-time big tool-making operation.

Higgins graduated from Case Western Reserve University in 1964, so Hack puts him at 58 years of age, young for Cooper Greens. Hack is 70, almost 71, and most of the male residents living here are eight or ten years older than he is. Half the women residents of Cooper Greens can look back on their eightieth birthday. How many would fess up to it though, is problematic. Generally, the women living here will not own up to their age until they're into their nineties. But then they bring it up at every opportunity.

Higgins was hired out of college by Pittsburgh-based Westinghouse, Inc., and shortly afterward he was transferred to a company plant in Meadville that manufactured industrial furnaces. That was sometime in the early seventies, as Hack recalls. Westinghouse eventually pulled out of Meadville and Hack had no idea of what Higgins did for a living afterwards. Until Hack became too old, he bowled, golfed, and played baseball in the County League, and their paths never crossed. Maybe Higgins was a model railroad enthusiast, or maybe he built tri-mast schooners inside champagne bottles.

Yesterday Hack lost two chess games to Carl; today he is winning. Yesterday was April 15th, income tax day, which at Cooper Greens passes quietly. Not long after Hack opened his first IRA, he moved his savings into another account. Technically, he did not roll the account over, and for his unfamiliarity with IRS jargon, he paid through the nose in taxes. IRS judges, Hack also learned the hard way, are covert, card-carrying members of the Judge Roy Bean Fraternal Organization of Egocentric, "Law west of the Pecos," adjudicators.

"It's your move," Hack says to Higgins for the second time.

Losing the game, Carl is taking long minutes between moves. When Hack woke up this morning his left knee was throbbing in time to a drum beat that reminded him of JFK's funeral procession. Advil did not help, and his patience is thin as gold-plating on the counter-displayed jewelry of "Big Box" stores.

"We're not playing Parcheesi," Carl replies.

Hack sighs loudly and stands up. "I need a Coke. You want one?"

Vaguely aware that he has been asked a question, Higgins indifferently shakes his head. When Hack returns, the board is exactly as it was when he left.

"Where'd you move?" Hack says, pretending he had failed to notice that Higgins had not touched a piece.

Higgins does not answer.

Hack begins whistling, and before long he is mashing together parts of two or three melodies, as he sometimes does, in a way that would befuddle, if not out and out bore, a jazz aficionado. A few seconds of Hack's incongruent whistling and Carl gives him a mean look, which Hack's concentration on the game prevents him from seeing. Carl eventually moves his remaining rook to a defensive position. Hack stops whistling, and immediately dusts Higgins' rook with his knight, putting Higgins' king in check.

"Your move," Hack says, as if Higgins was not paying attention. Hack resumes whistling.

Higgins studies the board for another five minutes, his brow furrowed deep enough to hold a pencil.

Hack stops whistling and shakes his head. "Your position's untenable," he says.

Hack is rubbing it in. "Untenable" is another of Higgins' favorite hoity-toity chess-playing words.

Higgins does not answer. Hack spots the TV remote lying on the window sill, retrieves it, and clicks on the TV. Hack stares down another of Higgins' dirty looks, but seconds later Hack turns off the TV.

"I just can't . . ." Higgins begins, expecting Hack to infer from his weepy voice that a healthy Carl Higgins would not be losing the game.

"Would you mind putting the set away?" Higgins says, backing onto the bed and winding into his usual fetal curl.

"Not at all," Hack replies congenially.

[21]

Kitty, visiting Hack in his room, is asking him biographical questions for an article about his upcoming birthday that she will compose for the monthly *Cooper Thymes* newsletter. The Thymes is the home's eight-page newsletter. All residents get their birthdays written up in *Cooper Thymes* – albeit occasionally too late to be appreciated, except, maybe, retrospectively by relatives. Hack considered asking Kitty if her questionnaire included a line for recording vitals, like pulse rate, but Kitty is serious about her write-ups and he was afraid she'd bolt the room in a huff.

"Do you prefer Tom, Tommy, or Thomas?" Kitty began.

Hack does not think of himself as a newsworthy person, birthday or not, and he is hard-pressed to respect the seriousness of her questions. "I prefer Tom, straight" he answers, "no letter h."

Kitty heavily pens the name "Thom Murtaugh" on the top line of her Xeroxed interview form where Hack can easily see it.

"And," she continues, "you'll be seventy-one on May third?"

"Sixty-one. How old are you, Dear?"

Naturally Kitty does not answer Hack's question, but Carl Higgins, who has not stirred until this moment, rolls toward them. "You know, Tom, you and I are almost the same age."

"Baloney!" Kitty blurts out. "He's blowing smoke, Carl. Tom will be eighty-one on May third."

Higgins rolls back toward the TV.

Kitty says to me, "You've lived at Cooper Greens since . . . ."

"I was committed on February eighth. Nineteen ninety-eight."

Kitty writes down the date. "Born?" she asks, her eyes intently on Hack's face.

"Indeed. And it didn't take a cruel slap on the butt to start my engine, either."

She sighs despairingly and looks away.

"In Meadville, at the City Hospital . . . as it used to be called."

"Hometown?"

Kitty, as Hack is answering, prints, SL, the letters standing for the borough of Snow Lake.

"Where did you live before settling in Snow Lake?"

"There was never a 'before Snow Lake,' Dear," Hack says.

Barely audible, Kitty says, "Explaining why you're such a bumpkin."

Kitty stops writing and gathers herself. "Vocation? I need to put down something like, oh, that you used to clean sheep pens, serviced portable toilets, uh . . . et cetera. That's assuming you weren't an idler all your adult life. Were you?"

Hack tilts his head up and feigns a look of superiority. "If you can't spell 'tool and die-maker,' Dear, write 'machinist'. But, I truly was a tool and die-maker."

Kitty carefully prints the words "tool and die-maker," and then looks expectantly at Hack.

"Bonded, of course," Hack says, nodding with certitude.

Kitty hesitates.

Hack notices and adds, "In fact, I was retired as a milling-machine laureate. All my trade magazines are addressed to Mister Thomas Murtaugh, Machinist Emeritus. You never noticed?"

Kitty scribbles something on her form. "Hun-uh, never."

"Let me see," Hack says, but she twists away.

"Out of curiosity, Thomas, why didn't you stick with baking?" Kitty's manner is somber.

For thirty-four years, Hack's parents owned a bakery. They opened it when Hack was eleven and sold it when they were in their mid seventies – some twenty years after Hack had left for fewer hours and greener pastures.

Hack answerd pointedly. "Because baking is damn hard work. And low paying. Ask one. Ask any baker. It's also dirty work. It's not–"

Kitty scoffs. "Dirty?"

"That's right, *Dear*. Baking is like mining coal. The flour dust, I mean. You *have* to shower after working every shift."

"I wouldn't know," Kitty says.

Hack nods. "You've watched a bird take a dust bath? That's exactly how it is. In a real bakery. Commercial baking is nothing like one of those . . . ding-a-ling cooking programs that you watch."

"Only–" Kitty begins, but Hack does not let her interrupt his whining about baking, as he knew she would.

When Hack finally peters out, Kitty says, "Didn't sleep well last night, huh, Thomas?"

"Like a baby," Hack says. "Only . . . remembering those miserably hot summer nights working at our bakery I am reliving bad times."

Kitty briefly considers Hack's reply, and then she asks, "Hobbies? When you're not reading tawdry novels?"

"Ping Pong. Table tennis. I could as easily be answering your questions in Chinese."

Kitty shows Hack a raised, skeptical eyebrow, and Hack explains that Chinese table-tennis players are the best in the world.

"You *know* what my favorite hobby is," Hack says, grinning.

"Yes," Kitty says, "I do. But I expected that you'd name something you're good at."

"You are cruel, woman," Hack says. "Put down . . . oh hell, say, watching baseball on TV."

Kitty nods, pens something, and, as if reading her own words, says aloud: "Hooked on soaps."

Hack pleads: "Anything but that."

Kitty stops writing. "That'll do it," she says cheerily.

"What'd you get me for my birthday?" Hack asks.

"The usual. A snot rag cut with pinking shears from a burlap sack."

While Hack is trying to think of a witty reply, Kitty says, "I see you're reading one of Tom Wolfe's latest." She is looking at a pocket book lying on Hack's dresser.

Two days ago, while Hack was sitting in the lobby reading a *USA Today* newspaper, a woman left a grocery bag of pocket books with Molly, Cooper Greens' receptionist, and Wolfe's novel, *The Bonfire of the Vanities,* was on top. Being in mint condition, and self-advertised as a number-one New York Times best seller, Hack snitched it for his private, bottom-dresser-drawer library.

"I just started it." Hack answers, "Have you read it?" Hack figures she has, or she would not have mentioned seeing it.

"No. But I've read several of his books. What do you think? So far?"

"It's interesting," Hack answers unenthusiastically. "But . . . he's not too smooth."

Kitty practically shouts a rebuttal. "Not smooth! Wolfe's in a class with Oates."

"If you say so," Hack mumbles.

"Not just me. Everyone who has ever read . . . . Read some of his other books."

Hack opens *The Bonfire of the Vanities* to a page where he had seen a list of Wolfe's published works.

Hack says, his eyes on the list, "Like, *The Electric Kool-Aid Acid Test*? What in the hell is that all about?"

Kitty answers dismissively. "The sixties California acid scene."

"Acid scene?"

Kitty explains that *The Electric Kool-Aid Acid Test* is a book about a group of Ken Kesey acolytes who set out to convert the masses to the religion of LSD. Kesey, Kitty reminds Hack, wrote *One Flew Over the Cuckoo's Nest*.

"I saw the movie," Hack says.

"You'd like Wolfe's Electric Kool-aid book," Kitty says crossing her arms authoritatively.

Hack promises to read *The Electric Kool-Aid Acid Test*, adding, "Provided, for a whole month, you don't lecture me on my literary inadequacies."

"Uh huh, and if you don't read it, don't plan on receiving anything from me on your birthday. If you get my drift."

Hack makes a big thing of agreeing to forthwith read Kesey's *The Electric Kool-Aid Acid Test*. "Hell," he says frowning sternly, "I'll write a book report if you want."

Kitty shakes her head, wordlessly scans her notes, and then begins writing at the bottom of her questionnaire. She finishes, reads the lines to herself, and then says, "Would you like to hear this?"

"I doubt it," Hack answers. "Yes," he adds. "Yes, please."

"Under the heading Birthdays," Kitty begins: "Tom Finbar Murtaugh on May 3rd. Tom has lived at Cooper Greens since April of 1998. A retired machinist, Tom, when he's not playing pinochle or chess, likes to watch sports on TV. Visit Tom in room B1006, and wish him a Happy Seventy-First Birthday."

"Barely adequate," Hack says nodding. "And cross out Finbar.'

"Too late,"Kitty says, putting away her notes. "Besides, 'Finbar" gives you stature, like a kind of cheap monogrammed breast-pocket hanky."

Kitty shuffles the forms on her clipboard, and says that she also has to interview a caregiver named

Patricia. Hack asks her if he knows Patricia, and she says probably not as Patricia is a decent sort who is not inclined to socialize with low-brows. "Besides," Kitty adds, "you're way too old – I'd say, four times her age."

Hack knows he has been set up, but he asks anyway. "How old is she?"

Kitty smirks. "One fourth your age."

Kitty leaves Hack's room, and Higgins asks, "How old are you Tom, really?"

Hack hears an irresistible straight line. "Well, that depends. You know, of course that a person's organs all age at different rates. My skin is sixty-one, but my brain's eighty-one. My prostate is somewhere in between. My kidneys are on unsure footing. I'd be surprised to learn that my liver is even still alive. It turns out that on the average I'm seventy one."

"That's about what I guessed," Carl says peevishly turning back to his TV program.

Cooper Greens, as usual when circumstances permitted, celebrated both Patricia Halsaver's birthday and Hack's at lunch on the same day, the fourteenth, a Friday. Small squares of a homemade, decorated cake were handed out. An ensemble of four dining room aides gathered between the tables where Patricia and Hack were sitting and sang the *Happy Birthday* song, finishing on words to the effect that we at Cooper Greens should also enjoy many more. Kitty softly added, after the Aides' emphatic ending line, "Happy birthday to you," the rhyming line, "You've become an old fool."

Kitty was right: Hack thoroughly enjoyed reading *The Electric Kool-Aid Acid Test*. Next he read *Radical Chic* and *Mau-Mauing the Flak Catchers*, two more of Wolfe's thirty-year-old books. Kitty dug them up. Had he finished reading *Radical Chic*, Tom Wolfe, not George Orwell, would have been his favorite author. Anyone, he reasoned, who could put down the "Beautiful People" of New York as slick as Wolfe did was copacetic in his book. Hell, he reflected, who doesn't feel concern for the unfortunate? Trumpets should sound every time someone stuffs a half-buck in a Salvation Army kettle? Hack begins to think that "Mason Dixon" is not a dirty Protestant expression after all, that unpublicized charity is not an evil tenant of depraved Masons, as he had always believed. Luoma, Hack knew, would have erected a shrine to Tom Wolfe.

[22]

Carl and Hack, chatting breezily in their room, are waiting for Higgins' wife to arrive and drive Carl home. Marie, and a Cooper Greens' physical therapist, stopped by earlier and wished Carl well.

Carl still drags one foot, and his voice sometimes fades. He has begun pronouncing words more clearly, however, and he is no longer the self-pitying kettle-head that he was for three long weeks after he arrived at Cooper Greens. He and Hack stopped playing chess weeks ago. Carl could beat Hack whenever he wanted, and – Hack presumed – the effortless winning bored him.

Clutching a folder to her chest and wearing her customary "ride-em-cowboy" outfit, Carl's wife flounces into the room. Inside the folder are Higgins' discharge papers, Hack assumes, and Hack is briefly depressed by the thought that he will be living the rest of his life, perhaps as long as five years, at Cooper Greens. Denny, one of Buster Mook's men, is waiting outside the door to their room: he will carry Carl's belongings to the car. Carl's wife, Hack decides, judging by the dour expression on her face, is less than delighted at the fact of her husband's discharge.

Hack offers Carl his hand. They shake, say unblushingly that they enjoyed each other's company, and, as dishonestly, promise to keep in touch. Hack watches from the doorway of, what for the moment is his room, until, bobbing along in his wife's backwash, Carl turns onto Maple Street. He does not look back. "So much for a lasting friendship," Hack says to himself.

Hack is soon over being a tiny miffed at Carl's apathy by remembering that he'll get the unencumbered use of his TV set, and that he'll be moving over to what was Carl's side of the room, the bed farthest from the door and nearest the window. Hack could have moved there when Toby was led unceremoniously to Elm Street, only on that afternoon he was so upset at losing Toby's companionship, so down in the dumps, that he could not bring himself to begin rearranging the closet they had shared.

An hour has passed since Carl permanently left Cooper Greens. Hack has moved his belongings in the closet, in the dresser, and so on, to the other side of the room, a deployment for which he knows he will receive static from Marie for not getting permission in advance. He is idly paging through a handsome cruise ship pamphlet, comfortably leaning against the headboard of his new bed – buffered by his pillow and the uncased pillow from Carl's empty bed – when Jackie Lybarger, Cooper Greens' Resident Services Manager, knocks softly on the door. A tall, thin, bony woman of forty or so, Jackie's unfriendly face – her mouth just naturally turns down – utterly belies her good-nature and non-stop high spirits. Hack invites her in., and she greets him warmly by name. She asks, "Can you spare me a minute, Tom?"

Hack looks at the clock on his dresser and frowns uncertainly. "Yeah," he answers after squinting hard for a second at his calendar. "But surely," Hack adds suggestively, "we'll need longer than a *minute*!"

Jackie does not even pretend to be amused at Hack's off-color flirting. "Your next roommate" – she edges forward to where her knees press lightly against the foot of Hack's mattress – "I have a particular person in mind." She smiles warmly.

The word "particular" gets Hack's attention. He assumes she has in mind a man who is somehow handicapped. His assumption, however, does not just miss the bull's-eye, his arrow of conjecture misses the whole target.

Jackie haltingly continues: "Are you . . . do you have any major reservations . . . I mean do you feel strongly about the, ah, the kind of person you room with?"

Some days, as Hack had previously mentioned, he cannot help but interpret an earnest remark as the straight-line of a comedy skit; it dovetails with his knack for concocting wild rumors, which, he is still thinking, will be a big part of his plan to roust Cooper Greens residents out of their blahs.

"Yes indeed," Hack says briskly to Jackie. "I'd much prefer rooming with a young blond, a feisty little chick, say, oh, one-third my age. By the way, how old are you, Jackie?"

Again, Jackie does not laugh at Hack's teasing. She does not get prissy on him either, however. "Oh, wouldn't you know it," she says, mockingly serious. "Cooper Greens no longer takes in young blond applicants."

"Okay then," Hack says, "how about a spiffy young redhead?"

Jackie's grin returns. "No sir. That's out . . . the red tape and all."

Surprised at her quick wit, Hack grins and nods his esteem.

"Brunettte?"

"Sorry, Sir, I can't help you there either . . . browns off Mister Harris."

"That's okay," Hack says, smiling again at Jackie's quick intellect, "he'd take a month explaining why she was inadmissible."

Jackie seems not to realize that Hack is making fun of Harris' stuttering, and he is grateful of that.

Hack flexes his Groucho Marx eyebrows. "Then, how about *you* moving in with me, Jackie?"

"Now that," Jackie says, "is *really* funny. The last I heard there are eight applicants signed up for admission. No, seriously, Tom, I'm here to . . . . What would you say to sharing your room with an African-American?"

Her question catches Hack totally off guard. He doubts if two hundred families of Negroes live in all of Crawford County, and not since he was in the Air Force had he spoken at length with a black person. When he played baseball, the opposition would sometimes field a black player, and he and Hack would half-heartedly nod at each other in passing. But for the last forty-odd years, that was Hack's intercourse of verbal exchange with a black person.

Hack's folks were not bigots. They passively disapproved of racial injustice, the same as most white folks, and they raised Hack and Danny to believe they were not superior to anyone, racially or otherwise.

Still, Hack was no John Brown when it came to defending the rightful place of blacks in Crawford County society. And he had passed on his share of crude jokes about Baptist preachers who over-imbibed, Rabbis who squeezed a nickel until the buffalo peed, and blacks involved in harebrained schemes that failed hilariously. Hack drew the line at jokes about nuns. In fact, he went to fist-city with some Protestant bastard over a man's joke casting a nun as a convivial sodomizing machine. A big guy stepped between the two of them and stopped the fight, but the Protestant horse's ass got the point.

Hack had never forgotten overhearing a fellow airman, a boy from West Virginia, say that he never met a nigger he didn't like but couldn't stomach niggers. It was a while before Hack caught on to what he meant. Whether they conceded it or not, Hack supposed that the bias of American whites was summed up in that airman's seemingly impromptu remark – the degree of prejudice of most white men anyway.

"I'm not sure," Hack answers Jackie meekly. He steps back to where he can sit on the edge of his bed. "Who . . . I mean, what's his name?"

"Aaron Blodgett."

The name Blodgett means nothing to Hack does not even tinkle a bell, and he shakes his head.

"I doubt you know him, Tom," Jackie says. "Mr. Blodgett was born in Meadville, but his parents moved to Philadelphia while he was a child. He retired from the Bendix Corporation in York."

"York, Pennsylvania? What'd he do there?"

"He was a technician, electronics I think. He's a widower, the same as you."

"How old is he?"

"Your age, seventy one." Jackie studies Hack's face and slowly nods. "But he looks *much* younger."

Distracted by the crux of her message, Hack barely catches her gibe. "He'll be the home's only black," Hack muses. "Won't he?"

"Yes, but not the first ever. Two Africa-American women lived here before I was hired in."

Hack takes in that news. "Did Kitty know them?"

Jackie nods. "She said they were both really lovely human beings."

"Sounds like Kitty. Is he . . . just elderly? I mean, how's his health?"

Incapable of automatically agreeing to the possibility of living out the rest of his life with a black-skinned, burr-headed man, whom he'd never even seen or heard of, Hack plays for time.

"He's diabetic," Jackie says. "Type two. He does not have to take shots."

She waits for Hack's next question, which, ignorant of the seriousness of Type II diabetes, Hack is unable to formulate. "Where's his family?" Hack says finally.

"His wife died last November, and he's been living alone ever since. They had five children, all girls. The youngest will be helping me with his admission. They live in Philadelphia. He moved back after his wife died."

"How did he happen to hear of Cooper Greens?"

"He was born in Meadville. And he was referred here by a cousin who lives in Meadville, a person related to one of the two women who used to live here."

Jackie waits while Hack considers her answers.

"What did you say his name was?"

Jackie tells Hack again, and he says, skeptically, "I don't remember any blacks from around here named Blodgett."

"He seems very nice; he certainly dresses nice."

Hack nods slowly, sighing as he does. Women, he tells Jackie, can no more judge the heart and soul of men than men can judge the heart and soul of women. "If I've learned anything in life," Hack adds, "it's the truth of that."

Jackie shrugs tolerantly. "I suppose your right." She does not budge from her anchor position at the foot of Hack's bed.

"Oh hell," Hack says finally. "Why not? If it doesn't work out . . . . When would he move in?"

"Tomorrow morning."

"Damn! You don't want me thinking it over, do you?"

"It's not that, Mr. Murtaugh. But I'll come back if you want more time. I need to know today, though."

"No reservations," Hack says after a good 10 seconds.

But in truth Hack does have reservations, doubts, anyway, not the least of which concern Mister Blodgett's hygienic routine. It is, however, a reaction – Hack's initial reluctance to a black man becoming his roommate – which he would come to think back on with colossal self-disgust.

[23]

Hack, after eating breakfast, scrounged the *Beacon* from a lobby sofa and caught up with yesterday's sports events while sitting on his bed. Outside it is cool, for the last week of April. The sky is cloudless, nevertheless, and the room is bathed in sunlight filtering through the window's Venetian blind. Yesterday, Denny, one of Buster Mook's men, dusted the blind, waxed and buffed the floor, washed the window inside and out, and touched up whatever else he was responsible for wiping down. Housekeeping always keeps our rooms spruced up.

Jackie Lybarger knocks lightly on Hack's door and simultaneously waves Aaron Blodgett into the room. The last time Hack checked – all of five minutes earlier – it was ten thirty-five. Nodding at his two visitors, he pushed himself off the bed, and stepped into his walker.

Blodgett, Hack estimates, is five-foot six-inches tall, if that. His hair matches in color and outline the well-trimmed burr of the distinguished-looking Negro shill on a box of "Uncle Ben's Rice." His complexion is more the mahogany of a sun-darkened Mexican fieldhand than the indisputable black of a simon-pure son of Africa. Glasses that darken in strong light shield his eyes. His salt-and-pepper eyebrows are full but not to where they would be called bushy. He is wearing a navy blue sports coat, a light-blue knit sports shirt, a pair of gray trousers with creases that would nick a bar of steel, argyle socks, and well-shined loafers. Hack is thinking that *he* sure as hell never looked as neat, that Blodgett could be modeling clothes in a Brooks Brothers Store front window.

Jackie, after introducing the two men to each other, tells Aaron that Hack has been a resident of Cooper Greens for over a year.

"Well over a year," Hack says to Aaron, smiling in a way to make it clear he is not complaining.

Some blacks, Hack learned while he was in the Air Force, are disinclined to initiate a handshake with a white man, so he makes his way to within an arm's length of his new roommate and offers his hand.

Blodgett smiles, sets the suitcase he's carrying on the floor, and firmly clasps Hack's hand. It is a large paw, Hack notices, not one accustomed to hard manual labor but not puffy soft either. Blodgett's teeth are perfectly aligned, and Hack is reminded of a piano's plastic white keys. "Pleased to meet you, Thomas," Blodgett says smiling.

Hack returns Blodgett's smile and releases his grip. "Make it Tom," he says.

Blodgett's smile lessens. "I don't have a nickname," he says. "I was Ron in grade school, but Aaron in high school. And that's what I've been ever since. My middle name is Horace, but I never liked it."

Hack nods and says softly, "Aaron Horace Blodgett." Louder he says, "are you from around here, Aaron?" Of course Hack already knows that Aaron is from Philadelphia, but as he intended it is a neutral, friendly question.

Blodgett repeats the gist of what Jackie had told Hack yesterday, and Hack nods earnestly, as if hearing the essence of Blodgett's answer for the first time. When Blodgett finishes, he asks Hack where he was from.

"The borough of Snow Lake, Hack answers. "It's twenty miles south of here." Naturally Blodgett has never heard of Snow Lake, and Hack concisely describes both the borough and the lake itself.

After Hack mentions several particulars about the lake, their conversation stalls and Jackie, gesturing at my old bed, says, "This will be your bed, Aaron. Do you mind if I call you Aaron? We generally go by first names here at Cooper Greens."

"No, not at all," Aaron says, turning her way. "It looks comfortable."

"If you like sleeping on a straw tick," Hack says. Then he quickly adds, "I'm only kidding, Aaron. The beds here are just fine, perfect for old bones."

Jackie tells Aaron that most times he would do

well to ignore Hack. She says, "Can I fetch you anything, Aaron?"

Aaron looks around and then says, "My other bag. And my–"

Jackie interrupts him. "The rest of your belongings are with Jolene in my office. I'm going right back to help her complete your paper work. We'll bring everything here."

Aaron nods amiably. Jackie leaves and Aaron hoists his suitcase onto his bed. While he's opening it, Jackie flashes Hack a questioning look. Hack shrugs in a way that he hopes eases her mind.

Hack says to Aaron, "I think you'll like it here. I mean . . . not that it's Camelot. But . . . you know what I mean."

Aaron's good-natured smile returns. "Well, I didn't expect that Cooper Greens would be the Shining City on a Hill." Just audibly, in an offhand way, he adds, "'Home is home, be it ever so humble.'"

"I guess so," Hack says. He favorably recalls Aaron's "Home is home" remark several days later, when he knows Aaron better.

Hack returns to his bed, makes a show of folding the USA Today newspaper to his liking, and pretends to read it.

Aaron, after opening, slowly inspecting, and then quickly closing every drawer of his dresser, begins unpacking. He carefully positions several articles on the top of his dresser, including a large white Bible with gold lettering on the cover and a yellow ribbon page-marker. He holds up a long-sleeved sport shirt and peers at our closet.

Looking at Hack, after turning enough that his movement catches Hack's attention, Hack says, pointing, "That's your half."

Our closets are not partitioned, and they are closed-off by sliding doors that overlap when one side is open. A one-inch wooden dowel, divided lengthwise exactly in the center by a narrow white painted stripe, runs the length of the closet just under the hat shelf. It used to be, I was told by Marie, that when the center of the dowel was marked by a piece of white adhesive tape, Buster Mook, almost monthly, had to settle a dispute between roommates over the placement of the adhesive tape, which seemed to migrate several inches one way or the other on its own. The shelf, solidly installed a few inches above the hanger dowel, is also plainly divided in the middle by a painted stripe.

Aaron opens his side of the closet and visually checks it over.

"Not all that big, is it?" Hack says, bearing out the obvious.

"I'll never be able . . ." Aaron begins. He does not finish his sentence.

Hack decides right away against offering Blodgett the foot or so of his half of the closet that he is not using. Two days later, he changes his mind.

"Some of us," Hack says, "don't completely

unpack. You can leave your suitcase on the shelf. If you want. Or Cooper Greens will store it. I gave my luggage to the Salvation Army." Hack stops himself from telling Aaron that his gift consisted of two barely reinforced, faux canvass suitcases.

Aaron hangs up four long-sleeved shirts, four short-sleeved shirts, a solid tan cardigan sweater, and a sporty green and white nylon wind-breaker, shaded exactly the same color, Hack decides, as the uniforms of Philadelphia's NFL football team. Then he begins filling his dresser drawers with underwear, socks, and handkerchiefs. From the middle of a stack of T-shirts he withdraws a large, gold-framed picture, studies it for several seconds, and heaves a long sigh before standing it upright on the top of his dresser. He turns back to his suitcase, to where Hack can see the picture. It is a photographic portrait of a family of seven whose matriarch is ornated with the mother of all noses, a bullfrog squatting right in the middle of her kisser.

Hack is pleased to see Aaron remove a cribbage board and two decks of playing cards.

Last, Aaron carefully aligns three pairs of shoes, facing in, on the floor on his side of the closet. Each pair is polished and stiffened with shoe trees. One pair, Hack sees later, is actually expensive-looking leather slippers.

Jackie, when she returns, is accompanied by Aaron's daughter. Jolene is lighter skinned and taller than her father. Hack estimates that she is almost his height (out of heels), making her around five-feet seven-inches tall. There is no doubting the fact that she is a true child of Aaron's wife, however. Her dress, belted and plain but definitely not cheap, has a turtle neck top and falls to several inches above her knees. It is a length and style, Hack decides, that is more fashionable in Philadelphia than around these parts. Hack makes Jolene out to be thirty-five years old, give or take a year. Jackie, at some point, had mentioned that she was Aaron's youngest.

Draped over Jolene's right arm, still attached to hangers, are a top coat, a rain coat, and a dress suit. Later, after energetically making room, she hangs those items up, one by one, in Aaron's half of the closet. It occurs to Hack while watching Jolene man-handle her father's clothes, that if her mother at one time was similarly constructed then Aaron must be a leg-and-butt man.

Jackie sets down her freight, a small, blue, duck-cloth bag, and introduces Hack to Jolene. Hack did not catch Jolene's last name, but he could tell it was not Blodgett. Hack is surprised when she unhesitatingly steps to where he is standing braced inside his walker and offers her hand. "Call me Jolly," she says. Winking, she adds, "And Daddy cheats at cribbage, so don't play him for money."

"Jolene!" Aaron cries. "You don't even know this gentleman. You shouldn't be saying stuff like that!"

Hack returns Jolene's wink. "That's probably why

he's wearing those shades," he says, "to cover shifty eyes."

Jolene slightly grins and nods indecisively. "Oh, Father," she says, "he knows I'm only funning. Don't you, Tom?"

Hack pretends to give Aaron a slow once-over. "Anyway, I'll keep my guard up."

Jackie asks Jolene to stop by her office before leaving. Jolene, who has begun fussing with her father's arrangement of his dresser-top items, says that she will, and Jackie briskly heads for her next destination.

"Now just what are you doing, child," Aaron demands as soon as Jackie leaves.

"This," Jolene mutters, "will never work, Daddy."

Hack cannot see what "this" is, but he sees that Jolene's arms are moving in and out and left and right as if she's setting places for a fancy sit-down dinner.

Aaron and Jolene continue to bicker. Afraid that he might be asked to rule on a father-daughter difference of opinion, Hack decides to leave. "If I don't see you again," Hack says to Jolene at the doorway, "have a safe trip home."

Jolene turns away from her father and says, "Nice to have met you, Tom. Please see to it that this old fool takes his medicine."

"My pleasure," Hack says, flashing Jolene a wide grin.

[24]

Hack, excited, is breathing hard when he reaches Kitty's room. She is chatting with Yvon Chafee, however, whose presence drains his enthusiasm. He mumbles a greeting of sorts. Yvon, sitting on the room's unused bed with her back to the door, turns and says, "I'm just leaving, Tom."

"It's okay," Hack says. I'll stop back later."

"No, really, we're done." Yvon rises and looks to Kitty for permission to leave.

Kitty slightly shakes her head. "No hurry, Vonnie."

Yvon, apparently deciding that Kitty's reply is counterfeit, turns and walks rapidly from the room. Hack plops down where she was sitting on the room's unassigned bed, which, for a good reason, has not been occupied since Hack moved in – that good reason being that Kitty's last roommate caught Kitty performing oral sex on her husband. Kitty and her roommate fought, and Kitty nicked the woman on her shoulder with a pair of scissors. Marie told Hack about it. The woman's husband was bootlegging screwdrivers – orange juice fortified with jiggers of vodka – to Kitty. That is all Marie would tell Hack.

"She seemed in a hurry to leave," Hack says to Kitty, cocking an eyebrow.

Kitty understands Hack's suspicion and shakes her head. "Yvon doesn't know about us. At least, no more than anyone else. Not from anything I've said."

Kitty, while Hack is mulling over her profession, says, "I hear you have a new roomie."

"How'd you come to know?" Hack asks stiffly, disappointed that she already knows about Aaron, that she did not first hear of Aaron from him.

Hack has insulted Kitty. "Oh, c'mon, Tom! How do you think I found out?"

"I wasn't thinking," Hack mumbles. "What else do you know about my new *roomie*?"

"I know he's an African-American."

"Ah. But, do you know his name?"

"Of course. It's Blodgett, Aaron Blodgett."

Hack pretends to weigh her answers. "So, Aaron's race is more important to you than his name?"

Kitty thinks of herself as a liberal of incontestable bona fides, and Hack's remark touches a nerve.

"No, of course not," Kitty snaps. "Put it in context, Thomas."

Hack frowns thoughtfully. "I'd have given his name first."

"Really, Thomas? I hadn't noticed a halo around your head today."

Hack decides a wise-ass rejoinder is not in his best long-term interest. "What else do you know about Aaron?"

Kitty's look softens. "Well . . . he's not very tall."

"He's a runt, a dwarf. What else?"

"I hear that he's the second coming of Cyrano de Bergerac."

Kitty means that Aaron is an adventurous romantic, but Hack thinks she is alluding to Cyrano's big honker. "Hell, you ought to see his wife," Hack says.

Kitty scowls and shakes her head uncertainly. "His cousin used to live here. That was before your time. His roots are in Meadville."

Smelling a rat, Hack says, "You're behind this, aren't you, Catherine Proctor? Jackie moving Aaron in with me?"

Kitty shrugs. "I was asked . . . ."

"Christ, Kitty," Hack says, "that was damned . . . you never thought to check with me first?"

"I did indeed. Oh, for a . . . long second. But then, I said to myself, 'Up ol' Thomas Murtaugh's bazoo.'"

"You would. Suppose, Aaron's gay?"

"It wouldn't break *my* heart," she says grinning. "Besides, I know better."

"How do you know better?"

"Know what better?"

"How do you know Aaron doesn't like men better than women?"

"He was married, and he has five kids." Kitty, after a moment, adds, "Besides, I laid his little black ass. And I'll tell you Thomas, Aaron could humble Man of War."

"No you didn't," Hack says, shaking his head.

"Didn't what?"

"Didn't give Aaron a boff."

"Oh? How do you know?"

"That's easy. If you did, you went back."

Kitty either does not understand or pretends she doesn't.

Hack says, "Ain't that what all you white swingers say, 'Go black and you'll never go back'?"

"I made an exception with you," Kitty says. "I was desperate. Stuck here in Cooper Greens and all."

"Uh-huh," Hack mumbles weakly.

Neither Hack nor Kitty speaks for a few seconds. "Help me up," Kitty says finally. "I have to pee."

Hack hobbles to a place alongside Kitty's recliner and offers his hand. Hack's assistance, as they both knew it would be, is more a well-meant gesture than real help. Kitty busses Hack lightly as she edges past.

"I gather I've been invited to leave," Hack says as Kitty closes the bathroom door.

"It's almost five o'clock," she answers loudly through the closed door. "Supper time."

"They serve supper here from five to six," Hank says to Aaron, returning his greeting. Aaron, sitting on the edge of his bed playing solitaire, is now wearing a knit, short-sleeve shirt and starched cotton work trousers.

Hack gestures at the TV. "Turn it on whenever you want. The controller's on the window sill. I always leave it there. I don't watch much TV. Sports. We can eat together, or . . . you know. Whatever you'd prefer."

"Good," Aaron says, nodding, "Jackie walked me past the dining room, but I've forgotten the way back."

"Whenever you're ready," Hack says. "I don't eat but a little at night, a snack. We're not served much. Soup and a half sandwich, so any time's okay with me."

"Shoot," Aaron says, rising and gathering the cards. "This hand's down the tubes anyway. Is there a dress code for dining?"

Our room is darker now, the lenses of his glasses are more nearly transparent, and for the first time Hack distinctly sees his eyes. His right eye is on Hack's face, but his left eye is angled severely inward.

"Yeah," Hack says after an embarrassing moment of speechlessness. "No shirt, no shoes, no service."

Aaron smiles. It is a slight, wry smile, suggesting, Hack decides, that his momentary awkwardness did not go unnoticed. "I'll wash my hands," Hack says.

Aaron leaves the bathroom. Hack bumbles his way into it, runs a little water on his hands, and they head for the dining room.

"You follow Philly baseball?" Hack asks, as they are trudging along. "I'm a Cleveland Indians fan."

"Not for some time," Aron says. "I used to go to a half dozen games every summer, but . . . I don't know, it became too big a hassle. And the Philly faithful are something else."

"As ill-mannered as Yankee fans," Hank says shaking his head deprecatingly.

Aaron agrees. "Yes, and they get more obstreperous every year."

"Get more– Hack begins, before Aaron cuts him off.

"Louder," Aaron says.

Hack slowly nods. "Though you have to admit, the Yankees are a hell of a team."

"The highest payroll in baseball," Aaron says.

Hank glances ahead to confirm that the man he glimpsed a second earlier waddling toward them is Bob Ford. Kitty introduced Hack to Ford some months ago, but they had never socialized. A thin, round-shouldered man, with hollow, blood-shot eyes, his gaze is glued to the floor. He is dressed as if the indoor temperature is in the fifties, hoping, Hack supposes, that people won't notice he is wearing a diaper, of sorts, under his pants. Luoma always addressed Ford as Ahab: "How's Ahab of the Yukon doing?" he would ask loudly whenever their paths crossed. "Keeping your powder dry?"

"That's Bob Ford," Hack whispers to Aaron, "the guy who shot Jesse James in the back."

Aaron barely nods, and Hack realizes the name Jesse James means nothing to him. "There was a movie . . . ." Hack begins, but he lets his voice die out.

They close to within ten feet of Ford, and Hack calls out his name. Ford is surprised, bewildered, and annoyed, in that order. "Bob," Hack says, "I'd like you to meet Aaron Blodgett. Aaron's my new roommate."

Ford nods but does not offer his hand.

Aaron smiles, not his glittering, white piano-keys smile, but a passable show of ivory. "I didn't get your last name, Bob," he says.

Ford's gaze slides from Aaron to Hack and then back to the floor. Finally he says, "It's Ford."

Aaron nods. His smile has disappeared. "I'm pleased to meet you."

"You're living here now?" Ford asks brusquely. The intonation of his question demands that Aaron answer him.

"I moved in today."

"Well, I'm on an errand," Ford says. He waddles past, giving us plenty of room.

After a few steps, Hack tells Aaron that Bob Ford is an irreversibly smelly little cunt – a personal quality of Ford's that Hack had just a moment ago found out.

After a few seconds Aaron says, "He's envies my height. I guess."

Hack disdainfully says to Aaron, "Exactly."

Turning onto Poplar Street, the two men nearly collide with Emma Pankhurst, Kitty's odoriferous, orange-haired pal, and two other women residents whom Hack does not know by name.

Pankhurst is ecstatic. "Oh, Tom!" she squeals. "I bet this is Aaron! I'm Emma Pankhurst!" She offers Aaron a chubby pink hand. "Only, please, Aaron, call me Panky! Everyone does." She withdraws her hand and waves it dismissively, as if to say "But why all this formality?"

Aaron nods, verifying his name.

Pankhurst's eyes, when she introduces her companions, never leave Aaron, and it is unclear which of her friends is June Gongaware and which is Opal Urbanick. Hack bluntly asks, and Pankhurst's feet settle back on the floor again.

June Gongaware, as enchanted at meeting Aaron as Emma Pankhurst, stops pushing her hair from her forehead and offers her hand. Opal Urbanick, whose pleasure at meeting Aaron is no less heartfelt than that of her two companions, offers her hand well before Gongaware turns loose of Aaron's mitt.

"Oh, I do hope you like it here," Gongaware implores excitedly.

"Yes," Urbanick gushes, "we are so happy you decided on Cooper Greens."

Aaron nods and mumbles words to the effect that he's glad to be at Cooper Greens. Seeing that he is less substantial than the shadow of a aged tree, Hack edges away.

Hack reaches Ash Street, which leads to the dining room, before Aaron can break away from the women, but shortly they are walking side by side again.

"Sorry," Aaron says.

"It's not your fault. The new kid on the block thing and all."

Aaron grins. "Somehow, I think it's the 'and all' as much as the 'new kid' business."

"Somehow," Hack says, "I think you're exactly right."

It is almost six o'clock when they reach the dining room, and only a dozen residents, in cliques of twos and threes, sitting at well-separated tables, are still eating. Kitty and Yvon Chafee are casually settled at a table nursing coffee from their personalized mugs. Hack steers Aaron and himself in their direction. As did Panky and her friends, Yvon goes air-headed at the sight of Aaron and acts like a groupie surprised by a rock star.

"Do you play cards, Aaron?" Yvon asks, as her fawning peters out. She cannot take her eyes off his face.

Aaron nods, but Kitty takes up another subject before he can elaborate. Hack keeps his nose out of the conversation, but he pretends to be interested. Eventually it comes out that Aaron favors pinochle over other card games, and Kitty right away schedules a session for two o'clock the next day in the dining room, matching Aaron and Hack against her and Yvon. Kitty, however, insists intractably that they rotate partners each game – determined, Hack knows damn well, that they all share equally in the pain of having Yvon as a teammate.

On the way back to their room, Hank asks Aaron if he played cards often.

"Oh yes," he answers. "It's . . . all we did . . . indoors when I was a youngster."

His answer sets Hack to thinking. When he was a kid, there were three movie theaters in Meadville. The largest, the Park, had two levels of ascending balconies. Blacks were permitted to sit in a half-dozen short rows of seats situated in the second balcony on either side of the projection booth. Those sections were called "Nigger Heaven," which, Hack presumes, was a common designation everywhere back then for that particular seating space in American theaters. Only a few times does Hack remember – once for an Abbot and Costello comedy – seeing any blacks sitting in Nigger Heaven.

Aaron says, "You're pensive, Tom."

"I'm what?"

"You're thinking about something."

Hack slightly lifts his head. "I think a lot. Deeply. It's my nature."

"Sure you do," Aaron says sensing that Hack's melancholy has passed.

"It never occurs to you that I'm thinking?" Hack asks.

A faint smile tweaks Aaron's lips. "It hasn't yet."

[25]

Most of the residents living at Cooper Greens are indifferent to world news, good or bad. Maybe one in eight knows that for over a month the United States and its NATO allies have been steadily bombing a part of Yugoslavia. For most residents, death is much more personal than bombs killing people living in Europe. Nor does the utter destruction of multi-story buildings and scenes of twisted, broken and abandoned vehicles impress residents.

Today, however, a news story is on the lips of every resident who can wobble up to a TV: yesterday, at a high school in Littleton, Colorado, two students shot and killed twelve fellow students and a teacher and then took their own lives.

"The last report," Aaron says glumly, "has the death toll reaching twenty-five."

The four of them, Kitty, Yvon, Aaron, and Hack, are sitting around a table in the dining room where they have met for their first card game.

"Just horrible," Yvon says forlornly.

Of course everybody is deeply troubled by the grisly happening at the high school in Littleton, and they all profusely agree with Yvon.

Kitty and Hack bicker over the reasons why the media's initial reporting of such events exaggerates the body count, but their heart is not in it.

Kitty shoves the box of playing cards toward Aaron. "Your pleasure."

"Kitty," Hack says to Aaron, "is a Constitutional scholar. She thinks it's okay to burn the American flag."

"I do *not* think it is okay," Kitty snaps, flashing Hack a nasty glance. "I just don't think it should be illegal."

"That's shaving it too close for me," Hack says, looking at Aaron.

Kitty and Hack often tangle over political issues. Aaron seems to understand that it is an ongoing squabble, and his dealing slows.

"It's your bid," Kitty says to Yvon.

Yvon finishes making up her hand and asks Kitty a question about an elementary bidding convention. Kitty explains, and Yvon, a puzzled look on her face, says that "skip bidding" has always confused her.

After another long wait, Yvon timidly offers a hefty meld bid. Hack turns toward Aaron and they exchange looks that are a milli-decibel short of audible moans.

Kitty wins the bid, and the women easily win the hand. As if scripted, the scenario is repeated four more times, and Kitty and Yvon win the game going away.

It is almost four o'clock when the first game finally ends – dragged out by Yvon's endless cortege of questions – so they call it a day. They do not leave immediately, however, and right away players from the other games begin shuffling their way. Each player wants to meet Aaron; Lon Fuller, the only male among them, is damn near as tizzy-eyed as the women.

"I hear you're a cribbage player," Fuller bellows at Aaron, all but daring him to not answer. Fuller will not look at either Kitty or Hack, still flustered, apparently, over losing his scuffle with Luoma.

"A dabbler," Aaron replies.

Fuller glowers. "Yeah, I'll bet. We'll get together and play sometime." He tilts his head at Edith. "I just hope you're not as lucky as this woman here."

Edith McGuire, standing alongside Fuller and beaming non-stop at Cooper Greens' newest resident, rolls her eyes but says nothing. Aaron smiles at her and says that he bets luck has nothing to do with it. Edith, lightly touching Aaron's shoulder, giddily assures Aaron that he is right.

On the way back to their room, Aaron asks, "How do you suppose that big fellow, the one with the cane"– Hack interrupts Aaron to tell him that the 'big fellow' was Lon Fuller –"knew I played cribbage?"

"News travels fast on the Cooper Greens' grapevine," Hack says. "Faster than a dirty joke at a convention of public school teachers. The women, in here, could survive longer without oxygen than without gossip."

"Is that so?" Aaron says amiably. "Anyway, I'm hungry."

Hack looks at his wristwatch. "Uh, I'm only eating a candy bar tonight."

It is after six o'clock when Aaron returns from eating. "Make a lot of new friends?" Hack asks from his bed, where he is leaning against the headboard watching TV.

Aaron rolls his eyes dismissively. "I've been invited to play bingo on Wednesdays, join a Bible study group that meets Thursday mornings . . . attend a karaoke sing-along on Fridays, listen to someone read the *Beacon* somewhere at . . . I've forgotten the hour. And–"

"Bingo is big here too," Hack interrupts, frowning as if Aaron had overlooked that ever-popular pastime.

Aaron is unconcerned. "Some of the women living here have it in their head that I'm a great singer. I don't know where they heard *that*."

Hack decides to test the thickness of his new roommate's skin: "Oh, that's just great. Turns out I'm rooming with the only black man in America who ain't got no rhythm. Can't dance, either? I suppose."

Hack is relieved when Aaron smiles.

"You mean, can I cut a rug?" Aaron waits for Hack's reaction to that fossilized slang term for fast dancing.

Hack says, "Is that what they called dancing when you were young?"

"No. I was respecting your memory of when *you* were young. Nope, I can't dance either. But I can easily leap over small buildings . . . garages, tool sheds, gazebos . . . ."

NBC News, returning from a commercial break, has begun reporting on NATO's ongoing bombing of Yugoslavia, and both men turn to watch as targets behind simulated cross hairs – buildings, bridges, vehicles – evaporate in bursts of gray-black billowing clouds. Hack's mind, however, is elsewhere, on the not-so-remote possibility that his new roomy, Mister Aaron

Blodgett, is a closet jokester. Hack decides that time will tell. Thinking back to when he had looked forward to the possibility, slim though Hack knew it was, of Joe Luoma helping him enliven Cooper Greens, his mind tilts heartily toward optimism.

They watch the TV until Tom Brokaw says that NBC's next offering will be a commercial, and Hack says, "So every night after school in Mentor you went back home to Philadelphia?"

Aaron's features take on a sad, thoughtful look, his first really unhappy face that Hack had seen. "On a trolley," Aaron answers softly. "Two different worlds."

"Still it's . . . different now. Isn't it?

Aaron slightly tosses his head. "People are still people. Some . . . but, yeah, a little different."

"Hey," Hack says, "I've thought of something else. Every Saturday we gather in the rec room at seven o'clock to watch reruns of the Lawrence Welk show on our big-screen TV. You sure won't wanna miss one of those hours of really hip music." Hack's pitch is a bit over the top – as if he really feels that way about Welk's music. His false passion sets Aaron to laboring over how to tactfully reply, probably sets him to thinking he'd rather suffer an amputation without anesthesia than sit through a Lawrence Welk offering. Weakly, he says, "I . . . always take it easy on Saturday nights."

Hack lets on his feelings are hurt, but he overdoes it, and Aaron's slight nod and sideways look tells Hack that he intends to get even.

The theme music of the *Wheel of Fortune* TV program comes on, and Hack asks Aaron if he ever watches the show.

"Sometimes. Do you?"

"Once in a while. Kitty likes it. And, speaking of Miss Proctor, I think I'll go see what she's up to. Straighten her out on the Constitutional right of U.S. citizens to bear arms."

Aaron. his mind on the TV program, "*Wheel of Fortune*," does not respond. Pointing at the TV controller on the window sill, Hack tells him to select any channel he wants. Aaron is trying to solve a word puzzle for which the program's designated letter-turner, Vanna White, has turned only two letters, and he barely nods.

A few seconds later Aaron bellows at the TV, "Hot . . . Plate . . . Window!"

"Hot plate window, you dummy," he yells again as the time allowed the contestant, a black man, runs out.

[26]

Kitty, when Hack reaches her room, is standing at the foot of the unassigned bed looking at the doorway. Evidently she heard Hack clomping down the hall. "Where's Aaron?" she asks, leaning to see past Hack.

"And a heartfelt hello to you too," Hack says.

Kitty walks up to Hack, hastily pecks him on the cheek, and says that she's happy to see him.

Hack lightly returns her kiss. "That's a little better. I invited Aaron along. But he said he'd rather spend the morning dragging a plank around the back parking lot."

"Of course he did," Kitty replies. "My nails are drying. Sit down."

Kitty carefully pushes herself onto her bed, then scoots backward until her shoulders are pressed against the headboard. Hack eases into her recliner, kicks off his slippers, and rests his feet on her bed.

"Well, what do you think?" Kitty says inspecting her fingernails.

"Think? About what?"

She gives Hack a surly look. "About the coming earthquake!"

"Oh, you mean . . . ."

As if he had just caught on, Hack enlarges his eyes excitedly and slants his head. "About Aaron? He's okay. So far. Hell, I just met him. What's your impression?"

"He's a little cutey."

"Cutey!" Hack blurts out. "Jesus Christ, Kitty, he's seventy if he's a day."

"Good looks are forever, Dear."

Hack points his chin up and slightly away. "Am I cute?"

Kitty turns again to inspecting her nails. "Not very, Thomas," she says apathetically. She shows Hack her fingernails, expects him to understand that their wetness will hinder their making love.

"Just thinking ahead. Greasing the skids. Verbal way-before-play."

She nods. "Not today. Want to watch TV?"

"Not especially."

"Well . . . want to hold hands by the window and watch the cars whiz by out front?"

"Yes . . . except, what about your fingernails?"

Kitty studies her fingernails again. "Right. We are not getting it on today, Dear."

They hear footsteps in the hall. The pace slows, and a door is opened.

"Probably old man Blair," Kitty says looking slowly around.

"That reminds me," Kitty says, her attention back on her nails. "Did you know Si Bloom?"

Hack reflects: Simon Bloom, a prominent Meadville physician, died last month at ninety-four years of age in Coral Gables, Florida, where he was living in retirement. "Yes, so?"

"He was a damn horse doctor," Kitty says.

"Yeah," Hack says, "I'd heard that he wasn't all that gentle. Anyway . . . I'm going to get bagged before my next prostate scrutiny."

"Think it would help?"

"Maybe. If I pass out before the goosing starts."

"Prostate's still sore, huh?"

"Yes, some. Bonifanti ordered me pills. But the damn side-effect is worse than the cure."

"The side-effect?"

"They make me sick . . . at first."

Kitty mumbles the cliché about the operation being a success but the patient croaking, "I don't know what to tell you," she says.

"That's okay," Hack says. "I've figured it out. Getting the ol' prostate massaged hurts worse than giving birth. I worked it out mathematically."

Kitty all but takes Hack's head off. "Nothing on God's green earth equals the pain of child birth!"

Until that moment Hack thought that Kitty had never delivered a baby. He is not rocked back by her sudden outburst, but he is surprised.

"I had two kids" Kitty says softly. "Both were stillborn."

Like many men, Hack is grossly inept at showing compassion. "I'm sorry," he mumbles finally. "I . . . didn't know."

Kitty stares out the window. "It gave me an excuse to drink. Anyway, that's what I did. The first . . . I blamed the father. I was a child, barely sixteen. Hell, I couldn't stay on the wagon for two kids, let alone one."

"Things usually work out for the best," Hack says insipidly, still groping for words of sympathy.

"Maybe," Kitty agrees. Kitty's eyes are moist. It is a dampness brought on by a melancholy that Hack had never before imagined of Kitty.

"What's on TV?" Hack says, after a long moment of silence.

"I don't know. Do you . . . think I'll . . . get to raise my children in Heaven, Tom?"

Her question stuns Hack. Kitty, as a Believer, is a skeptic, at best. Still, she obviously wants Hack to answer her.

Hack misplays her line-drive question. "Well . . . I, ah, never did too much believe in the significance of receiving the last rites. I mean, regarding . . . infants. I know what the Church says, but . . . I mean, I don't think God has Saint Peter certifying the credentials of the little nippers at the gate."

"It goes to the question of ensoulment, doesn't it?" Kitty asks the question softly more of herself than of Hack. "Christian ensoulment," she adds bemusedly.

"I don't follow," Hack says lifting his head to emphasize his confusion.

Kitty slowly nods. "When do we get our souls? When do we become human beings? That's the test, isn't it? At the instant of conception? After a slap on the butt? At Communion? She again expects Hack to answer.

"Damn, Kitty," Hank says, "you're the theologian, not me. Only God knows."

"You really believe, don't you, Tom?"

"Absolutely."

"I suppose," Kitty says, turning away, "that if your heaven is real . . . is genuine, we'll be adults when we meet up . . . my kids and me."

"I . . . wouldn't know," Hack says shrugging vapidly.

For a while, neither Kitty nor Hack speaks. Sighing, Kitty says, finally, that she's sorry, that she's over "it" now.

"What's to be sorry about?" Hack says. "I'd never be a good bartender is all."

"I could use a drink right now," Kitty says quietly.

"You could use a priest right now," Hack says.

Kitty looks away. After a good ten seconds she turns back, looks past Hack, and says, "You worked out mathematically how the pain of a prostate exam is worse than giving birth?"

"Yep," Hack answers. "Two pi as painful. Over six times worse."

Kitty shakes her head. "You're battier than I am, Thomas."

[27]

Aaron has lived at Cooper Greens four weeks. The first week he and Hack infrequently socialized, but since that first week they've been hanging-out together, non-stop, early morning to late evening.

Usually Hack is ready for breakfast before Aaron, but he is dragging this morning and is anxious for Aaron to finish dressing. "Helen," Hack explains, when Aaron asks Hack if he is feeling all right, "would have been sixty-eight today."

"I wish I had known her," Aaron says shaking his head sympathetically.

"Yeah. So do I wish you had. She'd have liked you . . . overlooked your many faults."

"In a glance," Aaron replies, looking through our window at the lawn outside.

Hack quietly studies him. "She didn't make it to her sixty-second birthday. We had a good marriage. Time is supposed to heal all wounds. Maybe. But the scars remind."

Aaron agrees. "They do," he says. "Would you like me to bring you something from breakfast?"

"Thanks, but . . . just give me another couple seconds and I'll be ready to go with you."

They eat breakfast together and afterwards Hack cuts away to return to their room through the front lobby. The woman who delivers the *Morning Beacon* leaves her extras on a chair sitting just inside the front door. This morning she has left three copies, and Hack takes one copy back to their room. Aaron, when he arrives, is sitting on his bed dealing himself a game of solitaire. He has one leg folded under him and the other dangling off a side edge, knees folded in ways that would leave Hack in tears. Today the *Beacon* consists of only one section, or Hack would offer Aaron the second part, Sports, usually.

Hack climbs onto his bed and scoots backwards against the headboard. Opening the paper to the sports section, he chides Aaron about the Phillies, tells Aaron how they blew another game in the ninth inning. Pretty sure that Hack is only teasing, Aaron indifferently asks Hack to show him.

"Just don't you worry about it," Hack says turning back to the front-page stories.

A couple minutes later Hack gives the screw another turn. "Cleveland won again."

The Cleveland Indians, Hack's team, is off to a fast start, winning every series they've played except a four-game set on the road against the Texas Rangers, which they split.

Hack finishes reading the paper, folds it twice to smaller sizes, and tosses it onto Aaron's bed. Aaron has begun grumbling softly every other breath, a sign he is running out of playable cards. Hack suggests they take their walk.

"In a minute," Aaron says, snatching up the paper and turning to the sports page. After a second, he tosses it back onto his bed. "I know your vision isn't weak. So, it must be your mind."

Molly, our receptionist, is talking on the telephone when Hack and Aaron pass by her station in the front lobby. Her baby was delivered healthy, and she has returned to work. They slow down, but Molly's mind is concentrated on her telephone conversation and she does not look their way.

The temperature, according to the *Morning Beacon*, will reach the low seventies today, but when Hack and Aaron begin their walk, at a few minutes after nine o'clock, it is still cool – chilly around the edges as the women at Cooper Greens liked to say. Aaron, after they take a few halfhearted steps, traces back to their room for jackets.

Buster Mook and two of his men are planting annuals in the little circular plots at the bases of the green, six-foot-high lamp posts lining Cooper Greens' front driveway. The flowers look to be marigolds and begonias but Hack cannot tell for sure from where they are looking. Hack yells at Buster, asks him how he sees summer shaping up.

"Hot and dry!" Buster yells back.

Aaron shouts that the farmers will not like that, and Buster grins and yells, "Cool and wet!"

"Like you know anything about farming," Hack says to Aaron, after they had drifted a piece from where they were opposite Buster and his men.

Aaron tosses his head in a direction away from Hack. "Oh, I don't know about that. When I was growing up–"

Hack interrupts him. "*Up?* When you were growing *up*?"

"One time," Aaron goes on as if he doesn't hear Hack, "I knocked a pot of tulips off the banister of our balcony. Just missed crowning the old woman entering the apartment below. Mama about killed me."

"It'd have been justifiable homicide."

"Probably would have, only Mama and the woman downstairs didn't see eye-to-eye on anything. And Mama wasn't about to make her day."

It has been four weeks since Aaron moved into Cooper Greens, and Hack has not once seen a glimmer of ill-humor distort his looks, except, of course, when he tries to neutralize one of Hack's concocted insults. Sometimes Aaron is all but snubbed by male residents – two that Hack is sure of – but Aaron never lets on. Probably, Hack figures, a practiced reaction. Aaron does not complain about the food, which, to be fair to

Cooper Greens, isn't all that bad – not when you take into account that Cooper Greens' consulting dietician apparently thinks that spice morphs old people into horny youngsters, and that all meat must be either baked or boiled until all sense of flavor has vanished. Aaron loses graciously at cards. He does not bitch about the weather – on a sunny day the temperature of our room would all but incubate a petrified dinosaur egg – or the sometimes lackadaisical attentions of Billie, our daytime aide.

During Hack's whole life, he had built only a few close male friendships, and almost none since sharing the last two years of a four-year hitch in the Air Force with another twenty-one-year-old male. Kitty tells Hack that he has the inclinations of a mountaineer. Mountaineers, she went on, are reclusive. But, then she said that islanders are friendly, gregarious types. Kitty denies it, but Hack is certain that she read that nifty little two-parter somewhere. Kitty is not a stickler about crediting the source of some of her clever sayings.

"So, you never hunted?" Hack says.

Hack's remark, coming out of the blue, surprises Aaron, and he gives Hack a confused look.

Most of the men living in the span of Cooper Greens are nutty about hunting. On the first day of deer season, schools close and most retail businesses in the boroughs shut down at least until mid-afternoon. People who live inside a borough, and happen to be in their home that first morning, expect, every half hour or so, to hear two or three sharp firearm cracks in rapid succession. Men and women rage on about nailing – or missing – a big buck, a big tom (male turkey), etc. Large turkey beards (wattles) are prized and showed off. Badmouth the National Rifle Association in a local bar, and you chance getting knocked on your butt.

"I never even owned a gun," Aaron answers after a moment, his eyes registering inquisitiveness.

"Neither did I . . . actually, get into hunting. You ever seen a deer that had just been knocked senseless by a car?"

"No," Aaron says wearily, "and I don't want to."

"I wish I hadn't," Hack says. "Once I was following a car that hit one. Never look at their eyes. You know that saying about 'looking scared as a deer caught in the headlights of a car'? That's a crock. Deer are too chronically dumb to look scared. If anything, they're trying to figure out what in hell the sun is doing wandering across the road."

They stroll silently a few more yards, and Hack says, "How do we prevent another massacre like what happened at that high school in Littleton, Colorado?"

Aaron sighs and shakes his head. "You tell me. I guess some people just have a wicked heart. It says that in Genesis."

Aaron has yet to attend any of the religious services transacted here daily, and naturally Hack has assumed that he is not a particularly devout person.

"In Genesis?" Hack says a tad skeptically.

Aaron's eyes measure Hack. "'For the imagination of man's heart is evil from his youth.'"

"Jesus Christ," Hack blurts out. "Are you putting me on?"

"Not so long ago," Aaron says, "I taught Sunday school."

Hack stops abruptly.

Aaron, after another couple steps turns and looks back. "You seem to be surprised."

"I am . . . you never let on . . . ." His wits return, and Hack says, "Not so long ago I *attended* Sunday school. Mass.*"*

"For almost thirty years," Aaron resumes, "I was an honorary deacon-in-training at Philadelphia's Franklin Street Church of the First Born."

"Jes—," Hack begins, before catching himself. "Well I'll be damned . . . I mean danged."

Aaron grins at Hack's awkward self-editing.

"You, Aaron Horace Blodgett, was a church deacon?"

Aaron's grin widens. "Now just why, old guy, do you think the fit is all wrong?"

"Because . . . you're too short, for one thing. Real deacons are tall, bony, scary looking suckers who never grin or laugh. You could be toting a fat bulldog under each arm, and you wouldn't frighten a baby cat."

"Clergymen" Aaron counters, "aren't supposed to frighten people. You had a point, earlier?"

"I did?"

"You asked if I hunted, and then you brought up the Littleton, Colorado high-school tragedy."

"I was just trying to begin a conversation."

"I don't think so," Aaron says, inclining his head to encourage Hack's answer.

Aaron is right. Hack had in mind the two of them debating gun control, something Kitty and Hack often quarreled over. Only, Hack assures himself, he absolutely will not become ticked-off at Aaron.

Hack is hesitant to argue his case now that he knows Aaron is a retired deacon. "Well," he begins, "I don't hunt either. But I absolutely cannot see the logic in condemning guns. I mean in arguing that guns should be outlawed. Makes as much sense as putting a gun in jail."

Aaron smiles good-naturedly. "Come on, Thomas, nobody blames guns themselves. It's just so dang easy to kill with one."

"So, stabbing a man to death is less a crime than shooting him? Can you even begin to imagine the pain of being stabbed over and over and over blood draining out of dozens of deep wounds"

"Hardly," Aaron says, "But . . . sometimes stabbing victims survive."

"Not often," Hack says looking downward and slightly shaking his head.

Minutes pass, and neither man speaks. After moseying along a few more steps, Aaron says, "But registering handguns does make sense."

"Book 'em, Danno!" Hack exclaims. "Then what? Register shotguns? Next, rifles? Meat cleavers?

Aaron shakes his head. "Oh, here we go. The 'slippery slope' argument. Someday, I hope a bright person explains to me exactly how that works."

"Anyway, it's not possible to write a gun law that bad guys don't ignore and lawyers can't hoodwink a jury about."

"So, people should be allowed to own . . . what? Weapons of mass destruction? Or for that matter–"

Hack tries not to sound angry: "Aaron, what in the deuce do you mean by *'weapons of mass destruction'*? If you kill–"

"I was exaggerating to make a point, I didn't really mean–"

"If you kill enough people with a rolling pin it would be a weapon of *mass destruction*. I'm sorry, Aaron, but I hate the way that darn expression gets tossed around. A nuclear bomb truly is a weapon of mass destruction. And germs can be. But a gun is a gun. Scissors cut paper, snip threads. Huh?"

Aaron sighs. "And a cigar is a cigar. Fair enough, I'll choose my words more carefully. But that still–"

Hank sniffs, "Please do."

Aaron continues genially. "Anyway, owning a gun should at least be a qualified right."

"Aaron . . . *all* our rights are qualified. Try yelling fire in a crowded theater. You know that's illegal.

Yeah, we can own land, but try building a mart on a plot where tiny puddles aggregate when it showers."

"Not that you'd *exaggerate*," Aaron says, rolling his eyes, "but they can't" – he holds up an index finger – "condemn it without just compensation."

Hack pretends to suppress a snicker. "In a pig's . . . rear end! See how much 'just compensation' you get for property that some EPA bureaucratic decides is a wetland."

"Yes," Aaron says, "I've heard that happens. But there are reasons and then there are reasons."

"The problem is that gun laws aren't enforced. A kid smuggles a loaded pistol into school and what happens? He gets expelled for a couple days. That's ridiculous. Parents have to be held accountable."

Aaron gives Hack another of his impish looks. "You didn't have any children, did you?"

"Dirty pool!" Hack exclaims.

"All's fair in love, war, and . . . roommates arguing," Aaron says laughing.

"You don't think parents should be held accountable?"

"It's not that simple, all the time keeping an eye on a child." Aaron shakes his head wistfully.

Their argument peters out, and they pick up the pace.

[28]

Aaron and Hack, their argument having regressed into a gentlemanly discussion, walk quietly onto the Home's back parking lot. Ahead they see Lon Fuller and Edith McGuire, arm in arm, rounding the far corner of the building and heading their way. Fuller's cane is dangling from his arm, the arm embracing Edith.

"It's Lon Fuller and Edith McGuire," Hack says softly.

Fuller, when he sees Hack and Aaron closing in, begins propelling himself every other step with his cane.

Aaron, lowering his voice, says, "What's your take on Fuller?"

Hack decides that the nature of Aaron's question is evidence that he and Aaron have fully bonded. "The same as yours," he answers. "He doesn't inform, he *pronounces*. He's a da . . . rn peacock, only he doesn't have the brains of one. What Edith sees in him, I will never understand. He and Luoma squared off in the dining room, to Fullers' . . . frustration. Women are so easily buffaloed when it comes to men."

"That's the one thing you've got right this morning," Aaron says nodding agreeably.

"I'm seldom wrong about anything," Hack says. His reply inspires another upward glance from Aaron.

They close to within ten yards of Fuller and McGuire, to where they are within earshot.

Edith is the first to speak. "Isn't this a beautiful morning?" she sings out.

"Splendid," Aaron replies.

Hack whispers a derogatory aside to Aaron: "*Splendid*?" To Edith he says, "The wind's a tad cool."

"Just gorgeous," Edith says nodding, her eyes fast on Aaron.

Fuller raises his chin importantly, reminding Hack of one of those old, low-angle mug shots of Italy's Benito Mussolini, Hitler's World War II ally. "When are we going to play our little cribbage game?" he asks Aaron. He stops, certain that his weighty question should not have to share even a second of time with the act of walking.

Aaron says, "Soon. I'm about settled in."

"Good," Fuller says. "I'll go easy on you." He glances at Edith, who is waiting at his side, her eyes engorging Aaron. "Same as I do for this little filly."

Edith grins. "I let him win," she says to Aaron.

"Sure you do," Fuller says, after comingling a snort and guffaw in one throaty sound.

"We'll get together," Aaron says inching ahead.

"Well then," Fuller says, "how about tomorrow?"

"Tomorrow?" Aaron says, hesitantly.

Hack stops and looks back. "Remember Aaron. Jake is coming by tomorrow."

"Oh, that's right," Aaron replies uncertainly. "I'll check back with you, Lon."

"I'm counting on it," Fuller says.

"I get you next," says Edith, her tone and look insinuating.

Catching Edith's predatory slant, Fuller glowers.

"No ganging up," Aaron says grinning.

"I'll see to it," Fuller ensures him.

Aaron, in a few quick steps, is back at Hack's side.

"And you claim to have once been a deacon," Hack says as if he has been woefully let down. He shakes his head slowly.

"Oh," Aaron whispers, "Jake *isn't* coming by tomorrow?"

"Then you agree," Hack says, after they have taken another half-dozen steps, "that gun control is not the answer."

"I have a more pressing problem," Aaron says.

[29]

Back in their room, Aaron says to Hack, "I hardly know that Fuller person. But . . . I don't like him."

"Welcome to Cooper Greens" Hack says. "Neither does anyone else living here . . . except that moron Edith. It must be all physical – only physical."

Sitting on the floor by Aaron's bed is a tape-sealed cardboard box. "We missed the UPS driver," Hack says.

Aaron bends down and reads the label on the box. "It's from Carolina, my oldest."

Aaron hoists the box onto his bed. It is bound with tape that has imbedded threads, and he has trouble loosening a flap.

"Here," Hack says, offering his jackknife. Knowing that resident-owned knives are contraband, Aaron hesitates before accepting it.

Hack's knife, manufactured by Zippo, the cigarette lighter company, is barely two inches long, unopened, and no one living or working at Cooper Greens knows he has it. It is universally assumed, hereabouts, that a man who does not carry a pocketknife sits down to pee – as Hack's wife would have characterized such a man. Once Hack watched at a wedding reception, of all places, as two male guests, wearing their Sunday-best, simultaneously offered the bride jackknives that they had whipped out of the front pockets of their pants, which the bride needed to remove a sliver from her new husband's palm.

Aaron hacks through the tape sealing the box on his bed, reaches inside, and lays a packet of snapshots on his dresser. Under the packet was a box of homemade cookies. Each of four flavors is enclosed in its own clear, re-sealable plastic bag.

Aaron lays the bags side-by-side on his bed and with a proud grin tells Hack to choose his poison.

Being partial to chocolate, Hack selects a dark, rich-looking pinwheel wafer from one of the bags.

"My favorite too," Aaron says; Hack passes him the bag.

"Umm," Hack says, taking a large bite. "Not bad."

But Hack does not pull it off: he is unable to contort his facial expression in a way to match the charity of his words. The cookie tastes awful, almost as bad as the grainy pumice that Hack's Mother periodically insisted her kids brushed their teeth with.

"They're sugar free," Aaron says.

"Hard to tell," Hack says.

"I'm used to them. I should have warned you."

"No, no, they're really good. Reminds me, though, Jolene said to make sure you take your medicine. How have you been feeling?"

Aaron chuckles and Hack realizes he has thoughtlessly compared the taste of the cookie he is chewing on to bitter medicine. Hack tries to verbally dance away from his goof but Aaron seems not to notice his silliness.

"Fine. Good," Aaron answers before directly addressing the matter of punctually taking his diabetic medicine. "I had a little spell a couple days ago. But I'm fine."

Aaron does not elaborate, and Hack says, "I guess I wasn't around."

Aaron slightly nods.

"Aaron, I don't mean to pry, but what in hell do you mean by, 'a little spell'"?

"I'm not sure myself," Aaron answers, opening the packet of pictures.

Aaron's smile is slight, and he obviously intends it to mislead Hack. "Sometimes, after I've overindulged, I sweat some . . . and grow a . . . bit weak in the knees. But it soon goes away."

Hack stares at Aaron. He shrugs and pulls a picture from the packet.

"Should I know–" Hack begins, but Aaron interrupts him. "There's nothing anyone can do. Besides, like I said, it goes with the territory."

"Okay, old man. But if there's something I should know that you're keeping from me it's your own damn fault if you swoon and recover with me giving you mouth-to-mouth resuscitation!"

Aaron's hand flies to his forehead. "Heaven forefend! Believe me. I wouldn't chance that for anything. If there was a remedy, I *absolutely* would tell you."

"I shouldn't have said that," Hack says, acting concerned. "I should never have mentioned the mouth-to-mouth thing. You'll probably start faking it."

Aaron laughs and promises that he will never again forget to take his medicine.

Wishing to hear what Aaron meant by "a little spell," Hack visits Kitty.

Stepping back from a kiss, she shakes her head. "Likely he went into a mild diabetic coma."

"A coma?"

"Not . . . prolonged, of course."

The possibility of Aaron losing consciousness is something else for Hack to worry about. When you're old, he thinks, worry comes easier than sleep after a big meal. If a windy night is forecast, an old person worries that his big front-lawn tree, which could shrug off the blow of a speeding locomotive, may not be standing in the morning.

Hack waits for Kitty to elaborate, but her mind is back on the crossword puzzle that she was working on when he arrived, and she doesn't.

"Something else," Hack says on his way from the room, "what does 'forefend' mean?"

"Forbid," Kitty says without looking up. "Why?"

"Aaron laid it on me. And I want to get even with the little peckerwood."

Hack visits their bathroom, and when he comes out, Aaron is writing a letter. It had been more years than he would care to own up to since he had written a letter – not counting the "How are you? I'm fine. Love, Tom" notes he penned on the inside of the Christmas cards that he mailed to Danny's family in Texas. Helen enjoyed writing letters, and Hank was assuredly pleased that she signed all of them, "Love, Tom and Helen."

Aaron pauses, and Hank says, "Thanking Carolina, I bet."

"Uh-huh." Aaron lifts his pen, reads what he's just written, and resumes writing.

"I'll help you with the spelling,." Hack says nodding purposely.

"Of course," Aaron mumbles his pen busy again.

"Wake me for lunch," Hack says, climbing onto his bed.

"Uh-huh."

"You're starting to get under my skin, Blodgett."

"Uh-huh."

Hack falls asleep immediately, as he often did when he sat idly for a few minutes in any half comfortable chair. Most of the residents at Cooper Greens are similarly disposed, the men anyway. More than once Hack had seen a man nod off in the middle of one of their so-called "block party" meetings, a gathering of residents under the jurisdiction of a particular nurse. A woman resident, mad as hell about finding a dust-bunny under her bed will be sputtering away when suddenly Harry Russard or Dock Mueller will begin snoring. Kitty rarely naps in the daytime. She claims that she does, but that's just a little fib to give her solo time.

It is ten minutes after eleven when Hack wakes up. Aaron is still writing. Hack washes his hands, and with a dampened washcloth plasters his hair down in the back of his almost totally deforested head. Aaron, when Hack leaves the bathroom, is proof-reading his letter.

"Shakespeare trembling in his grave?" Hack asks.

Aaron nods. "Tossing uncontrollably."

"Sure he is. Time to eat."

After a moment Aaron says, "Let me address an envelope, and I'll drop it off on our way."

Three women are eating at the table where Toby, Joe, Raymond, and Hack always ate, where Aaron and Hack eat now. Two, Mimi Kulic and Ruth Butterfield, are residents. The other, a younger woman, is a visitor. A visitor is charged six dollars to eat lunch or supper at Cooper Greens. They seldom visit for breakfast.

Mimi, as we pass by, says to Hack, "Oh, Tom, I'm sorry. This was the only table left for three people."

No problem, Hack tells her.

Unable to take her eyes off Aaron, Mimi says, "Phyllis, this is Mister Aaron Blodgett. Cooper Greens has been Mister Blodgett's home for the better part of a month now. It has been that long, hasn't it Aaron?"

"All but," Aaron answers, smiling and nodding.

Offering her hand, Phyllis says, "I'm Mimi's daughter. Isn't this a great place, Aaron! I bet you love it here."

"I do," Aaron says.

Ruth sees her chance and greets Aaron with a throaty "Hello," a greeting that Mae West would have died from envy at hearing. "We haven't formally met," she adds, offering her hand. "I'm Ruth Butterfield."

Hack listens to their clucking for a minute and moves on.

"Nice talking to you, Tom," Mimi yells after Hack.

Hack nods; he does not look back.

Aaron rejoins Hack, and Hack quietly says, "You milked it."

"It's my fault," Aaron says, glancing around cautiously, "that I'm movie-star handsome?"

"It's not your looks," Hack says, "It's your frilly clothes."

"My threads, you mean. Get with it, old man."

A kitchen aide brings their food, and they silently concentrate on eating.

They have nearly finished when Kitty stops by their table to tell us that Yvon will not be playing cards today, that Panky Pankhurst will take her place. Hank tells Aaron to wear a gas mask. Aaron gives Hank a puzzled look, and Kitty dresses Hank down with a stare that could crumble a brick building. "You'll understand," Hack says to Aaron.

Kitty assures Aaron that Panky is a good pinochle player.

"We'll slaughter 'em" Hank says to Aaron, "provided we're not as-fix-e-a-ted the first hand."

Kitty fixes Hack with another parched look and says, "Put your money where your big mouth is, Murtaugh."

Hack checks with Aaron. As if to say Hack should not have bothered, Aaron scowls chin to forehead exaggerating his annoyance.

"Two cents a point," Hack says to Kitty.

"Oh my. Big, brave, Thomas Murtaugh. How about a nickel a point?"

"Eee zee money," Aaron says, laying it on with a pursed-lip, nothing-to-it shake of his head.

"You're on!" Kitty squeals.

They all voice their eagerness to compete.

Kitty leaves, and Hack says to Aaron, "You realize, don't you, that we could easily lose by three hundred points. That's seven dollars and fifty cents apiece."

Hack's concern tempts Aaron's sense of humor: "Don't worry, I'll carry you."

"Ha! You can't even carry a tune."

That afternoon they played three games of pinochle. When Yvon plays, it's a wonder if they finish playing two games. Panky, for a reason that Hack could only guess, smelled like a heavily blossomed lilac bush. Thanks to Aaron's double-run in the second game, he and Hank were the financial net winners, splitting a dollar seventy.

[30]

It is Memorial Day, 1999. Hack and Aaron, back from breakfast, are lounging in their room watching TV coverage of a parade convened in the city of Erie, Pennsylvania. Erie, as the crow flies, is forty-six miles northwest of Snow Lake. A port city of some one hundred thousand residents, Erie's northern boundary is defined by a three-mile stretch of the Great Lake of the same name. Hack's mind is on concocting false rumors, a big part of his plan to stir Cooper Greens residents to liveliness, but everything he thinks up seems unplayable or potentially hazardous.

The parade is long and consists of similar assemblages over and over: a colorfully costumed high-school band playing a snappy marching piece; a troop of overweight, uniform-wearing male veterans trudging along to their own private drum beat; a beautifully re-finished vintage convertible carrying a flag-waving politician; and a gleaming, gold-trimmed, red fire truck with a town name ending in V. F. D. (Volunteer Fire Department) painted in sizeable block-letters on each cab door. The music played by the bands of the larger high schools is peppy and surprisingly harmonious. The music of the smaller high schools quavers as if the young musicians were struggling to keep step on a rolling ship. At the end of the parade, a dozen snazzy, gas-engine-powered go-carts chase each other in a figure-eight pattern before reforming as a rectangular flight and assuming their assigned place at the end of the parade. All the go-cart drivers are mature men wearing tasseled red fezzes.

"Ever eat blue pike?" Hank asks Aaron as a TV camera covering the parade pans the many piers, wharfs, large and small boats, and the occasional large buildings that line the shore of the lake.

Some years ago there was a fish native to Lake Erie called a blue pike. A small gamer, it was abundant until fished- and polluted-out of existence in the sixties – and declared extinct in 1972. Helen and Hank had dined at seafood restaurants in San Francisco, New Orleans, Boston, and Miami, and Hank knew that he had never tasted a morsel of fish as delicious as a bite of fresh-caught, deep-fried Lake Erie blue pike.

Aaron, half awake, says, "Did I ever eat what?"

"Ever eat Lake Erie blue pike? The best-tasting fish known to mankind. Bar none."

Aaron sighs, clearly wishing that Hank would tend to his knitting. "I'm not that fond of fish," he says.

"You don't like *any* kind of fish?"

"Not really. I like shrimp. And lobster. And Baltimore crab cakes."

"I love shrimp," Hank says. "When I was stationed at Keesler Air Force Base we were served shrimp on one Friday each month. Big fellers. All you could eat. Helped ourselves from piles of iced, boiled shrimp as big as . . . cucumbers. Once I got the damn runs I ate so many."

In the early 1950s, responding to the war in Korea, the Air Force sent recruits to Keesler Air Force Base in Mississippi to study electronics and to learn how to maintain military radar sets, a major application of that technology. Hack assumes Keesler is still an Air Force training base, but he does not keep up. Situated a few miles from the city of Biloxi, Mississippi, which is virtually on the Gulf of Mexico, Keesler summers were swelteringly muggy. Hack's barrack, which he shared with almost 80 airmen, like most homes in those days, was not air conditioned. Between the heat and the crowding, Hack doubted if the span of a daylight hour passed that summer when two student airmen were not trying to kick the living crap out of each other. Hack himself was knocked on his can contesting the ownership of a light bulb.

"I remember those shrimp," Aaron says shaking his head pleasurably. "I've never eaten anything as good since. We were so darn ignorant back then. Didn't know we were eating so high on the hog."

Hack quickly nods in agreement. "I could name a hundred things that I didn't have enough sense to appreciate when I was a kid." As an afterthought, he adds, "As far as I'm concerned anyone under forty is a kid."

"Amen," Aaron says.

Hack tells Aaron of the time an airman in his barracks looped a string over the erection of a fellow airman who was napping stark naked on the springs of his bed, tied the string to a side rail of the bunk above, joined several other airmen standing at attention by their bunks, and then one loudly shouted "Barracks! Attention!"

They both had several times heard the story of an airman similarly victimized, except the loose end of the string was tied to his brogan and the brogan dropped on his chest. The victim flung the brogan from his chest but caught up with it in mid-flight – or so the story went.

Biloxi's playground is a section of the north coast of the Gulf of Mexico, and the beaches there, and for miles east and west, are a stretch of heaven on earth, equal in sheer beauty to the miles of pristine beaches near Pensacola, Florida, some of the whitest and best-kept of any, in Hack's judgment, that he had ever swam from. It was a rare Sunday when most of the off-duty student airmen at Keesler, Hack included, did not head for those beaches, arriving in Biloxi city buses that had extensive routes from inside Keesler directly to the Gulf beach.

"That was the first time I ever swam in salt water," Hack says to Aaron after excitedly recalling that single fringe benefit of his otherwise aggravating duty at Keesler. "Do you swim?"

"Not really," Aaron says after a moment. "Anyway, Biloxi, Mississippi, wasn't exactly my kind of beach town."

Hack lets on he does not catch Aaron's meaning, but he does. It flashes through his mind that he never once saw a black person, man, woman, or child, swimming at any of those spectacular Gulf Coast beaches where he and other airmen frolicked at will. He also recalled once leaving the Base on a city bus and the driver, barely clear of the main gate, immediately pulling over and ordering a black airman to move to the back of the bus. Hack had never forgotten the driver's words: "It's the law here, boy."

Hack asks Aaron where he was sent after completing his training at Keesler.

"Offutt," he says.

Hack nods. "SAC headquarters. I'll bet that was fun duty."

Aaron chuckles. "Yeah, but Omaha was all right – especially after ten months at Biloxi. Where'd you go from Keesler?"

"Brookly Air Force Base," Hank says. "Ever heard of it?"

Aaron shakes his head, and Hack says, "Neither has anyone else. It's a little – or it was anyway – a little Material Air Transport base a few miles outside Mobile, Alabama. When Hack first saw his move orders, he misread the word Brookly, thought he was headed for Brooklyn, New York. He was grandly ticked off when he realized that he would be stationed only fifty miles away – in the Deep South, yet."

"Better you than me," Aaron says offhandedly.

"I guess so. After being stationed for six months at Brookly, I volunteered for duty in Korea."

It's Aaron's turn to be surprised: "I was stationed at K Fourteen!"

Hack, startled, shakes his head. "I was stationed at Seoul City Air Base, K Sixteen!"

"I'll be darned," Aaron says. "We were, what, twenty miles from each other?"

"At most."

"I was impressed with the Japanese people," Aaron says.

"But not the Koreans?"

"Well . . . Korea was a shambles, so–"

"Of course you were impressed with the Japanese. They don't think free love is immoral."

"And how do you happen to know that, Tom?"

Hack shrugs indifferently. "The usual. Scuttlebutt. Hearsay. The grapevine."

"Of course," Aaron says, flippantly mimicking Hack's attitude.

"Do you remember what we paid Korean barbers for a haircut?" Hack asks.

"Nope."

Hack misses the point of Aaron's clipped reply, which conciseness should have reminded Hack that likely a fellow black airman trimmed Aaron's hair, that most Korean barbers would not cut the hair of blacks.

Hack babbles on. "Ten cents. And a nickel for a shave. Hell, cigarettes were only a buck a carton. Eight cents a pack on the troop ship coming over.

"I never did smoke," Aaron says soberly.

"Big deal. Hell, anybody can not *start* smoking. Real men quit smoking. Like I . . . almost did."

Aaron utters a little grunt of disagreement. "I hadn't thought of it that way."

Marie, a stethoscope hanging around her neck, knocks lightly on our door. Entering before either of us answers, she says, "Vitals. Roll 'em up, gentlemen."

"Roll 'em up or roll 'em out?" Hack says squinting and turning an ear her way.

Marie shakes her head disgustedly. "Aaron. Do you want to be first?"

He shrugs. "Okay."

Hack says matter-of-factly to Aaron that Marie sometimes gets her thermometers mixed up.

"It only happened once, Marie says to Aaron. "I was taking Tom's vitals."

Marie checks Aaron's pulse rate and blood pressure, measures his temperature, and listens to his heart. She steps over to Hack's bed, on the way shaking another thermometer. She sticks it his mouth. "Have any problems breathing?" she asks Aaron, removing his thermometer. It is a routine question.

Aaron shakes his head. "What was my blood pressure, please?"

Marie pretends to study the thermometer. "Two hundred over one hundred."

"Of course," Aaron says.

Marie sterilizes the thermometer, drops it in her pocket, and says, "It's up a little. Both numbers. You and Tom weren't doing anything funny just before I came in?" She asks this question sternly, pretending that Aaron is to take her seriously.

"Really," Aaron says, flashing one of his toothy grins and shaking his head. "What were the numbers?"

"One forty-seven over eighty-two," Marie says. "Let's try your right arm."

Marie gets a slightly lower reading on Aaron's right arm. "A little better," she says. "One forty-four over eighty. Not good, but at least I know your heart's in the right place."

"I knew *that*," Aaron says, leaning back.

Hack braces the thermometer with his teeth and says to Marie, "Amazing you even found one."

"One what?"

"A heart."

Marie nods as if in total agreement. "Could be a truck just rumbled by."

Marie steps up to Hack's bed and removes the thermometer from his mouth. "Sixty-one. I'll call the meat wagon."

Hack murmurs disappointedly, "And you have the . . . whatchamacallits to call yourself a *nurse*."

"One thirty-six over seventy," she says, anticipating Hack's next question. "Excellent numbers for a sedentary old billy goat like you."

"I ain't old," Hack says. "You're just not around when I work-out."

"Neither," she says on her way from our room, "are the foothills of the Alleghenies, as we call the big hills around here, old."

"We're cosigning a grievance!" Hack shouts after her. "Both me and Aaron."

[31]

Once a week, usually on Thursday, Stephen Harris, Cooper Greens' CEO, brings his dog to work. Yang is a full-grown, forty-pound Shar-pei. Shar-peis, according to Kitty, were bred by the Chinese to be fighting dogs. She looks up that kind of stuff. In any event, Shar-peis look the part, remind Hack of strong-jawed Boxer dogs except most are more a dark solid brown than brindle in color. Pound for pound they may be stronger than Boxers. A groundhog 10 feet from his hole, once seen by Yang, is a dead groundhog. Still, Yang, not withstanding his innate predilection for attacking other mutts, squirrels, chipmunks, and the like, is gentle as a Spring lamb around humans. Harris lets him roam the halls of Cooper Greens. The residents greet him as if he is a favorite grandchild, and he laps it up.

Once, in the grip of a playful canine mannerism, Yang accidentally knocked Mary Joyce Winters down. A slight but lively woman, Mary Joyce was neither hurt nor did she report the incident: Yang, by that time, was everyone's pal. As far as Hack knew, that was his only serious misstep, not counting Yang's first visit to Cooper Greens when he felt obliged to irrigate three big potted plants strategically positioned on the floor of the front lobby. Yang's capacity for watering bushes, car wheels, and telephone poles was limitless.

It is mid-morning. Aaron is playing a game of solitaire on his bed, and Hack is about to enter the bathroom when Yang ambles into their room. Usually, Yang trotted indifferently past their door. Zeroing in on Aaron, Yang stops, freezes, and begins growling. His growl is not loud, but it starts somewhere inside his massive chest, and it does not falter. Hack had never heard him growl before – or bark for that matter. Later, when he asked around, Hack learned that no other resident had ever heard Yang utter a menacing sound.

"Yang!" Hack yelled, stepping from the bathroom and closing the door. "What in hell's the matter with you!"

Yang continues to growl, and Hack yells his name again. Yang finally turns his head away from Aaron and looks at Hank. His growl lessens and slowly fades. Hack whisks his walker in Yang's direction and commands him to "Git!" Yang looks one last time at Aaron and calmly turns and walks indifferently from the room.

Hack apologizes to Aaron. "Damned if I know what got into him. He's never done that before."

Aaron has trouble finding his voice, and Hack says, "Don't you like dogs? Animals can tell, you know."

"What the hell is he doing here?" Aaron says. It is the first time that Hack had heard him use a cuss word.

"He belongs to Harris," Hack says, "the guy who runs this place."

Aaron heaves his shoulders and exhales strongly.

"Harris also has a cat. Yin. Kitty explained the names to me, but I've forgotten their significance. Something about . . . balance or symmetry . . . whatever."

Aaron, veins visible on his forehead, looks at Hack as if he had lost his mind. "Something about, *what*?"

"Balancing life or some sappy damn thing like that. You know how she rattles on. I thought you'd seen Yang before?"

"I have," Aaron says, sounding as if he wants to pick a quarrel. "From a distance. I didn't know he had the run of the place."

Hack was not sure why Yang became so warped at the sight of Aaron. Kitty, when he mentioned the incident to her, said she once read – she has "once read" everything – that blacks have an odor different from whites. Her explanation confirmed, more or less, what Hack had feared: that Yang's reaction had a racial side to it. Unhappy at learning this, Hack rashly tells Kitty that she is full of crap. Kitty tells Hack to kiss her ass: exactly her words.

Aaron shakes his head, gathers the cards he has already played, and begins dealing a new game. When Hack finishes in the bathroom, which he was about to enter when Yang trotted into their room, Aaron is close to winning. Hack stops at the foot of Aaron's bed and watches. Aaron deals three more cards, and the game is over, the house winning again. Aaron turns the cards that are still in his hand face up. Tapping the red nine of diamonds with his index finger, he says, disgustedly, "It was this bugger." Aaron is talking to himself, not to Hack, so Hack dos not respond.

"Enough," Aaron says finally, sighing and looking up. "Enough is enough is enough."

"And," Hack says, "a rose is a rose is a rose. You ever own a dog?"

"All my life." Aaron says. He stands, sweeps the cards into a pile, and forms a deck.

"I'll bet you never owned a Shar-pei."

Hack's joshing does not amuse Aaron. "Is that what they call those brutes? You got that part right. All our dogs came from a pound. My favorite, Sentinel, was part setter. I guess. That rascal, he'd–"

"So'd most of ours," Hack says, butting in. "They'd have a beagle for a mother and a traveling salesman for a father. Or whichever. Helen, though, she always wanted a poodle, and I have to tell you about that."

Aaron pretends to look around. "I'll find something to read."

"For our twenty-fifth wedding anniversary I bought Helen two miniature, registered poodles, an eight-week-old black female and a six-week-old white male. Two hundred bucks apiece. From a kennel in Chesterland, Ohio. Just this side of Cleveland. I admit, I wasn't–"

"I get it," Aaron says. "Black and white combining into silver?"

"Uh-huh," Hack says. "Kind of makes sense, doesn't it?"

Aaron's lips purse, and he shakes his head. "Not to me."

Hack says, "I wasn't hot for owning one poodle let alone two. I got over it, though."

"Took a while, I suppose," Aaron says unconcernedly. He leans to the side and glances purposefully at the clock on Hack's dresser.

"A half hour yet," Hack says, certain that, in fact, Aaron does not have lunch in mind. "Anyway," Hack goes on, "I'm not done telling my story. We were returning from visiting friends in Guthrie, Oklahoma, and had stopped for the night at a motel in Jackson, Tennessee. Both dogs were with us so we asked the counter clerk for a room in back – where he couldn't see us carry the little beggars into the motel. I'm toting our luggage on a balcony . . . to our room on the second floor and a damn kid walked up behind us and snatched Helen's purse right off her shoulder. Scared the holy sh . . . crap out of both dogs. They tore loose from Helen, lit out, shot around the building, and across the road that ran in front of the motel. Duchess doubled back and was hit by a car. And killed. I took her body home in a black plastic trash bag, nailed together a little white cross, and buried her at the edge of our backyard. Helen tended the site until she . . . was clobbered herself. A friend, an old lady . . . even older than you . . . took in Pete when I moved here."

Aaron's face wrinkles and he groans in a comforting way. "Not easy, was it?"

"God no. You know how that little bas – that kid . . . who snatched Helen's purse, how he got away? Vaulted over the banister and onto the hood of a car parked six feet below."

Hack did not tell Aaron that the kid was a black youngster – and he probably didn't have to.

"It wasn't his first mugging, was it," Aaron says, slowly shaking his head.

"The police had been trying to catch him for a year. There wasn't much they could do . . . took our names. We left Jacksonville once the police business ended and did not stop until somewhere this side of Cincinnati. Which is about where Helen finally quit tearing up every ten minutes. To be honest, I did not hold up much better. I cry so damn easily anymore."

"I never used to cry," Aaron says. "Where I grew up, you just . . . didn't. Now, though . . . it broke my heart when I had to put Sentinel down. We lived alone together after Mother . . . after Opal died. He was fourteen, nearly blind, peeing on everything."

"Diabetes?"

Aaron nods. "You want a deck of playing cards? These are prejudiced . . . or something."

Hack pretends that he doesn't get the humor of Aaron's misapplication of the word "prejudiced." "I guess Sentinel was one heck of a watchdog?"

"No. That wasn't even his real name. I originally named him Julius, after Julius Irving."

"Ah, the Doctor."

Called Doctor J by fans, Julius Irving was both a flashy and a very good NBA all-star basketball player.

"Uh-huh. Sentinel was friendly and lovable but he was as useless a critter as God ever breathed life into – absolutely good for nothing. Jolly claimed that we misunderstood his true nature, that he wasn't worthless at all, but was an undercover guard dog. From then on, when I'd say something like, 'Where's Julius?' one of my girls would answer, 'pretending to be snoozing on the front porch, Daddy,' or another one would say, 'Slyly guarding the back yard, Daddy.' Sentinel was more rabbit than police dog."

"Reminds me," Hack says, once he stops chuckling from hearing how Sentinel had failed miserably to live up to his nickname, "of an incident concerning another of our dogs. We had a little mixed female that Helen named Mitzy. One time I heard her out back of our house barking her fool head off. And when–"

"Helen or Mitzy?"

"Yeah. And when I went out she was pointing like a setter, about ten or so feet from a big buck rabbit crouching at the edge of our vegetable garden. Mitzy sees me and barks louder. That damn rabbit never budged, didn't move an inch. In fact, it kept on eating. I told Helen that being faced down by a rabbit had to be the most mortifying thing that ever happened to Mitzy."

Aaron does not find my story of Mitzy's humiliation at all funny, and Hack says, "You had to be there."

Aaron says, "Did you ever own a cat?"

"One," Hack answers. "For a couple of years. It . . . just disappeared. I gather you owned one?"

"We had four . . . five, I guess, altogether. Every one of them ran away. Vanished, anyway."

"I liked cats," Hack said. "but Helen didn't. They are dumb, though. Lucky never did figure out that our kitchen door only opened from the latch jamb side. He'd sit and look at the hinge jamb and then at me, back and forth, but that was about it. Maybe he was just dumber than most cats."

"I doubt it," Aaron says grinning and shaking his head.

Hack nods agreeably. "For the right perspective on life, a man needs a dog to suck-up to him and a cat to utterly ignore him. I once read that in a magazine."

"Uh-huh," Aaron says. "Our kids threw in together and bought us a parakeet and a cage for our twentieth wedding anniversary. Chipper, we named her – or him, or whatever. It died, and Opal would not allow another one in the house. Said they were dirty. Of course there was much speculation in Mother's presence on why Chipper didn't live very long."

"Helen had a canary for years. That damn bird hated me. I'd walk by the cage and it'd stalk me like I was after its food. It never sang a damn note, not that I heard. Helen called it Sonny, and I called it Sonny the Dummy. Once we went shopping and left Sonny in his cage on our front porch. It rained while we were gone . . . I mean, it *rained!* When we got back, Sonny was lying flat on his back on the bottom of his cage with his feet sticking straight up. Honest. Exactly like in a cartoon. Helen ran and got her hair blower, and damned if she didn't coax the little Turk back to life. I held him while she dusted the little lice bag with hot air. You know the first thing he did when he came around?"

"Moved his bowels, I suppose."

"No, he started pecking my thumb! He didn't try to get away! He attacked my thumb!"

Aaron, laughing, rubs my nose in it. "Animals can tell, you know."

"Not birds," Hack replies feebly.

"I guess I'll wash up," Aaron says. "What's for dinner?"

"Macaroni and cheese," Hack answers as Aaron glides by him. Aaron is a picky eater, and besides fish, he does not like baked macaroni and cheese – among the dishes that Hack had learned he won't eat.

Actually, the main course is Swiss steak; macaroni salad is a side dish.

"What else?" Aaron yells from the bathroom.

"Lima beans," Hack yells back. He hates lima beans, and naturally assumes they taste bad to everyone.

"And?"

"And that's all. Rhubarb pudding for dessert."

"Right," Aaron says scornfully, emerging from the bathroom and drying his hands on a towel. He marches up to his bulletin board, reads the menu for today's lunch, and gives Hack a sour look.

They start to leave, and Kitty walks into their room.

"Hello, Dears," she says, her manner friendly. "The door was open."

"It's always open to you, Love," Hack says.

As if agitated, Kitty looks at Aaron and then says to Hack, "Did you hear that commotion last night?"

"Commotion?" Hack says, favoring Kitty with a look of skepticism. "What commotion?"

Hack glances at Aaron, but he's as puzzled as Hack.

"It happened on *our* street," Kitty says sharply.

"What happened on *our* street?" Hack says, mimicking Kitty's emphatic pronunciation of the word "our."

Kitty closes the door. "I was still awake. About midnight I hear screaming. 'Get out of here! You get *out*! *Get* out of here!'"

Kitty looks at Hack, at Aaron, and then at Hack again. She shakes her head. "Neither of you heard that?"

"No," Hack says looking quizzically at Aaron. "Did you hear anything?"

"Nothing" Aaron answers shaking his head.

Kitty continues: "It was Judy Klinginsmith yelling."

I tell Aaron that Judy Klinginsmith and Judy Pratt share a room. "The room of the two Judys."

Kitty nods and says, "I looked out from my doorway and see Janet, head up and tail-a-ri-sin', rushing into Judy's room. And then I hear, 'It's okay, ladies. Everything is okay. He's just confused.'"

"Janet," I say to Aaron, "is the grave-yard shift nurse for our wing. Janet Rae."

"Kitty introduced us one morning," Aaron says.

Kitty looks away and when she looks back says to me, "Thomas, who in the hell is telling this?"

"You are, Dear," Hack replies reverently. "And masterfully, too."

"Then please . . . ."

It takes a second for Kitty's feathers to unruffle. "The next thing that happens," Kitty resumes, "is Bertha leads Harry Cotterman out of the room of the two Judy's"– she glances sourly at Hack – "he's in his nightgown, holding the back of it against his butt with both hands."

"No shit? Hack deadpans, which costs him another sour look from Kitty. Aaron begins to grin, but he clamps it off and frowns at the floor concernedly.

After another pause, Kitty continues. "It seems Harry . . . dumped on Judy Klinginsmith's recliner. Apparently it was not an untroubled movement"– Kitty slightly smiles –"because his grunting woke up Judy – Judy Klingingsmith."

Anyone could tell that Harry Cotterman's Victrola needle sometimes jumped a music groove, but so far as Hack knew it had never skidded completely off a record. The next week, Cotterman was moved into Elm Street.

"Poor Harry," Hack says once he is damn sure Kitty has finished relating the story of Cotterman's accident.

Kitty's sympathy, however, is with the women. After a few seconds she says, "I'm going to lunch. You fellows?"

Hack nods. "We're on our way."

The three of us head for the dining room. As usual, Hack brings up the rear. Halfway there, Aaron decides he's not hungry. Begging off, he turns and heads back toward our room.

"Don't forget about tomorrow," Kitty says to me while we are sitting at her table waiting for an aide to bring our meals.

"*Tomorrow*? Hack says. "What's tomorrow?"

"The third Tuesday of the month," Kitty says. She glowers as if Hack had forgotten that tomorrow was December twenty-fifth.

"Already?" Hack says, slapping his forehead. "Are you sure?"

"Bern and I have a real, live author lined up."

It takes Hack a moment to realize that Kitty is referring to Bernice Goodson, Cooper Greens activities director. "This guy? He's coming here? To Cooper Greens?"

"*Yes*," Kitty answers irritably. "Here. To Cooper Greens."

Kitty has lived at Cooper Greens so long that she thinks of the place as a fine hotel and herself as a high muck-a-muck guest. "And," Kitty finishes, "he's a *she*."

[32]

Hack arrived at Cooper Greens' main recreation room, notebook in hand, at ten a.m., the curtain-call time for a meeting of the Cooper Greens Bookmark Club. Two rows of six folding chairs face a banquet table that has been set up four feet in front of the first row. Space is available at both ends of the rows of chairs for residents arriving in wheelchairs. Sunshine pours through the windows that line the room's outside wall. The smell of coffee is wafting from unwashed cups left in the room's pony kitchen sink.

Ordinarily, members of the Bookmark Club arrange their chairs in a circle with Kitty occupying the twelve-o'clock position and Bernice Goodson sitting in the chair immediately to her left. Today, when Hack arrives, Kitty is sitting alone in the middle chair of three that have been positioned behind the banquet table facing the chairs in place for an audience. She is talking to Panky, who is poised on the front edge of a chair in the first of the two rows of folding chairs. No residents arrive after Hack, and he is the only male to attend. He lets on that his presence is more happenstance than planned, but it truly isn't: Hack had begun to think about writing this book.

At five minutes after ten o'clock a tall, frizzle-haired woman wearing sneakers and a wrinkled, cotton, two-piece jogging suit strolls casually into the room. Dolled up, she could pass for forty years of age, but she looks closer to fifty. Either she is glaring or squinting; Hack gives her the benefit of the doubt. Bernice Goodson, holding together the throat of her blouse and pressing a small cardboard box against her bosom follows the visitor to the chairs behind the table.

This is the first time Hack saw Bernice since she had returned from maternity leave. She has put on weight. Her cheeks have filled out and her chin does not seem to jut out any more. Kitty says Marie is mistaken about Tom Hazlett, Buster's right-hand man, fathering Bernice's child. Marie, according to Kitty, does not have a clue – nor, Kitty went on, did Bernice herself have a clue. Hack keeps in mind, however, that Kitty is not above implying that other women have slept around as much as she has. Moreover, Hack knows Kitty thinks the spreading of internal rumors should be exclusively her function, and she likely resents Marie's nosing in.

Bernice waves at the table where Kitty is sitting, and Kitty, bubbly as a glad-hander at a fancy restaurant, rises to greet the book club's visiting author. "Sneakers and Togs" drops hard into the first empty chair, lets out a full breath, and begins staring past her audience at a four-shelf, open-faced, wood cabinet flush against the back wall. The repository for the books of Cooper Greens' "library," it includes an incomplete set of a vintage encyclopedia, perhaps two dozen hard-cover books – common doggerel that no owner ever wanted in the first place – eight or ten different size Bibles, and four shelves of soft-cover novels. She does not notice that Kitty had risen to greet her. Kitty cuts her eyes at the cluster of members, wrinkles her nose in a "well-smell-me" sniff, and sinks back into her chair.

Bern carefully walks to the chair reserved for her, the left-most of the three positioned behind the table, and sets down the box she is carrying. After removing half a dozen identical pocket books, arranging them in a display next to the box, and then shoving the box aside, she nods at Kitty and sits down.

Kitty rises and asks the audience to welcome Veronica Vale. Panky enthusiastically leads the applause.

"Veronica has just had her first book published," Kitty says when the applause stops. She gestures at Bern's display of books. "*Cayuga Captive*. It's an adventure romance."

Joetta Fisher, smaller but less wrinkled than most of us, and still nimble of mind, says that she didn't catch the title. Bernice repeats it loudly, separately pronouncing each syllable of both words: "Ka-yoo-ga Cap-tive."

Joetta thrusts her face forward. "I am not unfamiliar with the words, Bern. I didn't *hear them*."

Bernice nods at Joetta and addresses the rest of us: "Sounds exciting, doesn't it!"

Panky is moved to applaud and several others join in.

Bernice slowly sweeps her hand, which is holding a copy of *Cayuga Captive* from left to right and back.

Pictured on the cover is a shapely, full-lipped blond wearing a cut-off buckskin jump-suit – of sorts. The back of the garment ends an inch above the creases between the bottom mounds of her buttocks and her thighs. Her hair is woven into a single pigtail that falls almost to her butt. Hack cannot begin to figure what's preventing her sizeable boobs from falling out of the top of her outfit. Her getup shows marks and blemishes of rough handling. A beached canoe lies in the background.

Embracing the cute little sexpot is a giant of a frontier man wearing a fringed two-piece cloth outfit. His golden-bronze attire is obviously fresh from the dry-cleaners. The neck, a deep V cut, scarcely contains his dark, curly chest hair. His hat is an animal pelt, its dangling ringed tail once the aft-end of a raccoon.

Bern leans forward and tells VeronicaVale that Kitty started the Rolling Hills Bookmark Club.

Vale, still focused primarily on something behind the gathering of club members, could care less. "When," she says flatly, "did, uh, she do that?"

Kitty, who seems to be measuring Vale for a grappler's head-lock, says, "Over two years ago. We meet monthly . . . on the first Thursday."

Vale nods phlegmatically.

Kitty, staring hard at Hack, says, "Would you mind, Veronica, telling us a little about yourself?"

Joetta, waving a hand, says loudly, "You forgot the invocation, Kitty!"

Kitty glares at Joetta. Bern, before Kitty can reply, tells Joetta in so many words to stuff it.

"Well, she did," Joetta mumbles.

Vale says, "There's really not much to tell. Besides, my personal bio is of little matter."

Someone says, "We can't hear you."

A collective murmur confirms that sentiment, and Vale, in a slightly elevated voice, says, "I was born and raised in Crawford County. And I still live here."

Scowling, Joetta says to no one in particular that she still couldn't hear Vale. Panky, the next moment, says, "Oh how nice, Veronica. Where in Crawford County?"

Vale, as if the heat in the room is too much to bear, plucks at the top of her jersey several times before answering: "Our mail comes through the Bloomborough post office."

Cooper Greens' guest author, though clearly drained of all spirit, somehow finds the energy to tell us that her husband sells real estate and that she is the mother of two children, both students at Gannon

College in Erie. In her spare time, of which she does not have any, she putters in her garden. She cannot cook and is a "terrible" housekeeper. She taught herself how to write.

A woman sitting in one of the wheelchairs says, "Once I was engaged to a civil engineer." Smiling she adds, "He was uncivil."

Nobody laughs, and Kitty shakes her head dismissively. "Now," she says to Vale, "if it's not asking too much, Veronica, perhaps you could briefly relate the story line of Cayuga Captive?"

Vale nods. "However," she says turning and looking past Kitty at Bern, "you probably mean *plot*, not story line, Kitty."

"This'll be fun," Hack says to himself.

"You see, Kitty," Vale says, "a story line simply orders events. Usually, chronologically. I'd like to believe that Cayuga Captive isn't nearly as linear as all *that*." Cooper Greens' ersatz library again captures Vale's attention.

Kitty folds her arms across her chest. "Well, Ms. Vale, I barely know the difference between a literary plot and an onion patch, so you call it whatever you want. But kindly tell us what in the *hell* your book is about."

Vale shakes her head. "It's not a question of what *I* want to *call* it, Kitty. You see, there's an important distinction to be made between a story line and a plot. The difference is plain as writing, 'spots on the carpet,' meaning the carpet is soiled, and writing 'Spots, capitol S, is on the carpet.' See the difference?"

"Oh, bow-wow and bull-shit," Kitty snaps.

But Vale's attention has shifted away. Besides, Kitty barely mumbled the second syllable of her expletive and Hack doubts that anyone except he and Bernice caught it – and at that only because they both know Kitty.

"I've set Cayuga Captive in what is now New York State. On the south shore of Chautauqua Lake. It's seventeen ninety or thereabouts. You may remember–"

"The Cayuga," Kitty interrupts sharply "never settled that far west. I'm part Indian, part Cayuga myself, and I know damn well that's not right."

Hack knows Kitty is bullshitting about her ancestral stock, but he figures she's probably right about the westward migration of the Cayuga.

Vale says, "It's what we writers call poetic license, Kitty. Are you familiar with the term?" She smiles patronizingly at the rest of us.

Before Kitty can answer the woman sitting next to Joetta Fisher says to Vale, "It's called, what!"

"Po-et-ic li-cense," a woman behind Joetta shouts into the side of the head of the woman sitting beside Joetta.

"I didn't ask you!" the first woman says belligerently.

"Ladies! Ladies!" Bernice pleads.

The two women glare at each other but hold their tongues.

At least once that Hack knew of, it fell to Bernice to intercede in a struggle between two wheelchair-bound members of Kitty's Book Club, both of whom, wanting to park at the six-o'clock point of their circular gathering, charged into each other like bull moose in the sexual excitement rut.

Kitty begins another remark with an expletive, but Bernice cuts her off. "You were saying," she looks at Vale, "that the action takes place near Chautauqua Lake?"

"Yes," Vale says, glancing at a spot on the table in front of Kitty. "That is where the events unfold, the locale of my story."

Kitty says loudly, "The setting . . . she means."

Vale looks at Bernice, and Bernice says, "Let's, ah, everyone hold her comments until after Veronica finishes."

Vale nods at Bernice. "As I started to say, it is near the end of the eighteenth century, oh, say, the last decade. Three families of settlers are working their way west on horses and in two covered wagons when they stray north of Pennsylvania and are attacked by a roving band of Cayuga braves. The braves scalp and kill everyone except a fourteen-year-old girl whom all the braves take turns . . . ravaging. Moon Hawk, a son of Cayuga war chief Stone Packer–"

"That's bullshit!" Kitty shrieks. She pushes herself away from the table hard, nearly tipping over backward. "You ignorant bitch!" she says recovering. "You don't know a damn thing about native Americans. Not a goddamn thing!" She shoves her chair roughly toward the table. "Nothing! You know nothing about our culture!"

Bernice, jumping to her feet, steps between Kitty and Vale. "Give it a rest, Kitty," she says sternly. "Veronica is our *guest*. Her book is fiction, a novel. We can discuss historic issues later."

"I don't care if she's . . . Mother Teresa," Kitty says, straining to get past Bern. "No one that damn ignorant should be allowed to write a book . . . and see it published!"

Bern, who is tall as Vale, holds her ground. "Not now, Kitty," she orders.

Kitty sputters and for show, Hack suspects, tries several times to dodge past Bern. When she can't, she shouts at Vale, "Kiss my ass, you moron." She says to Panky, "Let's go. We're not listening to any more of her crap!"

Panky, after an ill-considered second of indecision, falls in behind Kitty, and the two women march from the room. Vale all the time has not moved except to slightly turn her head and stare absent-mindedly at the chair vacated by Kitty.

"She can be a pistol," Bernice says to Vale, shaking her head and sliding back into her chair.

Vale continues in the monotone that has been her mode of speaking: "Afterwards, Moon Hawk decides he wants the young girl for his concubine so he spares her life."

Someone says, "For his what?"

And someone else shouts, "For his girl friend!"

Vale, her attention again suddenly focused on our makeshift library, pauses.

Joetta, spunkier now that Kitty has left, says loudly, "And then what?"

After taking a second to sort out where she's at, Vale says to Joetta, "You don't want to hear how the movie ends do you?" She winks at the rest of us.

Joetta ponders the question for a moment and then says, "Well, it's not a mystery. Is it?"

"No," Vale says. "It's an adventure story, properly speaking." She adds excitedly in a hushed voice, "What is going to happen next?"

"It's already a movie?" a woman waving her hand in the second row asks.

Vale laughs. "No," she says. "I was only using a figure of speech."

"A what?" someone says.

"Who would like to ask Veronica the first question?" Bernice says. She looks at Hack. "Thomas?"

All eyes fall on Hack, and he says, "Is Veronica Vale your real name?"

Bern rolls her eyes, but Vale answers evenly, "No it isn't."

She does not elaborate, and Hack says, impatiently, "Well, what is it?"

"Veronica Vale is my pen name."

"I understand. But I know . . . I used to know a family from Bloomborough."

"I'd prefer," Vale says, "not to answer that question. I place great value on my privacy."

"You're that famous?" Hack asks.

Vale does not answer, and Bernice calls on Joetta, who is squirming with a question of her own.

Hack left the June 21, 1999, meeting of the Cooper Greens Bookmark Club not long after asking the only question he really cared to hear answered. Vale, by then, had told us that she had finished writing the manuscript for *Cayuga Captive* in her spare time in ten months, had done most of her research about artifacts and other "trivia" at the Meadville Public Library, and had chosen, for her prose style, an "omniscient third-person point of view," so she could "expound on her protagonist's innermost thoughts and fears."

She also slipped-in the fact that residents of Cooper Greens could purchase *Cayuga Captive* for $9.49, fifty cents off the cover price.

Hack sorely wanted to purchase a copy of *Cayuga Captive*, and give it to Aaron as a present just to watch him squirm accepting it as a sincerely offered gift. Of course, Hack did not have the ten bucks to spare. He had decided to conscript Aaron to help him loosen up Cooper Greens' residents; somehow, embarrassing

Aaron, seemed to Hack to be a good beginning, a perfect, bawdy prank for the opening of his book of high jinks.

[33]

Kitty's door was open an inch. Hack knocked lightly, but after a few seconds of silence he rotated his walker to leave.

"Tom?" Kitty finally says just audibly.

"I'll come by later."

"No. Come in."

Sitting on her bed, Kitty is staring through the room's window at the outdoor scene. She is still wearing her long-sleeve, go-to-meetings dress. Like many of the women living at Cooper Greens, Kitty wears winter-weight clothes year around. The cuffs on her sleeves are worn, and Hack has several times wondered what she would be buried in: she does not own an unblemished dress. Hack also wondered if he would be around for her burial. Buoyantly reflecting on his own mortality, he figured the odds were on his side. Kitty has a snit when she fails to get her way about most anything, and Veronica Vale had cavalierly dismissed her every criticism about the literary basics of *Cayuga Captive*.

"Boy, that Bern picked a looser," Hack says to Kitty.

"She picked an *idiot* this time," Kitty fires back.

Kitty heaves a sigh. In her right hand is a globule of damp tissue, which she is slowly kneading. Hack expects her to turn his way, but she doesn't. He stops midway between her bed and the empty bed that has been unoccupied ever since he moved into Cooper Greens.

"Okay my coming by?"

"Of course." Kitty dabs at her eyes. "I'm fine."

Kitty turns her head to the left and then part way to the right, and Hack realizes that she is scrutinizing her image on the other side of the windowpane that she is not looking at the scenery outside. Satisfied, apparently, she turns toward Hack and gestures at her recliner.

Kitty has obviously been crying, and Hack is at a loss over what to say. He was rarely able to console Helen, either. Most men, Hack included, feel it is unmanly to initiate a compassionate hug or to sympathetically kiss someone. Hack supposes that deep down, if the truth be known, many men are shaky about their own masculinity, uneasy over the thought that someone might glimpse a frail, feminine glint of their personality.

Hack admits to himself that he doesn't love Kitty – likes her a lot, but no more than that. Kitty is never dull or boring, and she looks after him. He nevertheless cannot honestly say he loves her, certainly not in the deep way he loved Helen. Helen, by and large, was singularly even-tempered. Rare is the day when Kitty does not steam-up over some trivial matter. Kitty must also dominate a relationship, which is why she and Hack often end up at sixes and sevens over nothing. Hack thinks Kitty likes him more than she lets on, but she is a hard person for Hack to read – favors him with oral sex unprompted, but unambiguously slaps his cheek if he tries to French Kiss her. He decides it is something that men, being men, can't understand.

"Oh hell, Kit," Hack says, backing into her recliner, "just because some horse's ninny wrote a book and it went to her head? One-shot celebrities are a dime a dozen. Some snot-nosed high-school kid is drafted by the Milwaukee Brewers, or another bottom-feeder baseball club, his hometown newspaper promotes the kid as if he's the second coming of Willie Mays. And the kid's head swells to the size of a medicine ball. And Vale – or whatever her name – is no different. Hell, I might be as big a pain in the butt if I ever make my mark." Hack pretends to sniff. "I know you would be."

Kitty's smile is brief. "Probably. But, that's not it, Tom."

"What is *it* then? You're pissed because Vale put you down? Tried to, anyway?"

Kitty's head whips left and right impatiently. "No! The woman is *stupid*. Just plain ignorant. She's a damn . . . Harpy. Reading her book would be like watching a skit of the Three Stooges."

"Both Joetta and Claudia bought a copy," Hack says.

"They're both morons," Kitty snaps.

"What is bothering you, Kit?"

"My God, Tom . . . her garbage about us Indians!"

Hack is dubious of Kitty's claim that she is part Seneca. Some of her stories simply do not add up, and he has a hard time believing she's so upset over Vale ripping on Indians. Joe Luoma teased her all the time about her putative Indian roots, and not too gently either, and she never became nearly as chagrinned. Plain and simple, Kitty's feelings were hurt because Vale abjectly disrespected her. Hack, however, pretends to believe her answer about Vale disparaging Indians.

"C'mon, Kit. You said yourself, Vale's a moron. Why in hell does it matter what she thinks?"

Kitty turns back to the window. "It matters because the ignorant bitch put all that crap about Indians in a book. And it got *published!*"

"I know, Hon," Hack says, "but my God, the IQs of people who read those sappy women's books would fit on two-digit Interstate Highway signs. How is that *Cayuga Captive* is any different from everyday pussy lit? How smart do you have to be to have an opinion? In fact . . . it probably helps if you're not too smart. Hell, most–"

"I'm sick of fighting it all my life . . . the endless bad-mouthing of us Native Americans."

"Fighting what, exactly? I have no idea what you're talking about." Hack did know, but he wanted to hear her say it.

"The negative stereotyping of us Indians. I'm as good as you or anyone else, Tom."

"Oh balls, Kitty! Stop jerking me off! You're acting like a damn teenager."

"I don't care," Kitty says, her voice whiny. "That's how I feel."

Hack encloses her hand, the one holding the damp ball of tissue, in his. She may be kidding herself about the reason for her distress, but her melancholy is genuine.

"You're as good a person as anyone I've ever known," Hack says, all but flinching at the triteness of his own words. "And, I mean it."

Tears again well in Kitty's eyes. "I've squandered my life. I could have done anything. Taught school. Written books. No . . . I became a drunk. You know what they'll inscribe on my tombstone?"

"Thirty-nine and holding?"

"Catherine Maud Wendell Proctor. Drunkard. Capital d-r-u-n-k-a-r-d."

Hack squeezes her hand. She tries to pull away, but he won't let her.

"Kitty," Hack says, "Look at me."

She does not.

"Please."

Her head turns slowly; her eyes downcast.

"You are *not* a drunk," Hack says forcefully, "and you haven't been for a long, long time. Stop calling yourself one. Now, I mean it, goddamn it. You keep it up and I'll blister your ass. Big time. Don't ever say that about yourself again."

Hack relaxes his grip. Kitty absentmindedly smoothes her bangs and then begins dabbing her eyes with a new tissue. After patting her bangs a final time, she lifts her head. "I'm sorry, Thomas. I'm being a . . . big pain . . . ."

Hack weakly shakes his head. "Sorry? Sorry, about what?"

"I know, but . . . . Hold me a minute, Tom. Please."

Hack moving toward her nearly falls into her lap. They both laugh. Hack cannot balance himself well enough to hug her, but he bends to her and they hold each other for several seconds.

Reading the look of uncertainty on Hack's face, Kitty says, "I'm good. Isn't it lunch time?"

"You're sure that you're okay?"

"Positive."

Hack gazes a long moment into her eyes. "I need to talk to Marie on my way back to my room," he says.

Hack stops at Kitty's doorway. She waves him on, repeats that she is feeling fine.

Medicines, At Cooper Greens, are stored in locked, six-foot-high metal cabinets situated inside nurses' stations. Each shift nurse ritually passes the only circulated key for a given cabinet along. Marie, when Hack arrives at our nurse's station, has the cabinet doors open and is straightening the vials, bottles, pads, and so forth that are scattered inside. Since it is the lunch hour, none of the four or five Cooper Greens' "regulars" are slumbering nearby in their wheelchairs.

Stopping at the counter of the nurses' station, Hack says to Marie gruffly, "How the hell long does a resident have to stand here before he gets a little service?"

Marie knows Hack's voice and does not bother looking back. "You'll get served," she says in a threatening tone of voice.

"I did *not* say '*served.*' Hack replies, "I said,'How long before I get *serviced*?'"

"Like you had a chance," she mumbles. Marie, stepping back from the open cabinet, studies her reorganization of its inventory.

After a few seconds, Hack, shamming a hard cough, says , "I feel cardiac arrest coming on."

"Not on my shift you don't, Murtaugh," Marie says in a syrupy voice.

Hack begins to moan, and Marie turns and says, "Okay, Pain-in-the-Ass Murtaugh, what is it you want?"

"First," Hack says, "I want you to stop calling me by my Indian name. Second, I have a request."

Marie grins and says, "But your Indian name is appropriate; it's a perfect fit."

"A lot you know," Hack mumbles.

"Never mind," Marie says, exhaling a long sigh. "What do you want?"

"To see Bonifanti again."

"About what?" she says, all humor gone from her voice.

"You don't need to know."

"You can tell me, I'm a nurse."

"Rectal mange."

Marie thinks over Hack's answer and then says, "Prostate bothering you again?"

"No. Still."

Marie locates a pad of forms and begins filling in the top sheet. "You a Pepper?" she asks as she's writing.

Marie wants to know how often Hack gets up to urinate during the night. Theoretically, members of the all-male Cooper Greens Dr. Pepper Club stumble out of bed every night at ten, two, and four o'clock to relieve themselves. Toby Roofner came up with the name, which he filched from one of those old Dr. Pepper wall ads that promoted the hours of ten, two, and four o'clock as the ideal times to slurp down one of their soda pops.

"A charter member," Hack answers. "Sometimes I have to go more often. But I can manage. Joe Luoma used to say that if there truly was a God he'd have equipped men with petcock valves. You know what a petcock valve is?"

"No. And if it has anything to do with something Joe Luoma brought up, I don't want to know."

"A petcock valve is used to drain excess water from a car radiator. What'd you think it was?"

"A faucet on an automobile radiator," Marie answers smartly.

"The pain's getting worse is why I need to see Bonifanti."

After more questions, Marie says she'll let Hack know, that is, inform Hack later of the date and time when Dr. Bonifanti will visit.

Aaron is standing in the doorway of our room. "Ready?" Hack says to him.

"Starved."

"I have to pee first. What's for lunch."

"Chitlins," Aaron says, stepping out of Hack's way. "Do you like chitlins?"

Of course Hack knows chitlins are not on the menu, so he says, "Hot dang, pork butts. My favorite."

Hack relieves himself, washes his hands, inspects his teeth, cocks his head at different angles to the mirror and decides that the span of his baldness is no greater than it was the last time he looked. In other words, he goes through his usual bathroom routine. Aaron, when Hack joins him, repeats his question.

"I like chitlins fricasseed," Hack answers excitedly. "Fricasseed, stir-fried, and smothered with truffles."

"Truffles?" Aaron says. "That explains your chronic halitosis, anyway."

For almost the first time since Aaron moved in, they eat lunch without a queue of female residents mincingly approach our table to compliment Aaron about trivia: apparently the novelty of a black man residing at Cooper Greens is finally wearing off.

Either that – or women believed Hack when he began telling them of Aaron's unusual devotion to weaving decorative macramé's. Helen, Hack remembers, used to weave macramé slings for flower pots, and in the summer a person couldn't, as they say, swing a dead cat on the Murtaugh's front porch without knocking a couple of her slings off their hooks. Hack always explained this mania of Aaron's – that's what he called it, his mania – with great sincerity, leaving Aaron to squirm through a denial without denigrating the wholesome pastime of macramé weaving, which is popular with a few of the hardiest women living here.

"Except to eat and to play an occasional game of cards," Hack would cheerfully tell one of Aaron's fawning devotees, "that's what he spends all his waking hours at. Usually alone in our room."

If a listener nodded understandingly, Hack always added, "In the corner between his dresser and the back wall."

We're eating our dessert, bread pudding topped with a tangy raisin sauce, when Lon Fuller and Edith McGuire walk up to our table. Aaron, if an aide accidentally serves him dessert, always wolfs it down.

Hack chides him, but he might as well rebuke a tree stump.

"Blodgett!" Fuller says piercingly, "about our cribbage game. It's been a good three weeks! I'm still waiting."

"Oh my," Aaron says, dabbing a corner of his mouth with his napkin, "It has been that long?"

"Three weeks yesterday," Edith pipes up, moving from behind Fuller to a place at his side.

"We're going to get together yet," Aaron says. "I've just been so darn busy settling in and all."

Aaron glances at Hack, hoping that he'll rescue him. All but praying that he will, Hack thinks.

"He never stops," Hack says to Fuller, and then, addressing Aaron: "You're hardly half way done with that slip cover for my throw-pillow. You promised it last Thursday."

Fuller's face, as if he is suddenly unsure of Aaron's masculinity, slowly takes on a troubled look. Edith smiles and nods approvingly. Aaron does not know what to say.

Hack turns back after pretending to cough into his handkerchief. "I'd at least like it by the middle of next week," he says to Aaron, warmth intoning his words.

Fuller, his eyes still angled suspiciously on Hack, says to Aaron, "Well, let me know." He looks at Edith, the sour look on his face suggesting that all the time they were talking she had been standing on his foot.

"I don't know whether to thank you or not," Aaron says to me in a low voice as soon as Fuller and McGuire leave the dining room.

Hack is wounded. "I do you a favor and you don't know whether or not to *thank* me?"

"Yeah. Some favor. Fuller thinks I'm gay."

"Well . . . I'm still uncertain myself. Anyway, it's for your own good."

"My own good? Like a slipped-disk would be for my own good?

"Um, close," Hack replies, his manner thoughtful.

Aaron, still a shade annoyed, asks, "You ever had one?"

"A slipped disk? Yeah, many. But not since the music business upgraded from seventy-eight records to thirty threes."

Aaron groans. "That is really bad, Thomas, even for you."

[34]

Bernice Goodson, our activities director, has decided to experiment with the scheduling of her Sing-A-Longs in the afternoon instead of the evening. If her plan works, she won't have to stay late on Wednesdays. Hack does not expect it will, however, as many of the women who live at Cooper Greens, not to mention a fourth of the male residents, are hooked on afternoon TV soaps.

So, Hack and his friends cannot play pinochle in the dining room today. They could make other arrangements, but neither Kitty nor Hack takes the initiative. Hack cannot speak for Kitty, but he holds back because he is exhausted from dragging through game after game with Yvon. Yvon, Hack reasons, is a nice enough person, but somehow playing a game of cards disjoins every cell in her head.

"I owe Jolly a letter," Aaron says, as he and Hack walk into their room. "I guess I'll start it."

"Jolly is your youngest?"

"Uh-huh, you met her the day I moved in. Carolina's my oldest."

"Carolina must be about my age," Hack says after a moment of squinting as if trying to add up numbers.

"Ha. Not even half your age. She'll be forty-two on August nineteenth."

"You have five kids?"

Aaron nods pleasurably. "Five girls."

"All basketball players, same as their old man?"

"Better. All five. Jolly and Trudella played together on the same high-school team. They won their league that year."

Hack is honestly impressed. "Yeah? Nowadays fourteen-year-old girls are better athletes than we were in our *twenties*. A couple years ago Snow Lake's high-school softball team made it to the state finals. I couldn't have hit their star pitcher's curve with a tennis racket. All five of your kids live in Philadelphia?"

Aaron opens his box of stationery and removes a sheet. Buster Mook has foraged a folding TV stand and extended the legs so Aaron can easily write on it – which he does while sitting on the edge of his bed.

"No," Aaron says after arranging to write. "Marigold, my mid-middle girl, and Carolina and Jolly live there"– his voice falls off –"the other two . . . haven't really settled down yet."

"That's okay," Hack says. "I was only beating my gums. It doesn't matter."

Hack visualizes the Blodgett family picture on Aaron's dresser. All Aaron's daughters, he knows, are plain; to put it nicely, and Hack had jumped to the conclusion that the ones Aaron said had not settled down were not only unmarried but also un-pursued.

Aaron begins to write, but after finishing a sentence, lays down his pen. Pivoting to face Hack, he leans forward and rests his forearms on his thighs. "Oh heck, Tom. Frankie and Trudella are both in prison – like the . . . place by . . . Bradford."

"Oh my," Hack hears himself say. He doubts he has ever before used those two words together in a sorrowful way. "That's awful," he adds. "I mean, I'm really sorry, Aaron. I don't mean . . . I mean I'm sorry for *you*, Aaron."

Aaron sighs and removes his glasses. "I know, Tom." He fetches his bifocals from the top drawer of his dresser, momentarily holds his pen in a writing position over the sheet of stationery, and resumes writing his letter to Jolene. Pulling up, he says, "Both are fine, wonderful Christian girls. Do anything for you. They . . . got on dope . . . marijuana, crack. God only knows what all. I tried hard to be a good father."

Looking past Hack, Aaron shakes his head. "I just don't know, Tom. Once you're hooked, it's . . . a tape worm living in your belly. Always starved."

"Of course I never met your wife," Hack says, searching for words of consolation. "But I cannot imagine how *anyone* could raise kids today, certainly not any better than you and Opal. Drugs . . . sex. And there's so damn much totally vicious crap on TV."

"A . . . junky will do anything for a fix. What's the answer, Tom?"

Hack shakes his head. "Maybe someday there'll be a vaccine . . . or something. I don't know."

"I hope so," Aaron says dispiritedly. "Nothing else seems to work. I know that."

Aaron covers his skewed eye with his hand. His other eye finds the sheet of stationery to be an object of some interest. He removes his hand, shakes his head slowly, and resumes writing.

Hack makes his way to the window. "Guess I'll take another walk," he says. "When my mind finally takes in the scene outside."

As Hack is leaving, Aaron asks if he wants company. Hack cannot for a moment decide if Aaron is thinking about who it is the walk will benefit. Hack bungles his answer and then spends the next ten seconds insisting that he really does want Aaron's company on his trek.

"Naturally," he finishes, "I'd prefer the company of a winsome young platinum blonde."

"Oh really?" Aaron says. A hint of his usual toothy grin returns."And just what in the world would you do with one?"

"Unlike you," Hack says, his attitude high and mighty, "the possibilities are endless."

"Like, take a picture for your bulletin board? For your wallet? Take her to a Cooper Greens' intergenerational? You could read a primer together. She could help you with the big words."

[35]

Hack and Aaron are watching the news program *Early Edition* on the CNN TV channel. The lead story, a change from the endless reports of atrocities committed by opposing forces during the war in Yugoslavia, is about Hillary Clinton's hankering to represent the State of New York as a U.S. senator.

"She's able," Hack says, when Frank Sesno, co-anchor of *Early Edition*, finishes reporting that Mrs. Clinton has formed an exploratory committee, "but I don't like it."

"Oh?" says Aaron, his look suggesting that Hack had just said he favored abolishing sunshine. "Why?"

"Because she's screwing a good, native New York Democrat."

Aaron grins. "Are you talking about Hillary or Bill?"

"I'm a Democrat," Hack says, barely returning Aaron's grin. "Have been all my life, but I couldn't vote for Hillary."

"Because she's a woman?"

"No. That's not it at all."

"So, you'd vote for Giuliani?"

"No. I just wouldn't vote."

Aaron shakes his head. "What's your unhappiness with Hillary?"

"Nothing against her, personally. It's us Democrats. Big names count for too much.

"Big names?"

"Qualifications don't matter, celebrity matters. Too many Democrats are personality junkies. Anyway, she'll run. She's got the hots for it. Bad."

Aaron chuckles. "The hots? You're *sure* we're not talking about Bill?"

"Positive," Hack answers blandly. "Kitty says that greed is the worst of all sins, and it . . . well maybe it is. But I'd put my money on ambition."

"Two of the seven deadly sins of damnation," Aaron says nodding. "Still, I'd sure like to have seen Bobby in the Oval Office for eight years."

They are comparing the relative political assets of JFK and RFK when Kitty strolls into the room, her manner foretelling them that she is about to ask for a favor.

"Tomorrow," she says, "is Bingo day."

"So?" Hack says.

"Bern asked me to try and interest more men in playing."

Hack makes a face and looks at Aaron. "Bingo is for women. My wife played." Hack shakes his head and frowns: playing bingo would cast doubt on his manhood.

Aaron is more tactful: "Oh, goodness. I don't think so, Kitty."

"I've never won anything in my life," Hack says.

"Helen was just a big void? Kitty says.

"No . . . but she was lucky, not me."

"Not I," Kitty murmurs.

Aaron says that he and his wife, when it came to games of chance, were under the same dark cloud as Helen and Hack: Opal sometimes won; he never did.

Hack and Aaron continue to protest. When they lapse for a few seconds Kitty, indifferent to their objections, explains how the game of Bingo is played at Cooper Greens. "Cards only cost ten cents apiece, and you can play up to three each game. Ten games are called, each typically paying the winner a few dollars. Fifty cents is put aside from the cumulative bets of each game for a number called the Pig. The following week, if a player bingos on that number he or she wins the set-aside money. It takes up the better part of an afternoon, and at worst you're only out two or three dollars. At *worst*," Kitty adds emphatically.

"Can I run a tab?" Hack says looking about helplessly. "That's at least twelve bucks a month. I'm not a Rockefeller."

"Only play one card, Thomas. You can afford the ten cents. And you're bound to win *some* games." After a brief pause, she adds, "Well, maybe not."

"I don't know," Hack says glumly. "An afternoon of Bingo and I'll fall behind on my letter writing."

Kitty looks at Aaron and shakes her head, "he's so full of it."

"And besides," Hack says, frowning as if he is consummately worried, "Aaron writes a letter home every day, and I have to help him with punctuation. He doesn't know a period from a comma. Thinks "My Country Tis of Thee" should end in a question mark."

That's not it," Aaron says, "I just don't know what "Tis" means."

Kitty snorts and says, "One thing's for sure, I'll never stop by here for a humorous pick-me-up."

Aaron nods. "How about this one: 'Hack couldn't spell ink if he was spotted the letters I and K.'"

Aaron's offer is a slight twist of an old put-down joke, but Kitty's chortle is long, loud and so sincere sounding that Hack isn't sure if was sarcastic or not.

Kitty says to Aaron, "Can I count on you?"

"Not so fast," Hack says, looking at Aaron. "We're conferencing on this."

Kitty understands, however, that Hack has tacitly agreed to play. "At two o'clock in the dining room," she says. "Bring markers to cover the numbers on your cards . . . the ones that get called."

"Only the number *one* gets called?" Hack asks querulously.

Kitty looks disgustedly at Aaron. He nods, and says, "I'm not playing if Hack is."

Bern Goodson is pacing back and forth in front of a regular, four-place dining table that has been moved to the head of the dining room. An aide, sitting behind the table, is staring at a spherical wire cage half filled with numbered wooden balls. What's left of a stack of Bingo cards is sitting to her right. Next to the stack is a blue, imitation leather pouch, the kind banks loan to business customers for depositing receipts or toting cash. Stuffed slipshod inside the pouch are what appear to be a five-dollar bill and a dozen or more ones. Lon Fuller is sitting with Edith McGuire at the table where the two of them always eat together, and Kitty is sitting with her friends, Emma Pankhurst and Yvon Chafee, at the table nearest to where Bern will call the game. Kitty sees us, slightly nods, and turns back to her friends. Aaron, while Hack makes his way to an empty table, purchases four cards. He keeps two cards and hands two to Hack.

Bern stops pacing and looks at her watch. "Another minute, people," she says. She resumes her slow, absent-minded, back-and-forth stroll. The players begin talking among themselves again. Hack looks at his watch: it is exactly two o'clock.

Bern after a few minutes stops pacing and says loudly, "Okay people . . . let's begin!"

The chattering, unbroken to that point, stops as abruptly as when someone suddenly mutes the audio on a TV. Random kitchen clattering becomes audible.

"Are there any first-timers?" Bern says. "Any newcomers?"

Joetta Fisher, who is sitting at the table next to where Kitty and her two friends have settled in, stands and wildly waves her hand. No doubt a veteran player, her friends let on that her gesture is terribly funny. No one else admits to being a first-time player.

"All right then folks" Bern says. "Remember, ball N fifty-four is missing, so right away, everybody! Cover N fifty-four. N as in Nancy, five four"

The players cover the number N-54 on their cards. Aaron and Hack exchange brow-wrinkled looks, and Hack raises his hand. "Uh," he says when Bern sees him, "Aaron forgot to bring our number markers."

Aaron aims his thumb at me, looks away, and shakes his head showily.

Kitty says to Bern, "I *told* them!"

The crisis ends when a woman player offers Hack and Aaron a handful of small buttons that she has pawed from an eight-inch round tin box on the floor under her chair.

The emergency over, Bern says, "Who wants to select the Pig today?"

Four or five players rise erratically to their feet, and the honor of selecting the numbered ball that will be the "Pig" goes to withered-but-nimble Joetta Fisher.

"You picked the last time, Joetta," a woman complains. Another woman huffily agrees. Joetta ignores both women. Turning her head toward the rest of us, she reaches through the trap door atop the cage of numbered balls, pulls one out, and hands it to Bern.

"Everybody!" Bern says loudly. "The Pig is number B sixteen. B one six." Returning the ball, she says, "Did everyone get the Pig number?"

Gary Moyer, shaking his head, says loudly, "Did you say fifteen or sixteen?"

Moyer is badly stooped. His center of gravity falls somewhere in the space under his forward slanted chest; when he's standing he'd fall on his face without his walker for support; Kitty says his inclined body is evidence of advanced osteoporosis. His voice, however, is strong and commands attention. Once, alone with Kitty, Hack referred to Moyer as Ichabod Crane, and he was instantly stabbed with one of her icy stare-downs.

"Six-teen," Bern says to Moyer.

Moyer is still uncertain.

Bern loudly repeats the number, this time holding up ten fingers and then six fingers. At the same time, the woman sitting at the table next to Moyer shows him a bingo card and agitatedly pokes a finger at the number B-16. Moyer nods congenially.

"Any more questions?" Bern asks. Several players shake their heads. "The first game will be single Bingo, one line horizontally, vertically, or slanted. Okay?"

Several of the players nod.

"Then here we go people!"

The aide spins the cage, and when it stops she opens a small door covering the chute. A ball rolls out. Bern inspects it and shouts, "O seventy-five. Under O seven five."

The number O-75 is not on any of the four cards purchased by Aaron.

On the eighth number called by Bern, two women bingo.

"Not already!" Lon Fuller says loudly. He glares at the winner, the woman sitting nearest to where he and Edith are playing.

Together, Aaron and Hack have covered a total of seven widely scattered numbers.

Hack says to Aaron, "Even I could pick better cards."

"You want the other players to think we're ringers?" Aaron asks.

"What's a 'Ringer,'" Hack whispers.

After a moment, Aaron whispers back, "three points in Horseshoes."

"As if I didn't know," Hack mumbles.

The two winners split the proceeds, less fifty cents that is put aside for next week's Pig. They net two dollars and change, apiece.

After the aide returns from paying the winners, Bern orders us to clear our cards, and like a stern schoolmistress she looks around to make sure everyone obeys. While she's explaining the form of the next game, Fuller bawls, "I did not forget."

Snickering, Aaron whispers, "He forgot and cleared N fifty-four."

Moyer turns half way around in his chair and glares at Fuller. Moyer is so bent over and turns so slowly that he reminds Hack of a long-armed construction crane swinging a heavy load across a site. Hack cannot see his eyes, but from his bearing he knows they're cocked as if he were looking over lowered reading glasses. He turns back, and says to Bern, "What game is this again?"

Hack needs two more numbers to win the Red Cross game when someone bingos. Aaron's best card needs four more numbers. The payout is the same as the first game.

Fuller, the next game mistakenly thinks he bingoed, and when Bern invites him to check the numbered balls that she had set aside after announcing each of the winning bingo numbers, instead of simply rectifying his goof he marches away in a huff. Surprisingly, Edith does not follow Fuller from the room.

No one at Kitty's table wins, nor does anyone bingo on the Pig number: next week's Pig, therefore, will be richer by several dollars. Bern tells the players to leave their cards where they are sitting, that Mary, the aide, will gather them after everyone leaves. Hack assures Aaron that they did not blow their standings as Bingo pros.

"Ready?" Hack says to Aaron. Spotting Edith McGuire bearing down on them, Hack turns loose of his walker and sits back down.

Aaron, who does not see Edith coming, looks at his watch, nods, and begins to rise. "Well, that wasn't too bad."

Edith stops inches short of bowling Aaron over. Smiling excitedly, she asks him how he did.

"No luck," Aaron answers shaking his head.

"Me either," Edith says. She pretends to whimper.

Edith McGuire is an airhead. She is, however, still an attractive woman. Her hair, cut pageboy style (Kitty's description), is thick and dark, slightly gray-flecked, and always perfectly arranged. Her face is neither wrinkled nor puffy with age, and she does not trowel on the make-up. She has a little whore's belly and could lose a few pounds around the hips, but that's nitpicking. Her clothes are flashy and too coed-ish, but Hack has yet to see her wearing a blouse that was spotted with dribbled food, a common sight around here. When men are nearby, she acts like a skittish teenager.

"It's so nice out today," she says, staring dreamily across the room at the scene visible through the windows of the dining room's one outside wall.

"Beautiful out," Aaron says, his eyes tracking Edith's gaze.

Hack could be another chair at the table.

"I believe I'll take a walk," Edith says, smiling and hunching her shoulders lazily. "Would you walk with me, Aaron?" Her little-girl pout explains what a bummer it would be if he refuses.

Aaron's smile, as it does when he's considering one of my less than sparkling suggestions for killing time, begins a slow fade.

"Well I . . . I guess so. Yes, that . . . that'd be just fine."

He looks at Hack and says, "Think you can you make it back to the room alone old fellow?"

Edith leaps to Hack's defense. "Tom is *not* old!"

"I'll manage," Hack says petulantly.

"I better make a pit stop first," Aaron mumbles.

Very concerned, Edith says to him, "You had better do what?"

"I better take care of some personal business first."

"Oh. Mind if I tag along?"

Hack lays his hand on Edith's forearm and says softly, "Aaron has to urinate."

"Oh," Edith says.

[36]

Hack pushes a wheelchair-bound player from the dining room to a Cooper Greens exit door through which he will leave the building for a smoke, as will Hack himself. It is three forty-five. If Hack goes to his room, he will doze off. He has already napped once today, and if he dozes off again he'll be awake most of the night. Damned Aaron, he knows, conks out at ten p.m. and, whether he naps in the daytime or not, sleeps for seven straight hours. One thing, Aaron does not snore at night; at any rate Hack does not hear him with his "ears" (hearing aids) removed.

Deciding to visit Marie, Hack heads for his unit's nurse station. On the way, he passes Violet "Bushel Butt." He has not visited Elm Street since before Joe Luoma died in April, and Violet wants to know where he's been.

"In the john," Hack answers without slowing.

Violet's grin becomes an up-yours smirk that lasts as they slowly pass each other.

Marie is sitting at the desk inside the nurse's station that serves some sixteen rooms, including Hack's and Aaron's, working on her shift report. "Hi, Nursey," Hack says, "Working overtime?"

Marie has on her glasses, which usually hang from a cord looped around her neck. Billie is standing behind her, ready to offer up the events of her own first-shift activities. Three residents, two women and a man, their wheelchairs backed against the wall opposite the front of the nurses station, are chin-on-chest sound asleep.

"What do *you* want?" Marie says sharply, glancing at her watch.

"I decided to favor you with the pleasure of my company," Hack says. "Since you're not busy."

"I haven't heard yet from Dr. Bonifanti," Marie says, removing her glasses.

"Likely, you haven't even called her."

"Likely not." Marie masks a yawn with the back of her hand. "Where's Aaron?"

"In our room playing with himself. I was embarrassed and left."

Marie sighs and brushes aside my remark. Billie smiles timidly.

"He's with Edith McGuire."

"*With* Edith?" Marie says, raising an eyebrow.

"Yeah. Think we can trust the little squirt? He's hyper-sexed, you know."

Marie pretends to be shocked. "I didn't know *that*," she says in a low confidential voice. "Do you suppose he caught it from you?"

"Likely. They're taking a walk. Tell me a joke."

"I don't know any," Marie says, looking around for any nearby people. "Did you hear the one about the undertaker who hung himself?"

"Yes. And I laughed so hard that I wet the mattress in my crib. Besides, he wasn't an undertaker, he was a plastic surgeon."

"I guess I heard a recycled version," Marie says shrugging. She masks another yawn with her hand.

"Whoa!" Hack blurts out. "Let me see that again!"

Marie smiles and presents her left hand, palm down. On her ring finger is a tiny diamond engagement ring.

"Why, you horse's pa-toot! You didn't tell me!"

Pulling her hand closer to his face, Hack excessively admires the stone's pin-point of sparkle. "Congratulations!" He exclaims. "Dang, who's the lucky guy?"

"It's only been a week," Marie says pulling her hand back. "Henry Spear. Do you know Henry?"

"Hank Spear! Of course I know Hank. From Trundel Mills. Salt of the earth."

Hack reviews his knowledge of Henry Spear: Henry Spear is a stubborn old farmer who has yet to spend all of the first dollar he ever earned. He's my age, maybe older. He goes to our church, St. Bernadette's.

Helen once told Hack that he could not keep his eyes off her legs.

"Guess you've been seeing each other for a while?" Marie nods. "For . . . months."

"Hey!" Hack says, after a moment of groping for another matrimonial topic. "I get to kiss the bride!"

"I'm not a bride yet," Marie says, rising and offering Hack her cheek.

"No you *don't*," Hack says. He takes her head in his hands and presses his lips hard against hers. In the process, he nearly loses his balance.

Grinning, Marie pulls away. "Now, you've got lipstick on."

"Good. Wait 'til Aaron sees. He'll turn green as a dill pickle."

Billie has been watching silently and Hack says to her, "I suppose you knew all along." Billie emphatically nods.

Hack asks Marie, who has returned to her chair and resumed writing a report, if a date has been set.

"Not yet. Goodbye, Mister Murtaugh." Slipping her glasses back on, she adds, "I'm busy."

Linda McNutt, who was sleeping in her wheelchair by the nurse's station when Hack arrived, is now awake – probably roused by his joshing Marie. As Hack is leaving she queries him about Aaron's well-being.

"I'm sure you heard about his bad accident," Hack says over his shoulder. Hack shakes his head sadly, pretends not to hear her answer, and hobbles off.

[37]

Yesterday Hack resumed reading Tom Wolfe's *The Bonfire of the Vanities*. He had not cracked a book since Aaron was moved into his room, and Kitty had been after him. At the beginning of chapter seven, where he picks up again, Peter Fallow is waking up with an industrial-grade hangover. Hack cannot remember who Peter Fallow is, and he is thumbing through chapter six hoping to spot a contextual reference when Aaron returns from his walk with Edith McGuire. Marching straight into the bathroom, he steps out some ten minutes later with a confused look on his face. He asks Hack in a detached way if he'd been waiting long, meaning had he been waiting a long time for him to arrive so they could eat supper together.

"Well over an hour, "Hack answers mechanically.

Aaron of course knows better but he reminds Hack, nevertheless, that patience is a virtue, quoting exactly (it sounds like to Hack) a biblical mention of the Devil's testing of Job.

On their way to supper, Hack asks Aaron if he enjoyed his stroll with Edith. Aaron does not immediately answer, and Hack says that the hard questions come later. Finally, Aaron allows that their walk was "interesting." Hack mulls over Aaron's reply and decides Aaron would rather he changed the subject. "Did you hear about Marie?"

Aaron shakes his head.

"She's engaged to be married."

Having drifted a yard or so ahead, Aaron turns and waits for Hack to catch up. "No kidding." Aaron smiles for the first time since returning from his walk with Edith. "That's wonderful. I like Marie. Do you know her fiancé?"

"Yeah. Slightly. Henry Spear. He's a farmer. His wife died . . . some years back."

"He's older than Marie?"

Hack grunts disdainfully."Fifteen years, I'd guess. Maybe twenty."

"When's the wedding? Have they decided?"

"Not yet, is what Marie told me."

Hack and Aaron are still a few yards from the dining room when Kitty and Panky Pankhurst saunter through the door on their way out. They see the two men, and Kitty, obviously feeling good about something, sings the first two lines of the refrain of the minstrel *Old Dan Tucker.* "'Get out the way old Dan Tucker, You're too late to get your supper.'"

Aaron looks at Hack. He nods and says to Kitty, "Care to hear my version? Get out the way you old . . ."

Kitty scowls, and Hack asks her if she knew that Marie had become engaged.

"To Henry Spear," Kitty answers, nodding. She doen't sniff, but it' is clear that Hack has disrespected her endless knowledge of social events taking place at Cooper Greens. "I'm familiar with Hank Spear," she adds. "He won't beat on her anyway."

"He better not," Hack says. "He does, and Marie'll kick *his* butt."

"She might at that," Kitty says.

Aaron has drifted closer to the dining room where Panky, who has followed him, is solemnly elaborating on how she cheated death from an agonizing gout attack on her big toe – or an equally deadly mosquito bite. Left practically alone with Kitty, Hack says softly, "It has been two weeks, Dear."

Kitty nods. "Tonight?"

"How well do you know Edith McGuire?" Aaron says to me. He and Hack have finished supper and returned to their room. Aaron barely spoke while they were eating.

"I don't know her at all," Hack answers cautiously. "She's a looker, though. Why?"

Aaron slightly shakes his head, acts as if he is uncertain over what to say next. Hack settles his back against the headrest of his bed and turns on the TV. Aaron says something that Hack cannot understand, so

Hack mutes the audio. Aaron glances at their door, which is two-thirds closed, steps between the room's two beds, and backs onto his. He again weakly shakes his head. "I almost didn't escape with my life out there this afternoon."

Hack makes certain that Aaron is alluding to his walk with Edith McGuire: "Out there?" "With Edith?"

Hack nods, but as if he anticipated hearing something of a private nature, says nothing .

"You know that recess in the wall near the middle of the west wing?" Aaron asks.

"I don't think so."

"Behind those two big lilac bushes."

"Oh. Where the gas company put in a meter?"

"Yes. That one."

"I guess it's still there." Hack says uncertainly.

After several seconds Aaron says, "She . . . wanted to, right then and there."

"Wanted to?" Hack says. Hack knew what Aaron meant, but that's what popped out of his mouth.

"You know . . . Tom . . . what I'm saying."

"I guess so."

"She said she'd never "been" with a man . . . like me. I blew it. I said I'd never been with a white woman either. I meant that I did *not* wanna start now. Only, she took it the wrong way. I wasn't . . . ."

Hack shrugs in a way to mean that Aaron's hand was on the tiller, on the lever attached to his sea-going ship's rudder.

"She was very dogged."

"Like . . . busy little hands, dogged?"

"And then some."

"Uh . . . what . . . happened?"

"Nothing. I . . . stopped it. The next time, though . . . I don't know, Tom. I was . . . starting to swell."

"Go for it!" Hack says. "Stop acting like a Benedictine monk."

But Hack's enthusiasm, he admits to himself, is a bit put on. It bothers him to see a white woman coming on to a black man. He supposes it is deep-seated envy, a vague sense of physical inferiority that depreciates his whiteness. Does that make him a racist? He hopes not, but he does wonder. He knows this irrefutably, he has never liked another man as much as he likes Aaron. Not even Toby.

"No . . . I won't. For a lot of reasons," Aaron says.

Aaron does not particularize, and Hack says, smiling, "Change your luck. You know what they say."

"Yeah." Aaron says after a moment. "And *they* also say funny things about . . . the anatomy of Oriental women."

"Hell, you're both adults," Hack says.

Aaron expels a full lung of air. "I don't know. I'd feel like I was cheating on Opal. Can you . . . believe that?"

With all the sincerity he can muster, Hack says, "Aaron, you have never told me a thing that I did not believe." Aaron seems to barely hear Hack.

"Seriously. Never. You're a dad-blamed saint . . . you little peckerwood. For a year I felt the same way. That I'd be cheating on Helen. But, hey . . . time has a way of wearing a man down."

Aaron nods slowly and then suddenly stops. Hack wonders if Aaron suspects he is sleeping with Kitty.

Wheel of Fortune ends, and Aaron, holding the TV remote, asks Hack if there is a program he'd like to watch.

"What's today? Thursday?"

"Thursday the eighth, all day."

Hack tells Aaron that on Thursday there's nothing on TV that he enjoys watching.

Aaron begins clicking the controller, finally stopping on the Discovery Channel.

Cooper Greens residents pay sixteen dollars a month for a basic TV package that includes twenty-six of a hundred or so available channels. Hack's service is in his name, but Aaron unfailingly reimburses Hack half the charge on the first day of each month. Aaron even insisted that Hack accept his pro rata share for the week he lived at Cooper Greens in April.

Evidently the Pittsburgh-based cable company's main broadcast dish is not aimed north because Cooper Greens does not receive Pittsburgh transmissions, which are all sent from south of Cooper Greens. That is Aaron's theory anyway. This matters to Hack because he cannot routinely watch TV broadcasts of Steelers football games that are transmitted by Pittsburgh's pioneer station KDKA. It's Hack's certainty that the best three hours on TV, other than a Yankee-Indian baseball game, is when the Pittsburgh Steelers are kicking the health out of the Dallas Cowboys at – at Three Rivers Stadium on a snowy Sunday afternoon. The Philadelphia Eagles were a pathetic, three and thirteen last season, a fact that Hack reminds Aaron about every chance he gets.

The program on the *Discovery Channel* is on deciphering ancient stone markings, and Hack quickly loses interest. Aaron, however, is spellbound. Hack removes his hearing aids and picks up where he left off reading *The Bonfire of the Vanities*.

Aaron, whose attention has remained steadfast on the television set, suddenly improves his posture and mutes the audio. He addresses someone at our door, and Linda McNutt, the woman who was dozing in her wheelchair when Hack chatted with Marie yesterday, cautiously wheels herself into our room. She is followed by three more women in wheelchairs – a regular caravan of the walking impaired. Hack pushes his hearing aids back into his ears.

"We're so glad to see that you're feeling better, Aaron," Linda says.

"We were worried," the second woman says.

"Very," the third woman, genuinely concerned, chimes in.

If the fourth woman, who has stopped in the doorway, said anything, Hack did not hear her.

Aaron, his tiny smile contested by a frown, mumbles something amounting to praise of their thoughtfulness for stopping.

"He's started watching TV again," Hack says earnestly to Linda. "That's a good sign."

Linda agrees excitedly. "Oh, it certainly is."

Her companions all gushingly concur.

Aaron by now has caught on, and the glare he aims at Hack would penetrate a gladiator's shield. Hack is smiling tenderly at Linda, however, and he hardly notices.

"I'm ashamed to admit this," the second woman says, "but I'm not sure exactly when you had your accident, Aaron."

The third woman, her face drawn, asks, "You fell, didn't you Aaron?"

"I'm . . . not sure," Aaron answers uncertainly, his narrowed gaze still focused on Hack.

His eyes narrowed, Hack nods at Linda. "He was unconscious a good half-minute."

"Oh," Linda says, "that had to be scary."

"But not for Aaron," Hack says. "Personally, I hadn't been as frightened since the night I walked on the berm of a road against traffic pouring from a NOW meeting."

Linda stares at Hack blankly, but he decides not to tell her that N O W stands for the assertively intolerant National Organization for Women.

"Well," Linda says to Aaron after a few seconds of frowning uncertainly, "we're very happy to see that you're feeling better."

Her three friends, as if their heads are ganged to a length of rebar, nod rapidly.

Linda once more assures Aaron that she and her companions are elated to see him up and about and then hands him a large greeting card. "We've all signed it. And, Aaron, we mean every word!"

Aaron, smiling weakly, reaches for the card. On the front, in a large, swirly script, are two words: "In Sympathy."

"Oh that is a beautiful card," Hack says, leaving his bed and stepping into his walker. "You ladies made it, didn't you?"

A number of Cooper Greens' female residents fabricate holiday and birthday cards from artwork that has been cut from used cards of similarly well-meant expressions. Bern Goodson holds classes, and the make-over cards are quite attractive.

Beaming, Linda allows that that was indeed the case. "Be sure to save us all your greeting cards, Thomas," she adds looking past Aaron at me.

"I most certainly will," Hack says.

Hack works his way around Linda while Aaron is reading the message printed inside his card. Apparently, it is quite long; Hack can't help but notice that it is surrounded by dozens of signatures.

"I've got to run, ladies," Hack says, pausing in the doorway. "You folks have a nice long visit." Hack cuts his eyes briefly at Aaron and slightly nods. "But don't stay too long, please."

A step into the hall and out of Aaron's sight, Hack says loudly, "See you later, Aaron. *Don't* over do it."

Hack boasts, tells himself that making Cooper Greens a more cheerful place to live out one's life, at least on a small scale, is working even better than he had hoped. So what, he thinks to himself, if it takes two of us. He and Aaron are not getting older, they're getting better. "Or so," he tells himself, "I've heard elders remark about themselves – in TV and magazine ads."

[38]

Hack and Aaron have finished breakfast and returned to their room. Aaron is writing a letter and Hack has resurrected his interest in reading Wolfe's novel. It rained hard during the night, judging by the many shallow puddles on the rear parking lot. Neither Hack nor Aaron brings up the subject of taking their usual morning walk.

Marie marches briskly into their room. "Doctor Bonifanti will be coming by tomorrow," she announces.

Aaron nods agreeably; Hack presents her an irritated look. "What time?"

"Nine thirty."

"What this means," Hack says to Aaron, "is that Bonifanti, if we're lucky, will arrive here sometime before noon."

Marie gives Hack a spiteful look. "Doctor Bonifanti is usually punctual." She says to Aaron, have you checked your feet? Lately? Has he Tom?"

"God, I don't know, Hack answers. "If I see him removing his socks I clear out."

"Yes," Aaron says, nodding twice at Marie. "Ah . . . you know. More or less."

"You can bet it's not more," Hack says brusquely to Marie.

"Is there swelling? Itching? I haven't trimmed your toenails since you moved in."

Although Helen would sometimes voluntarily trim Hack's toenails, he knew that nurses at Cooper Greens were duty-bound to see that every resident's toenails were regularly trimmed. Hack was still uneasy, however, over asking one to do something that he could at least marginally do himself. Hack presumed Aaron felt the same way.

"I haven't seen anything unusual," Aaron answers.

Marie is openly skeptical. "Tom, is he still sneaking cookies from vending machines?"

Surprised to hear of his pussyfooting to weasel cookies, Hack tilts back and fixes Aaron with his practiced faux mean look. "I don't know. Most likely he is."

"Only twice since I've been here," Aaron says firmly to Marie. "And the last time was weeks ago."

"I'm sure Doctor Bonifanti will want me to draw blood," Marie says, clearly suspicious of Aaron's answers.

"Honest," Aaron says. "I feel fine."

Marie crisply tells Aaron that in the case of diabetes, feeling "fine" does not cut it. She asks Hack if he has any questions, and he shakes his head. After she leaves, Hack tells Aaron that he, Aaron, acted as embarrassed as the time he was preaching and his tally whacker tumbled through the fly of his pants. Nodding contemplatively, Hack adds, "Jolly told me about it."

Hack's silliness does not strike Aaron as funny. "Of course she did," he mutters.

Aaron is playing solitaire on his bed, and he and Hack are kibitzing, when Dr. Bonifanti walks into their room at a couple minutes before ten o'clock. Marie follows her in. Hack has already explained to Aaron why he is sure to like Dr. Bonifanti as she is not only pretty but also a runt, which half-pint stature Aaron will readily appreciate. Her hair, it seems to Hack, is a shade blacker than it was her last visit. She is definitely more self-assured.

After sparingly greeting me, she says to Aaron, "I'm Doctor Bonifanti."

Aaron meekly returns her salutation.

"Who," she asks the window, "wants to be first?"

"Aaron," Hack says. "And then please order him from the room. I don't want him watching you check me out." Hack is kidding, but Doctor Bonifanti takes him seriously.

Hack, mumbling that he is only teasing, looks at Aaron. Aaron shrugs and agrees to be her first patient.

Dr. Bonifanti tells Aaron to sit on his bed. "How have you been feeling? I finally received your medical records from Dr. Gruenthal's office. It has been over a year since your last eye examination. I'll set up an appointment. There's an ophthalmologist in Meadville."

Aaron nods unenthusiastically.

"How's your weight?"

"The same, a hundred-fifty pounds."

Marie thumbs to a sheet on her clipboard, reads aloud the figures of Aaron's last two weigh-ins, and dates of the measurements.

"Good," Dr. Bonifanti says. "Are you exercising regularly?"

Hack, pretending he cannot suppress a snort of amusement, cups his hand to his mouth. Aaron ignores him. "Pretty much," Aaron answers. "Tom and I hike around the building every day."

Dr. Bonifanti glances at Hack's walker. "That's not enough. You should be hitting the PT room for a good half hour every day."

Hack fakes another guffaw.

"I know," Aaron says sheepishly. "I'll get with it."

Dr. Bonifanti methodically checks Aaron's blood pressure and pulse rate, which Marie records, looks into his eyes, ears, nose, and throat, and listens to his heart. "Are you're taking your Glucotrol regularly?" she asks him, slipping the stethoscope into a pocket of her smock.

"Yes Ma'am."

"There's a new medicine I may start you on called Rezulin. It makes better use of your body's natural insulin. I want to see your blood sugar first, though . . . get an A 1 C test."

"A what?" Aaron says.

"A comprehensive," Dr. Bonifanti answers dismissively. "Show me your feet."

Aaron removes his slippers, leans back on his elbows, and holds his feet out. Dr. Bonifanti lightly scores his left sole with a throw-away tongue-depressor offered her by Marie. His foot slightly moves. She scores the other sole and gently pokes the stick in the area by his toes. Looking quizzically at Aaron, she says after a bit, "Get your nails trimmed." To Marie she says, "A 1 C Diabetes."

Dr. Bonifanti hands Marie the tongue depressor and Marie tosses it in Aaron's waste basket. Finding a label, Marie writes on it and then presses it onto a vial.

Dr. Bonifanti moves to the foot of my bed, curiosity distorting her pretty face. "Marie said you wanted to see me?"

Hack is slow to answer. Unable to easily overlook her urban abruptness, he wonders why she does not see that all the residents of Cooper Greens' are basically slow-witted country folk. "Yes," Hack says after a long sigh. "My prostate's giving me fits again. And I can't urinate easily."

"Easily?" Dr. Bonifanti says.

After a moment, Hack says, "my stream is weak."

Dr. Bonifanti nods slowly. "And . . . giving you fits? How?"

"It hurts . . . worse than before."

"The Naprosyn isn't helping?"

"No," Hack says shaking his head. "It never helped. I stopped–"

"Doctor!" Marie cries out suddenly.

Aaron, who was sitting on the edge of his bed when Dr. Bonifanti left him, has fallen back and is laying half on his side and half on his stomach. His face is buried in the bed's quilt. Marie is struggling to simultaneously roll him over and lift his legs onto the bed.

Dr. Bonifanti rushes to help. They turn Aaron to where he's lying flat on his back in the middle of the bed. Marie slips his pillow under his feet. In at most twenty seconds –Hack was gathering his wits, and he wasn't sure how long he was out – Marie says cheerily, "Good morning, Aaron!"

Aaron tries to sit up, but Dr. Bonifanti, one hand firmly on his chest, orders him to lie still.

Another few seconds pass, and Aaron says, "I fainted, didn't I?"

"Yes you did," Marie says clearly concerned.

"Darn," Aaron says. "I should have said something. I thought I was over it. That's the first time in a long while." He sighs. "I . . . taking shots upsets me."

"So we gathered," Marie says. She sneaks a wide-eyed look of relief at Dr. Bonifanti.

"I'm all right now," Aaron says, sitting up. He briefly stares out of our window before turning back to look at Dr. Bonifanti and Marie. His tiny smile is apologetic.

"You're sure?" Marie says to him, ready to offer her arm for support.

"I'm sure," Aaron says, patting her arm.

That afternoon, Aaron told Hack this story about himself: Years ago, a carbuncle – big around as a half-dollar, Aaron claimed – developed on the back of his neck. His family doctor decided, during one of Aaron's office visits, to lance and drain it. Helped by his nurse, the doctor prepped Aaron's neck. Aaron, of course, could not see what they were doing. The doctor momentarily turned away, and at that point Aaron decided he'd better fess up to the fact that he sometimes fainted while getting a medical shot. Grinning, the doctor explained that he had already shot anesthesia into the infected area. Aaron thought this over for a second and passed out.

Dr. Bonifanti, after studying Aaron for the better part of a minute, nods at Marie and then resumes asking Hack questions. "You said the Naprosyn isn't helping?"

"Not really."

She stares off thoughtfully a few seconds, and then – as if Hack had a choice – says, "I'd like to examine you again."

Her digital examination this time is as thorough as before, and when she finishes Hack is half blinded by the tears in his eyes. After slowly removing and disposing her latex glove in a plastic bag offered by Marie, she tells Hack she wants another biopsy.

"Hell, you just got one," Hack says irritably.

"That was nine months ago."

"I gather that . . . there's been a change?"

"Yes. Besides the swelling, I can feel a tiny nodule that wasn't there before."

"Great," Hack says disgustedly. "Exactly what I wanted to hear."

Dr. Bonifanti finds a particular page in Hack's medical chart and then tells Marie she'll have her office contact Dr. Egli. "Hope will call you," she says.

Before it dawns on Hack that "Hope" is the first name of a woman in Dr. Bonifanti's office, Hack thinks she said "Hope will call on you," and for a moment he wonders what in the hell kind of faith healer is treating him.

Dr. Bonifanti and Marie have left the room for only a few seconds when Aaron walks in. Marie, when she left Aaron's side to help Dr. Bonifanti minister to me, had unfurled our privacy curtain, and Hack was not aware he had left until she re-bundled the curtain on her way out. Aaron has a curious look on his face, but he simply stares at Hack without saying anything. Hack finishes buttoning his shirt and says offhandedly, "Doctor Bonifanti's a little cutey, isn't she?"

"What'd you find out?" Aaron says, after Hack breaks the silence.

"I've got a pimple on my prostate. Apparently you are doing all right?"

"I guess so. What else?"

"She wants a biopsy . . . wants to examine a tad of my prostate."

Aaron is suddenly lost in thought. "I had it done . . . three years ago."

"Me too. Hell . . . months ago."

"Then," Aaron says, "you know the program."

"I'm afraid so."

When Hack does not elaborate, he says, "I'll go with you, Tom."

At Aaron's kindness, Hack struggles to avoid showing the emotion he feels, and his answer is a small unworthy nod.

"But, only if you want," Aaron adds meekly, wondering, Hack presumes, if he's crossed the line in the matter of judging Hack's courage.

Hack assures him that he'd like nothing better: "Really. I'd like you to be with me."

Aaron nods and slightly grins.

"Hey!" Hack says, with false-hearted enthusiasm. "It looks like I'll have to ask Buster to hang an Off-Limits-To-Aaron-Blodgett sign on all the vending machines around here."

Aaron snorts, insists that Marie got carried away in relating his conversance with our cookie vending machine.

"I don't think so," Hack says. "But I hope the hell you're not BS-ing me."

Aaron, after moving to a place in front of his bulletin board, says, "You ever attend an Intergenerational?"

"No," Hack answers. "Children don't cotton to me."

Aaron explains to Hack why that might be. "Maybe you kid them too much, Tom. Most children don't know you're kidding, especially when you use hyperbole."

"There you go again," Hack says. "Using a big word you can't even spell."

"Hyperbole?" Aaron says. "It means exaggeration." Disheartened at my ignorance, or so he would like Hack to believe, he sadly shakes his head.

Plain and simple, Aaron is offering Hack advice. Hack did not at first understand, but once he did, he took it to heart.

"You're way over his head," Kitty says, glancing at Aaron and then fixing her gaze on me. "Good morning, Dears," she adds.

Having turned to face me, Aaron did not see her enter our room. He says to her, "Scrooge, here, insists that children don't like him. I can't imagine why, can you?"

"Oh heavens yes," Kitty says, "Give me a tablet and I'll write down my reasons. Number the pages."

Kitty asks Hack what Dr. Bonifanti had to say, and he tells her she ordered Aaron to get off his duff and onto a treadmill. "The little sneak's been tapping vending machines for cookies. Did you know that?"

Kitty shakes her head. Still the focus of her attention, Hack says that Dr. Bonifanti felt a pimple on his prostate and wants a biopsy.

Clicking her tongue, Kitty says to Aaron, "Tom wants me to believe that'll hurt."

"It will," Aaron replies. "*Slightly*."

Kitty walks to our window and looks at the sky. "It's time for lunch. What are we having today, fellows? Either of you know?"

"Road-kill possum," Hack says. "Why do you care? A hummingbird couldn't survive on the scraps you eat."

Aaron turns back to his bulletin board, taps a square on our July calendar of events, and tells the two of us that today's lunch menu calls for New England Boiled Dinner, Parker House rolls, and tapioca pudding.

Aaron and Hack take turns washing their hands in the bathroom sink, and the three of them leave for the dining room.

A few steps away from the door of our room Aaron says to Kitty, "We can lose him if we pick up the pace."

Kitty says, "I should have worn my Keds."

Hack says softly, "Up yours. Both of you."

[39]

All the resident rooms of Cooper Greens have call-lights over their doorways, and many are illuminated in the hallway where Hack and Aaron are plodding along. Aaron comments on the unusually high number of lit call-lamps – were on our way to breakfast – and Hack is sorely tempted to remind him, as a currently popular saying has it, that "shit" happens. Only, it is early and Hack is inhibited by morning willies – over and above his somewhat spotty respect for the fact that Aaron was once a practicing Protestant clergyman. A few doorways down the hall, Susan Bender, glumly shaking her head, steps out of one of the rooms. Susan takes Billie's place on weekends. Hack calls to her, and she waits for them.

"Busy morning," Hack says. "Must have been the sauerkraut for supper."

"You haven't heard?" she says. Susan is flabbergasted that Hack and Aaron haven't an inkling about something the entire world is tuned in to, notwithstanding the obvious fact – her deference suggests -- that Hack and Aaron are a couple of doddering old goats.

Aaron and Hack exchange frowns, and Aaron says to Susan, "Haven't heard what?"

As if indignant that she has to explain, Susan, in a hushed voice, says that John Kennedy's plane crashed in the Atlantic Ocean. Implausible though it sounds, it does not instantly occur to Hack that she means JFK, Jr., not his father. Aaron later told Hack that he had exactly the same reaction. They dismiss their moments of confusion as the collateral damage of old age.

"It's all over the TV," Susan says, beckoning us to follow her back into the room that she had just left.

Dan Rather, ordinarily CBS's evening news anchor, is explaining that young Kennedy, a licensed pilot, had intended to make a daytime flight. But for a reason Hack and Aaron missed hearing, he was held up and did not leave until evening. In the meantime, threatening weather had moved in.

Hack and Aaron watch the TV for a number of minutes, until Rather reports that the Coast Guard has recovered wreckage and flotsam that is likely from Kennedy's plane. At this news, Aaron and Hack, as if cued, turn and leave the room. Susan had already quietly left.

They continue on to breakfast. "I'm afraid that's it," Aaron says, his face sober. "Now all we can do is pray."

"Pray he's already in heaven. Is that Kennedy family snake-bit or what? He's still a kid. Was a kid, I mean."

Aaron nods. "Suffer the little children to come unto me," he says softly. They walk a couple more steps, and he says, "I've forgotten how the rest goes."

Kitty, Panky, and Yvon, lingering over coffee, limply wave to us as we enter the dining room. Their faces are sullen. Yvon is clearly the most unhinged. When they leave, Kitty swings by the two men's table and tells them that neither she nor her friends will be playing cards this afternoon.

Aaron and Hack eat and leisurely drift back to their room. On the way, they discuss the tragedy that is on everyone's lips. At some point – their conversation is anything but centered – Hack wonders aloud at how history would have treated JFK's presidency had he served two full terms. His remark sets the two of them to arguing the policies of President Clinton's administration.

Aaron, as does President Clinton, favors tariff-free trade among the U.S., Canada, and Mexico. Hack, for years a union machinist, does not. Aaron thinks the U.S. should not have interfered in Yugoslavia's domestic problem; Hack disagrees. The Democrats and Republicans are at odds over the best way to spend down this year's budget surplus: Aaron wants the money returned to the people in the form of tax relief; Hack thinks it should be used to reduce our national debt. Aaron accuses Hack of being a closet Republican, adding that he has been an "FDR Democrat" his whole life. Hack tells Aaron that he is also a life-long Democrat. By the time they reach their room, the quarrel has deflated to where they are arguing over their heroes' personalities, and Aaron has Hack boxed in a corner trying to deflect criticism of President Kennedy's rainbow of extra-marital adventures. By now, both men are a bit testy. Hack reminds Aaron that he voted for Clinton, and Aaron curtly reminds Hack that he voted for Kennedy.

"At least Kennedy didn't lie about it . . . about his affairs." Hack has already reluctantly conceded that JFK topped the list of America's womanizing presidents.

"Nobody knew about them!" Aaron exclaims, mystified that this point has escaped Hack's awareness. "Not while he was still president. Did you know he slept around back then?"

Hack admits that he didn't know: "No, but I bet the White House press corps knew."

"Kennedy would have lied, too," Aaron says earnestly, "wouldn't ever have admitted that he was . . . with other women."

"I don't think so. Kennedy had better values. He didn't take advantage of women. Hell, even Tricky Dick could have gotten lucky in the Oval Office."

Deaf to Hack making light of Richard Nixon's prospects as a White House sexual rounder, Aaron says evenly, "I'm not sure what you mean by 'better values.'" Had Hack chosen his words more carefully, Aaron's voice likely wouldn't have been so frosty.

Hack realizes that he has inadvertently, and unfavorably, compared the quality of a Protestant upbringing to that of a Catholic rearing. "I didn't mean it that way," he says tamely. "Not the way you took it."

But in truth he did. In his heart, he believes – unshakably knows – that Catholicism is morally superior to all other religions, but above all to Protestantism.

"I meant," Hack continues explaining, "that when it comes to women, Clinton doesn't have any sense of respect."

Aaron for a while does not reply. Finally, he says that if he had a son he would not have held either man up as a role model.

"Take it to the bank," Hack says resignedly.

Hack thinks their argument has played out, but a moment later Aaron says, "At least you admit Clinton is much the smarter of the two men."

Hack stops abruptly. "I cannot believe you said that. Absolutely, I cannot believe you said that."

Hack is not as shocked as he pretends. He does, however, have strong convictions about human mental power. Analytical ability, it is Hack's belief, tends to inhibit persons from readily expressing themselves verbally. Therefore, Clinton, by his theory, is not the deep thinker the press represents him to be; he is quick with words but not a cut-to-the-chase diagnostician like Kennedy had been. As a machinist, Hack, naturally, did much concentrated thinking untying technical knots.

Hack says, "Clinton's quick, like a sharp accountant, but there's–"

"He's brilliant," Aaron says. "Our smartest president since FDR."

Hack snickers disdainfully. "You know that for sure?"

"Even Republicans concede that."

"Proving my point," Hack says stoutly. "He's quick to chew up a half slice of bread . . . but he won't touch a heel . . . of a quarrel, I mean. Just once, I'd like–"

"You think he should, what, be a chess Grand Master, too?"

"Yes," Hack says, after a moment of thought. "That's good, Aaron. Perfect. Clinton probably knows more about chess than Bobby Fischer. But you know what? I'll bet he couldn't beat Howdy Doody to save his tail. There's a big difference between talking a good game and playing one."

"Exactly who we need running the country," Aaron says interrupting. "A nerdy chess player."

While Hack is considering whether to educate Aaron in the basics of his own private theory of human intelligence, Edith McGuire walks into the room. She is wearing a red, snug-fitting, spaghetti-strap top and white, stretch pedal pushers that are straining mightily to keep her butt well encased. The hems of her panties stand out as if they were underlying sneaker shoelaces.

"The door was open," Edith says, smiling at Aaron. "Isn't that awful about John John?"

Clearly Aaron is not thrilled to see Edith. "Hello," he says timidly. "Yes, terrible."

"I haven't seen you for a while," she says. "You either, Tom."

His eyes downcast, Hack says, "I've been sickly. And poor Aaron's not getting around like he used to. He finally saw Dr. Bonifanti last week."

"Oh," Edith says, silently staring at Aaron. "I didn't know." She waits for his explanation.

Some women, Hack is convinced – provided a fabrication is sincerely uttered – will believe a cock-and-bull story no matter how out-and-out absurd.

Hack grimaces. "It's his feet. The bottoms are turning purple . . . as a bouquet of . . . fuchsia, I think my wife would have said. Doctor Bonifanti told him to keep off his feet as much as possible."

Edith nods caringly and turns back to Aaron. "Do they hurt?"

"No," Aaron says, shaking his head at Hack and then at the floor. "No. Not that I can tell."

Hack says, "It's his diabetes. When I was a kid we called feet like Aarons' snowshoes. You know how mean kids can be. My brother had it in one foot. He's a diabetic, too."

"Is there anything I can do?" Edith asks, an anxious look on her face.

"Nothing," Aaron says. He glances at Hack ill-humoredly. "Nothing that I know of."

Hack says to Edith, "He's not a happy camper. In fact, he came down with snowshoe feet the first time while he was camping out. It's totally curable. If I could only get him to take his medicine. And sunbathe – soles to the sun, of course." Hack points at their window. "Show her Aaron."

Aaron, cutting his eyes at Hack, shakes his head. Hack squints at Edith. "It embarrasses him," Hack says, sneaking in a grim nod.

Edith is quiet for a few seconds, and then she says to Aaron, "It sounds a lot to me like psoriasis. Is that what it is?"

"Oh no, no," Hack says. "It's nothing like psoriasis. Latent pink eye is known to spread, especially if you're diabetic. That's Doctor Bonifanti's diagnosis anyway."

Edith, Hack suddenly becomes aware, is closer to the door than she was a minute earlier. She again asks Aaron how she might help ease his suffering.

Aaron sighs tiredly and shakes his head.

Hack interrupts Aaron's answer, which had become disconnected stuttering. "He's especially fond of grapefruit." Hack says this softly, as if he did not want Aaron to hear him. "In fact . . . any citrus fruit. But no berries . . . nothing with tiny seeds. And especially no goosefoot roots."

"Certainly not," Edith says, nodding thoughtfully. She turns to Aaron. "If you need anything, anything at all, Dear, you let me know."

Edith leaves, and Aaron, once he's certain she's out of earshot, snaps, "And I don't care for grapefruit, either."

"It's my favorite fruit," Hack says.

[40]

Hack and Arron have returned from their morning walk, and Aaron has begun writing a letter. Sitting with his back to the door, he writes one almost every day. If he sits facing the door, aides and nurses wander in and interrupt him with inconsequential questions.

Hack turns from watching, through their bedroom window, a crow picking at the entrails of a dead rabbit, and he is startled to see Jolene, Aaron's youngest daughter and another African-American woman standing silently just outside their doorway. The second woman, beyond all doubt another child of Aaron's wife, appears to be a few years older than Jolene. Both women are wearing dark pants suits, heels, and white blouses. Brightly colored scarves are tucked in at their necks. Jolene places her index finger across her lips, which partly conceals the equivalent of one of her father's toothy, hundred-watt grins. She edges quietly to a foot or so behind Aaron and covers his eyes with her hands.

"Oh my," Aaron says, laying his hands over the ones on his eyes. "No idea."

Hack senses nervousness in his voice. Later Aaron tells Hack that he thought his covert visitor was Edith McGuire.

"Take a guess!" Hack says enthusiastically.

"I just . . . have no idea." Aaron lays down his pen and pulls gently at Jolene's hands.

"I'll give you a hint. It's someone you know."

"You are so helpful, Tom."

"No," Hack says, winking at Jolene, "it's not Marie."

"I didn't think it was. It's a woman, though."

Hack says, "She's a real looker, too," and Aaron noticeably stiffens.

Jolene shoots Hack a tickled smile and then abruptly uncovers her father's eyes.

Aaron cautiously turns his head. "Oh my goodness!" he exclaims when he sees who it is. "Jolly!"

"And look, Daddy!" Jolene says, sidling to where Aaron has a clear view of their room's doorway.

"Carolina!" Aaron cries. "Oh my, oh my! How long has it been?" His smile is full power, as big and bright as Hack had ever seen it.

Aaron and his daughters embrace as a threesome. His eyes become moist. Both women assure him that his grandchildren (and a half-dozen persons Hack had never heard him mention before) were all enjoying good health. He tells them that he is also doing well.

Jolene lays hold of Carolina's arm, nods at me, and says, "This is Daddy's roommate, Tom Murtaugh."

"Nice to meet you Tom," Carolina says. "Daddy has written so much about you."

"Keep in mind," I say, squinting unhappily, "that he's monstrously jealous of me."

Carolina grins, and Aaron, his big toothy smile all but etched on his face, tells her that he no less envies Sasquatch, the imaginary ape-like being that allegedly inhabits America's northwestern forests. (Usually when Hack tells someone that Aaron is jealous of him, Aaron counters with words to the effect that he envies Hack in the same way that he longs for a aggressive diarrhea.)

Carolina laughs, and says to me, "It's Carolina *Stainbrook*, Tom. I'm his oldest."

After we exchange nice-to-meet-you expressions, and so on, Hack tells her that he was about to leave. She says that she and Jolly will be here until tomorrow afternoon. "We'll be getting together," she assures Hack.

Hack has not quite reached the door, when Jolene, says, "Tom, you're eating with us today." Jolene obviously means it – is not just honoring an unwritten and usually unfulfilled posturing of etiquette.

"Gosh, I don't think so," Hack says. "It's awfully nice of you to ask me Jolly, but you folks need time together. Alone."

"It's a done deal," Jolene says with a stern look. "Besides, we wouldn't know where to go."

"Yes," Aaron says. "If it wasn't for that one reason we could just leave Tom here."

"Daddy!" Carolina exclaims.

"I'm used to it," Hack says to Carolina. "The last kind word he said to me was, 'How do you do.' He's taken over the room . . . worse than sharing quarters with a black bear just out of hibernation."

Hack no more gets the words out of his mouth than he feels his face beginning to color. Aaron sees, and, nodding determinedly, as if Carolina had asked, says, "Yes, he is indeed a closet racist."

"Some bears don't even hibernate," Hack says weakly, his Irish gift of gab failing him utterly. "Grizzlies don't . . . at all," he mumbles, roughly in the direction of his dresser.

Jolene giggles. "We know better, Tom. Know that you're not at all that way."

"God, I hope you know."

"We do," Carolina says dismissively. "Let's say we leave here at . . . twelve o'clock?"

"Okay. Fine by me," Hack says, feeling a sense of relief. "I'll come back here at a quarter of."

A step into the hall Hack realizes that he has two full hours to kill, so he decides to visit Kitty. Passing Marie on the way, he tells her that he and Aaron will be eating lunch out. She orders Hack to make a note in the sign-out book and have Aaron's oldest sign for him. Hack asks if she's heard from Dr. Bonifanti's office regarding a date for his prostate check. Not yet, she says. "Dr. Egli is attending a doctor thing out of town."

It's almost two weeks since Dr. Bonifanti examined Hack. The pain, on its own, has lessened: the physical condition of his prostate seems wholly unrelated to anything Hack does – or eat, or drink. Anyway, he has not fussed over the delay. When Hack first gets the urge to go, he still has to hurriedly relieve himself. His urine sputters out on different trajectories in three or four modest streams, and he is never sure which one to aim. Sometimes he pees on his trousers and sometimes on the floor. Most often, he hits the inside of the commode, however, if not the commode water itself.

"Sit down to pee," Kitty once advised Hack disgustedly when he told her about his gallivanting urine.

"Yeah," Hack replied. "You'd tell everyone that's how I always pee."

[41]

Kitty, sitting in her recliner writing on a tablet, does not hear Hack arrive. She is wearing the robe Hack gave her for Christmas, and her hair is still matted from sleep. Her feet are stocking-less, which is not like Kittyr. Hack waits quietly until her pen stops moving and then he lightly taps the door frame with a leg of his walker. Kitty looks up. Her,"Yes?-and-don't-bother-me-look," is not open to interpretation.

"I'll return later," Hack mumbles. Kitty nods indifferently. But as he is leaving, she apparently has second thoughts and invites him to stay.

Part of the tablet on which Kitty is writing has been used up, and the consumed sheets are folded behind the tablet's cardboard stiffener. About the time Hack is close enough to make out her cursively written words, she flips the sheets back into place and turns the tablet over. Making his way to the unassigned bed, Hack asks her good-naturedly if she's writing a book.

"You know," Kitty answers, "I've been thinking, Thomas. If that witless Veronica Vale, or whatever her name, could write a book and get it published, so could I."

Hack backs onto the bed. "Definitely. Take it to the bank, Dear. How many times have I told you that?"

"Goodness, Tommy," she says, chuckling, "I could become the Grandma Moses of American literature."

"Like I said," Hack tells her.

"Grandma Moses took up painting at eighty," Kitty says, "after she became too frail to continue farming. Did you know that?"

Hack, with an effort, represses the urge to make a dumb remark, to tell Kitty that she could say that her parents were of Welsh royalty, that her oldest brother was a "renowned" house painter. Or, as bad, tease her about her qualifying age. Mention of the A-word, he knew, would end their conversation then and there.

Hack shakes his head. "Hard to believe, eighty years old, huh?"

"That's right," Kitty says fingering the tablet. "Read this, Tom."

"What is it?"

"It's a children's story."

"A kid's story? That's great," Hack says with spirit. In truth, he is thinking that of the women he knew, Kitty is the last one he could imagine writing a children's book.

"I've finished three chapters. I'm building the plot as I go. Letting events take the story wherever . . . "

"You can do that?" Hack asks. "God, I had to work

from blueprints."

Kitty dismisses Hack's concern with a quick shrug. "I know, dear. But writing a book is . . . far different from running . . . a lathe."

"No shit! Hack exclaims, less than thrilled at her not-so subtle putdown. "Boy, I learn something new every day."

"Seriously," Kitty says, indifferent to Hack's sarcasm, "writing is a creative activity. I don't doubt for a moment, Tom, that it takes lots of smarts to be a good machinist. But it's not the same thing. I make something from nothing; you start with a plan."

Hack reaches for the tablet. "The only difference," he says, "is that your plan is in your head and mine is a diagram on a sheet of paper. You just don't write words down without any forethought at all, Dear. Besides, whoever conceives of the plans I work from – me often – is making something from nothing." He encloses the words "something from nothing" with quote marks, which he represents with curled number-one and number-two fingers of both hands.

Kitty offers Hack the tablet. She would like to argue the point but even more wants to hear his opinion of her writing.

Hack remembered this much of Kitty's effort, which is dressed up a little:

Jessica, the main character (apparently) is a young, unmarried, elementary-school teacher living alone in an apartment near the school where she teaches. She has three pets, a dog, a cat, and a parrot. The dog, named Holly, is a short-haired female dachshund "with a face, in its own way, sweet as a possum's." The cat is a tabby named Boots. Boots is not only lazy he's also impudent. The parrot's name is Clementine. "Clem" is always grumpy and has this quirky habit of saying everything twice. The three animals communicate in Fauna, a language that predates Neanderthal. Humans can't hear Fauna, even when spoken loudly. (When I suggested she explain that her animals converse in Fauna at supersonic frequencies her brow knitted disapprovingly.) Clementine, the parrot, is not only glib in Fauna she also understands English. She becomes upset, pouts, and won't eat when Jessica lines the bottom of her cage with a boring financial section of a newspaper. When Jessica is away, Clem runs the place, and if either Boots or Holly steps out of line, the next time Jessica lets Clem out of her cage to exercise she secretly nips the offender on the butt with her "powerful beak." Mostly, what Boots and Holly do is roughhouse. Neither animal understands more than a half-dozen words of English – unlike Clem whose vocabulary is "exceptional" – nor is their Fauna anything to write home about. When the story opens, Holly, the pooch, is anxiously awaiting the arrival of Jessica, who, every school day, walks home at noon and lets Holly out, scratches Boots belly, pours herself a glass of milk and fixes herself a half sandwich. As it turns out, Holly has misjudged the time – it is overcast and the sun is hidden

– and the person she hears climbing the steps to their apartment is not Jessica but the building's super. That person, a Mr. Sidney, is often unshaven and has a long face, sunken cheeks, and wispy, untrimmed eyebrows. Attached to his belt is a large ring of keys.

Hack presumes Mr. Sidney is the villain, but that's all Kitty has written.

"Excellent!" Hack says, returning the tablet to Kitty. "Clever. Very imaginative. Rich with tension."

Kitty's face cringes unhappily, and Hack fishes with different bait. "I mean, that is really good stuff, Kit. Keep it up."

Obviously, Hack does not choose the right bait. Either that or he is not fishing deep enough. In any event, Kitty is no longer the confident aspiring author she was a few minutes earlier.

"What about the writing?" she says, seeing through his off-white praise. "The writing itself?"

Frankly, Kitty's sentences, in Hack's opinion, often do not smoothly connect. Each one alone reads sensibly – Kitty could teach grammar – but they do not congregate clearly into framed paragraphs.

"It sounded fine to me," Hack says. "Only, you might want to run it by someone with a better ear. Remember, I'm the guy who thinks *The Bonfire of the Vanities* is herky-jerky."

Hack does not give her a chance to argue. "Look, Kit, I already said I was impressed, and I am, honest to

God. There are rough spots that need polishing, a little going over with steel wool. A paragraph or two that I'd reorganize a tad. I'm a barely literate, ex tool-maker, so dammit take what I said for whatever it's worth."

Kitty's scowl of a second earlier fades completely. "I'm sorry, Tom. And I do respect your opinion. You know that."

"I hope so," Hack says. "You want me to just totally bullshit you?"

"No," she says. "No I do not. Not at all. I don't know though," she adds with a tiny chuckle, "maybe I do."

Hack hobbles close to where Kitty is sitting and kisses her on the forehead. She tilts her head back and smacks her lips as if returning his kiss.

"I'd better be going," Hack says. "Two of Aaron's daughters are here, and we're eating lunch together. The four of us."

"Oh, how nice," Kitty says, laying the tablet down. "I think I'll wait and read this cold-turkey tomorrow morning. When did they arrive?" She steps into her bathroom, and Hack answers her as he leaves.

Just outside the exit door near Kitty's room is a backless, four-foot wooden bench constructed of milled oak two-by-sixes fastened lengthwise side to side. The bench faces north and gets little direct sun; Hack had never seen it occupied. Several of these benches are scattered around the grounds of Cooper Greens; all are anchored permanently to concrete footings buried deep in the ground. Deciding that the bench near her exit door is where he'll spend the next forty minutes, Hack retraces his steps. The air seems warmer to him than when he and Aaron took their walk together earlier, but the wind has died down and it's hard to tell for sure. Hack looks at his watch and decides that he has a good twenty minutes to kill before making his way back to where Aaron and his daughters will be waiting.

Hack's forehead is beaded with sweat when he reaches his room. Aaron notices and wants an explanation.

"I've been jogging," Hack answers, winking at Jolene.

"See what I have to put up with," Aaron says to Carolina shaking his head forlornly.

Jolene points toward my TV and says, "What do you think, Tom?"

The TV sits on a high stand in a front corner of the room; the stand is a minimal, boxy structure with a phony walnut finish. Originally a small end table that was left at Cooper Greens by a resident who passed on, Buster Mook has added legs to it so that Hack and Aaron can easily watch TV lying on their beds.

Property abandoned by one-time residents is temporarily stored in a shabby, barn-like building – once called by a nurse the Bates Motel, which name caught on – just off the back parking lot. Goodwill Company drivers get stuck with carting off the really ratty stuff. Hack suspects Mook and his men "borrow" many of the items of any worth.

The storage building is where Aaron and Hack, after they came to really know each other, temporarily hid Bob Ford's new recliner while Ford was at lunch. Ford is the jerk who snubbed Aaron his first day here. (And he still snubs him.) Returning from eating, and likely contemplating some serious nap action, Ford after gaping for a long minute at the place where his chair should have been, lit out for the front office hellbent on reporting that a dastard had made off with his brand new lounger chair. Likely, the person to whom Ford reported the thievery merely figured that his senility had finally become full-blown dementia. That is what senility usually translates into.

Later that day, while Ford was away still trying hard to convince an executive that his chair had really vanished, Hank and Aaron, with help, returned it. Even though Aaron wrestled with the chair damn near all by himself, Hack's knees ached for two days afterward. Mook himself loaned the two of us a dolly, that is, he made sure Hack and Aaron would run across one when he heard of their plan. They were also lucky to find the door of the storage building unlocked. Unfortunately, during the hubbub they could not risk asking questions about the strange circumnavigation of Bob Ford's chair without implicating themselves, and Hack never did hear how Ford explained the sorcery that had transpired. Had Hack been nearby while Ford struggled to explain, he'd have subtly expressed an opinion about

Mister Ford's readiness for Elm Street.

Hack looks in the direction that Jolene is pointing. Sitting on a shelf of his TV stand, near the top, is a brand new VCR.

"Well I'll be darned," Hack says. "Now, how do you suppose that got there?"

Jolene laughs. "The tooth fairy slipped in and left it while you were out, Tom." Both women, smiling broadly, watch Hack closely.

"That is really nice," he says. "It's a Sony, too."

"Four video heads," Jolene says proudly.

Hack does not have a clue, but he lets on that he is very impressed.

Carolina, who is standing near Aaron's dresser, pulls open the bottom left-hand drawer. "Look here, Tom," she says, no less pleased with herself than Jolene. "I hope you like football!"

Inside the drawer, neatly arranged with their edge labels up, are some two dozen video-tape cartridges.

"I love football," Hack says, stretching the truth a little.

"Daddy's a Philadelphia Eagles fan," Carolina says. "I think he's taped every game they've ever played." Grinning, she adds, "But he only saves the ones they win."

Hack pretends to study the drawer's contents for a few seconds and then says, "Hmmm, twenty winning games. That's what, thirty seasons of taping?"

"Hey!" Aaron says. "They've faltered a little since

trading Cunningham, but this season . . . this season we at least win our division again, may even go all the way."

Hack shoots Jolene a dubious look and mouths the words "faltered a little." She laughs, and in a low, but clearly audible voice, says to Hack, "We humor him." In her regular voice she adds, "Do you think we had better get going?"

"Give me a minute," Hack says, heading for the bathroom.

"We'll wait in the lobby," Aaron says. "It takes Tom a while to figure out sink faucets."

[42]

Jolene and Carolina, arriving in a shiny off-white Lincoln Towncar, pull up to the exit across from Kitty's room. Larger than recent models of Lincoln automobiles and blunt nosed, Hack makes it out to be five years old. To Carolina's delight, he pretends the reflection of the sun from the hood of the car blinds him.

Carolina offers her father the ignition keys. Aaron declines her invitation to drive, and Hack exhales loudly as if relieved.

Carolina climbs into the front seat on the driver's side, Jolene slips into the passenger's seat, and Aaron and Hack settle into the back seat. As they leave the parking lot, it occurs to Hack that for the first time in his life he is alone in the company of blacks, and he briefly feels uneasy.

"Which way, Tom?" Caroline says as they are about to turn from Cooper Greens front driveway.

Hack has in mind a restaurant located on the highway leading to Meadville."Turn right," he says.

Brushing the car seat's dark upholstery with his finger tips, Hack says, admiringly, "what color is this Carolina? Forest Green?" Hack had no idea of Forest Green's hue, but he had once heard Marie use that description.

"I don't remember Tom. It's . . . a car color."

"Anyway, it's beautiful. This is a ninety-seven? Or a ninety-eight?"

"No, a nineteen ninety-six."

"Honest? How many miles?"

Caroline's head slightly bobs several times. "Thirty-eight thousand . . . six hundred and . . . change."

"I'd have honestly guessed twenty thousand, maximum," Hack says.

Aaron, looking out the window on his side, says, "All my girls are finicky, but Carolina is the worst." He raises his voice: "Isn't that right, Jolene?"

Jolene giggles. "Yes. And most of the time she's a big pain in the you-know-what, Father."

"Gracious," Hack says, "I wonder who she got that from."

Smiling, Jolene twists to where she can comfortably look at Hack. "You were born here, Tom?"

"In Meadville. At City Hospital. As it used to be called."

She encourages Hack with a nod.

"But I've lived in Snow Lake all my life. My folks owned a bakery. I helped when I was a kid, but then I became a tool-and-die-maker. That's about it."

"You . . . and your wife didn't have any children?"

"No, we weren't blessed."

"If 'blessed' is the right word," Jolene says glancing mischievously at Aaron before turning back around.

Aaron does not notice, and Carolina says, "Has Daddy told you about himself?"

"A little, Hack says. "Like . . . oh, that he was a choir boy. And a Boy Scout. And a war hero. And, uh . . . a kindhearted, understanding father. And other stuff."

Both women slightly chuckle. "Not always," Jolene says. "Not always, Tom."

"Go on," Hack says, pretending to turn up the sensitivity of his hearing aids.

"For sure he wasn't always an understanding husband and father," Carolina says, her delight equaling Jolene's.

She says to Jolene, "Tell Tom about the night Daddy came staggering home, frazzled, and ended up in the wrong apartment."

Hack interrupts Aaron when he protests. "Well, well. Here he has me believing he's been Dudley Do-Right of the Mounties his whole life. Now you're about to tell me he kept falling off his horse?"

Jolene nods rapidly twice, and then says, "You tell him, Carol. I was only five years old."

Aaron, shaking his head disgustedly, turns and again stares out the window on his side.

"We were living in a second-floor apartment," Carolina begins, "in Philadelphia. One night Daddy came home stoned and walked into – wandered into I should say – into the apartment next door."

"Yes, wandered into the wrong apartment," Jolene adds emphatically. "We lived in a duplex, a . . . reverse mirror image, or something like that, of the one next door. Daddy made it up the stairs fine, but once inside he turned left thinking that was where he'd find the bathroom, instead of turning right."

"Uh-huh," Hack says nodding. "The bathrooms were back-to-back – no doubt shared the same plumbing."

"I guess so," Carolina says, looking at Jolene.

Hack quietly reminds Carolina to turn left at the next intersection.

"Anyway," Carolina continues, "Daddy ends up in the Turners' kids' bedroom. Tookie . . . Mister Turner's wife, heard him stumbling around, and she woke up her husband."

Carolina pauses and says to Jolene, "What was Mister Turner's name? I've forgotten."

Jolene says, "Clarence, wasn't it?"

"No it wasn't Clarence," Aaron snaps. "How much farther, Tom?"

"Oh, a long way yet," Hack answers.

"Anyway," Carolina goes on, "Mister Turner grabs this, ah, handy kid's baseball bat, which he kept by the head of the bed, and gave Daddy a terrible whack across the shoulders. In the dark."

Aaron turns and looks through the window on my side. "Drunk as I was," he says rounding his shoulders and gritting his teeth as if still feeling the pain, "*that* hurt."

Jolene giggles. "You were in bed for two days."

"I never took another drink."

"Fa - ther . . . ." Carolina says accusingly.

"Maybe once."

"Tell Tom about that *once*," Jolene says.

Aaron, his gaze again fast on the sights drifting past the window on his side, says, "Not much to tell. I got arrested . . . busted as my adoring daughters called it . . . for public intoxication. And spent the night in a drunk tank."

"And . . ." Carolina says.

"You talk about a sorry lot of humanity. Tom's been there, done that. Take over, Tom."

"See how he is," Hack says. "Lies like a Persian rug. I have never–"

"It opened my eyes," Aaron says.

"For sure, Father," Jolene says.

"I'll bet it did," Hack says, nodding his head as if seriously concerned. "Uh, we're nearing the restaurant."

Carolina slightly turns her head to give Hack her ear.

"There it is," Hack says after a few more seconds. "On the left. It's the only one in these parts that serves chitlins. Aaron's favorite."

"See how *he* is," Aaron says.

They finish eating and while Aaron and his daughters are nursing second cups of coffee Hack visits the men's room. Jolene, as he is leaving, stops him just outside the doorway.

"How is he, Tom?" she says. "He never tells us anything."

Hack makes a snap decision not to tell her of Aaron's "spell," as he called it. "He seems to be doing all right," Hack says. "He never complains."

Jolene nods. "He won't, either."

"Did he tell you the doctor changed his medicine?"

"Yes. Do you know why?"

"Just that something better came along."

"That's what Daddy said. He doesn't always tell us the whole story, though."

Hack says, "As far as I know, that was the only reason. He doesn't exercise enough. Get on him for that."

Jolene promises to "land" on her father "with both feet."

Her remark draws Hack's attention to her feet, which are measurably larger than his own. Seeing that Hack noticed, she says, "You should have seen Mother's."

Jolene grins, but Hack still feels his cheeks warming.

[43]

Carolina carefully steers her Lincoln to the front of the restaurant, and once all of us have climbed inside and buckled up she suggests we return to Cooper Greens by a different route.

Hack nods decisively. "Good idea, Carolina. Aaron hasn't seen the area either, not that I know of. If you're interested, we could drive through a neighborhood of better Meadville homes. They're not that common, here."

Both women want to see an upscale Meadville neighborhood, and they explore several streets of a neighborhood developed on Meadville's only true plateau. Several times they catch the unwavering attention of housewives puttering in their front yards; some casually greet them but most stare slack jawed. Leaving the neighborhood, Hack tosses a question up for grabs, "Ever hear of Talon zippers?"

"Sure," Aaron says.

Both women reply that they have not.

Jolene, however, is uncertain: "Do I mean zipper zippers or something else," and Hack tells her that he is referring to the tiny sliding devices that sometimes replace buttons. "When I was a kid," he says, "they were called slide fasteners. They used to be fabricated in Meadville – by the trillions. Talon had several plants here. I apprenticed in the tool room. We could drive past if you want."

Aaron says he'd like to do that, would like to see where Hack had majored in "Monkey-wrench 101." Everyone seems mildly interested, so Caroline drives around the city block enclosing the now-empty buildings that once housed Talon's corporate headquarters, its big essential machine shop, and the main zipper production building.

Completing the loop, Hack says, "Our hospital's pretty new. The fair grounds are a little north of town, but there's nothing going on there now. People hereabouts claim that the Crawford County Fair is Pennsylvania's biggest. Some years back" – Hack leans forward – "the Anheuser-Busch people sent one of their beer-wagon teams of Clydesdale horses. Ever been close to one? I mean, close to a Clydesdale?"

Carolina shakes her head. "But I've seen them several times in TV ads."

"Like standing beside an elephant," Hack says to Aaron.

"Like you'd know," Aaron counters.

Leaving the Talon complex, Aaron says, "Let's see where Tom last *worked* . . . ascribing a novel meaning to that word."

Hack says, "Let's drive by my last job site just to humor the old guy sitting back here. You ladies, I'm sure, are dying to see a tool-and-die shop."

They head for Hack's last place of employment, driving slightly out of the way to take in part of the campus of Allegheny College. Hack says, as they cruise by, "Allegheny's supposed to be first rate academically. Maybe it is. How do they tell?"

Back-tracking from Hack's last place of employment, they follow Meadville's one street that is wider than two driving lanes, through the downtown district. They pass the big building situated at the corner of Park Avenue and Chestnut streets that once housed the Park Theater, and Hack is reminded that Aaron, when he was a kid, would have had to watch movies from the Park's "Nigger Heaven." Aaron sees Hack's dejection, which Hack tries to cover with a historical observation: "At one time, as late as the early fifties, there were three theaters in Meadville, the Park, the Academy, and . . . a small one on Water Street. The Mead I think it was named."

It is four o'clock when they pull onto Cooper Greens' main driveway. Carolina stops the car under the portico. She and Jolene will return tomorrow morning, so their farewells are brief. Hack thanks them for buying his lunch, probably overdoing it, and they thank him for being their navigator. Aaron and Hack watch until the Lincoln reaches the beginning of Cooper Greens' driveway. They wave, and Jolene, from the passenger's side window, waves back a few seconds later.

Entering the front lobby, Hack says to Aaron, "Home sweet home." Aaron nods, but his mind seems to be elsewhere.

The lobby of Cooper Greens extends inward to Ash Street. Ash Street connects to Maple Street, and Maple Street intersects Beechwood, the hallway on which Aaron and Hack live. They have turned from Ash Street onto Maple when suddenly Aaron says weakly, "Wait a minute."

They stop, and he grabs a handle of Hack's walker.

"I don't feel good," Aaron says feebly.

Kneeling, Aaron's hand slides down the front leg of the walker. He momentarily supports himself on all fours, and then, by slowly pivoting on one hand, allows himself to sit on his butt. His chin slowly comes to rest on his chest. His forehead is beaded with sweat. Hack shouts for help, but an aide, who had been following them, is already at their side. "Get a nurse!" Hack yells. "Find Marie!"

The aide, a young girl, races off. Twice Hack tries kneeling, but the pain in his left knee cuts like a knife. He again yells for help, and an aide from somewhere runs toward them. The aide, an older woman, drops to her knees and puts her arm around Aaron's shoulders.

"What happened?" she asks Hack.

"I don't know. He just . . . kind of slid down."

Other residents gather, and shortly, Marie, turning onto Maple from the same direction in which the aide embracing Aaron had appeared, rounds the corner in full stride. "Get back," she commands, and everyone backs up a half step or so. Marie looks at Hack, and he shrugs. Lie back, she commands Aaron. At the same time she tells the aide to unbuckle Aaron's belt, and soon she has a span of Aaron's stomach exposed. Marie produces a syringe from the pocket of her smock, attaches a needle, and injects Aaron with what, Hack assumes is insulin. In moments, Aaron attempts to sit up. Marie, however, will not allow it. Wait, she orders him. She tells the young aide, who has been watching at the edge of what has become a crowd of eight or so people, to fetch a wheelchair.

Hack shakes his head. His concern borders on disgust. At any rate that's what he wants Aaron to think. Aaron is sitting dejectedly on his bed, where he has propped himself against its headboard, apparently no worse for the wear. Marie has left and Aaron and Hack to themselves.

"You aren't ever going to learn," Hack says, trying for a tone that scolds.

"I'm learning," Aaron mumbles. "That . . . scared me."

"Can I get you anything?"

"No thank you."

"Talk about the blind leading the blind," Hack says. "We'll both end up in a gutter along the road."

"In the proverbial six-foot ditch," Aaron amends.

Neither man speaks for several seconds, and then Aaron tells Hack that he will not be eating supper. Hack had not planned to eat supper either, but he thinks Aaron should eat something.

"I'll bring you back a sandwich," Hack says.

"No," Aaron says after a bit. "I'd better eat. I'll go with you."

Aaron leaves his bed for the bathroom, and when he comes out, he says to Hack, "Tom, promise me you will not tell my girls about . . . this."

Hack does not answer right away, and Aaron says, "I'd really appreciate it."

Hack tries to stare Aaron down, but he cannot deal with the pleading set of Aaron's eyes. "If that's what you want," Hack says finally.

While Hack and Aaron are halfheartedly eating supper, other diners, all the dietary aides, and many kitchen workers – almost the home's full afternoon staff – visit our table to ask Aaron how he feels. He smiles and answers each person the same way: "I'm fine. Nothing serious."

To the first woman who stopped, Hack said that Aaron would do anything for a little attention. She thought Hack meant it, and he had to excessively explain that he was only kidding. He did not try that again. "Sometimes," Hack told himself, "I can be an awfully dumb ass."

Jolene and Carolina return to Hack's and Aaron's room the next morning at nine o'clock. Hack makes up an excuse to leave the room. Jolene promptly tells him that she and Carolina are "on their way to Philly." Hack is the beneficiary of a warm farewell hug from each woman.

"You keep after him, Tom," Jolene says; Hack promises that he will.

Later in the day Hack examines the strange tilt of his bed pillow and finds a quart jar of jelly beans under it. Taped to the lid of the jar is the note: "With love. Hide from Daddy."

[44]

Aaron is visiting the laundry room: his blue short-sleeved shirt came back with a large bleach mark under the front pocket. Hack is lying on his side of his bed reading. Marie says from their doorway, "Buddy will be driving."

"Tomorrow?"

"Yes."

"Aaron's going with me."

Marie nods. "Be in the lobby by eight forty-five."

"Tomorrow morning," Hack says to Aaron when Aaron walks into the room.

"Your procedure?" Aaron says after a moment.

Hack repeats Marie's instructions.

The sky is motley gray and the wafting breeze is cool. Buddy, sitting behind the wheel of the Cooper Greens' van, has reverse-folded a *Region Shopper* newspaper and is scanning the ads. A tabloid, the *Shopper* typically advertises second-hand goods – everything from used golf clubs, to refurbished merry-go-round steeds, to "good" used tires, to spruced-up doo-wop era cars. Buddy rises to help Hack enter, but Aaron is with him and Hack waves him off. It's cold inside the van: Buddy has the engine running and the air conditioner on full. Hack asks Buddy if his father was a fat Eskimo. Buddy grins and turns down the air.

Buddy tells Hack and Aaron that he'll take a back road to Meadville, a bumpy but shorter route that he would not follow with more passengers than only the two of them. Nervous, and therefore sillier than usual, Hack tells him to avoid driving by farm pastures because cows frighten Aaron. And then he compounds his silliness by saying that Aaron believes cows are milked by pumping their tails. Buddy, obviously a kindly man, pretends Hack has cracked two good ones.

Hack is admitted to the hospital as an out-patient, and then wheeled by a volunteer to the same room where in December Dr. Egli snipped three smidgens of tissue – three benign organic bits – from his prostate gland. Aaron follows them. He tells the red-coat pushing Hack's wheelchair to warn the nurses about Hack, to explain that Hack forgets he is ancient and senile. An elder himself, the red-coat flashes Aaron a perplexed look. Aaron leaves Hack and the red-coat, and heads toward a waiting room reserved for the family members of patients undergoing surgery. The same genial orderly and the friendly nurse who assisted Dr. Egli on Hack's last visit are on duty. Dr. Egli arrives at the scheduled time, and he and the nurse proceed as before.

A neatly barbered, twentyish, white boy pushes Hack to the lobby.

"How'd it go?" Aaron asks. He is truly interested.

"I don't know," Hack answers, "he didn't tell me anything."

Aaron shakes his head. "It figures."

Buddy, walking rapidly toward Hack and Aaron from an outside door, says to Aaron, "I'll bring the van around."

"We'll meet you," Aaron says.

Hack uses the wheelchair arm rests to pull himself onto his feet. He politely refuses Aaron's offer of help. Hack's attention is focused on his throbbing prostate – or nearby region, he isn't sure – he had all but forgotten about his tender knees.

Hack asks Buddy by what route he plans to return to Cooper Greens. "It doesn't matter," Buddy answers, meaning it is Hack's choice. Hack suggests they return by way of Snow Lake, a roundabout trip of five extra miles. "Fine," Buddy answers, and for the first stretch of their return trip they follow heavily traveled U.S. 322, the road that connects the city of Meadville to the borough of Snow Lake – and beyond. Five lanes wide, one a center turning lane, U.S. 322 is lined on both sides with sundry retail businesses, including two gas stations, taverns, a furniture store, automobile dealerships, a Wal-Mart, a Smoker Friendly store, and on and on. Aaron and Hack share a front seat, as they did riding into Meadville, so they have a good view of the unfolding scenery.

A mile or so before reaching the eastern edge of Snow Lake, they pass a hard-to-miss billboard with a recreational water scene featuring a beach populated with frolicking swimmers. A water slide and sun-bathing raft are anchored some twenty yards offshore. Pymatuning Lake, reclaimed from swampy land, is the largest lake in Pennsylvania. The sign informs motorists, that it is twelve miles ahead. Most of Pymatuning lies inside Pennsylvania but sizeable acreage extends into the state of Ohio.

"I suppose you've been there," Aaron says. His gaze follows the billboard as we cruise past.

Hack explains that for two years in the fifties he moored a small sailboat on Pymatuning Lake, but managed to sink it when he sailed into a submerged stump and split open a seam at the prow. The stump, maybe breast high, was one of many dozens that were a residue of the land's original clearing project.

"Well," Aaron says after a moment, "Then you and the skipper of the Titanic have common very apt experiences for your résumé's."

"Yeah," Hack sniffles, "A flair for conscripting nearsighted landlubbers for crews."

"Of course," Aaron says nodding sternly. "How many were in your crew?"

"Not counting myself? Oh, I'd say, a muster of . . . one."

Buddy says over his shoulder, "We'll be going to the Pymatuning area for a picnic, once public schools are back in session."

"Us residents you mean?" Aaron says.

Buddy nods, and Hack says to Aaron, "I'll sign us up if you want. Have you ever seen ducks walk on fish?"

Aaron gives Hack a funny look. "Have I ever seen *what*?"

Hack explains that near the middle of the two- or three-mile road that stretches across Pymatuning Lake there is a spillway where people chuck slices of bread to gatherings of fish. The fish throng after the bread, and the ducks, also hungry for their share, reach the bread by walking on the swarming, solidly packed fish. Aaron is dubious.

"Honest. It's a feeding frenzy. Like one you've never seen."

"Is he joking?" Aaron says to Buddy.

"It's true," Buddy replies over his shoulder. "You'll see more billboards farther along."

Aaron uncertainly asks, "What kind of fish?"

"Carp. No game fish. You ever see a walleye or a bass in the spillway?" Hack asks Buddy.

Buddy shakes his head, starts to reply, but Hack interrupts him. "Aaron's never fished," he says, adding as if to clarify his remark, "he's from Philadelphia. The city, not the institution . . . I don't think."

Buddy sniggers. "Never fished?" he says to Aaron.

"I was born in Meadville. But my folks moved to Philadelphia when I was only two years old."

Buddy, his attention on driving, nods.

"Sure," Aaron says to Hack, "I'd like to go. What's the name of the lake again?"

"Pymatuning. Pie-ma-tuning. It's an Indian word."

"Meaning?"

Hack has no idea of what the word Pymatuning means. "It means large pond where ducks walk on fish."

"Of course," Aaron says disgustedly.

"It was named after an Indian brave . . . Chief Pymanutia, as I recall."

"Of course," Aaron skeptically says again.

They drive a little farther and Hack says to Buddy, "What's a Spatterdock? Some kind of duck?"

Buddy lightly shrugs.

Hack looks at Aaron. "I remember the word from reading about Pymatuning when I was a kid. Do you know Aaron?"

Aaron shakes his head.

"I hardly expected you would," Hack says, rolling his eyes skyward. "I'll check with Kitty."

"You do that," Aaron says. "I can't wait to see how long before you work the word Spatterdock into a conversation. And, what exactly is a spillway?"

"Spillways channel water around dams. For different reasons. The water of the spillway at Pymatuning runs under the road that crosses the lake.

Remember those old porcelainized, cast-iron bathtubs with claw feet? Before my time, but you likely–"

Aaron scoffs. "Do I remember? We had one in our apartment in Philadelphia."

Hack nods appreciatively. "Well, the back of one of those tubs is exactly what the inflow end of the Pymatuning spillway looks like. Only, it's about twenty feet across. The pool of created water is one heck of a big tub of fish – all churning around waiting for people to throw them bread. The outflow from the pool of water is, oh, maybe eight feet across and five feet deep. I'm not sure."

Fascinated, Aaron says, "Yes, I would very much like to go."

"I'll sign us up, Hack says. "The first time Father took me and Danny to see the spillway we'd been there maybe ten minutes, watching from the railing where the water goes under the road and damned if a kid doesn't fall in."

Aaron recoils. "Fall in. Seriously? How in the world . . . how old was he?"

"Three, four maybe. His father was standing right there."

"Hard to believe," Aaron says, shaking his head.

"I know. Anyway, the father begins screaming for someone to save his son because he, the father, says he can't swim. The kid sinks out of sight. Two men jump in after him. I don't know how, but one comes up with the little tyke some ten feet downstream. You should have heard the cheering. It was a Sunday crowd.

"The boy was okay?"

"Yeah. He coughed and, you know, spit up some water. But that was about it."

Aaron says, "That was a really long time ago, huh?" His voice trails off. "If, as you say, you were just a lad then."

"Nineteen thirty-nine or nineteen forty. I'm not certain."

Aaron says, "That . . . carelessness has haunted the father all his life." He shakes his head. "The man who saved the child? That must have been something, jumping into that . . . stream of slimy carp."

"Yep," Hack says. "He was a true hero. You'll see the place for yourself."

We're cruising back to Cooper Greens at Buddy's usual five-miles-per-hour under-the-speed-limit pace. Tillable farm land lines both sides of the road, and fields of multi-colored forage crops, which are sometimes separated by newly turned, street-wide bands of rich-looking brown dirt, leave Aaron spellbound. Sometimes a couple dozen cows and one or two horses graze the pastures lying beyond the fields of crops. The pastures themselves end abruptly at impenetrable walls of tall, thin maple trees a tenth of a mile or so from the road.

Buddy, as he pulls the van to a stop under the Cooper Greens' portico, proudly informs us that we are back in time for lunch.

Kitty is waiting for Hack and Aaron in their room. Aaron, after washing his hands, takes his leave, saying on the way out that he'll save me something to eat. Hack turns his way, to where Kitty cannot see his face and mouths the words, "No sweets."

"What did you find out?" Kitty asks Hack as soon as Aaron clears the doorway.

"Shit. Not a damn thing. Doctors won't tell you anything"

"What's your intuition tell you?"

"I don't have a gut feeling. I'll just have to wait until I hear from Dr. Bonifanti."

"Think you'll feel like playing cards?"

Hack lets on it is not an easy decision before saying that he'll give it a try. "I might be a few minutes late," he finishes, milking it further.

"Go eat," Kitty tells him.

Hack hurries through lunch, finds Marie, and tells her he needs a favor. Dr. Bonifanti, he explains, will get the results of his prostate test on Monday, meaning, Hack goes on, to say that, he'll be sweating it out over a span of four long days and five long nights. "Could you not prevail on Dr. Bonifanti," he begs of Marie, "to get the report by Friday?"

Marie telephones Dr. Bonifanti's office on the spot. Dr. Bonifanti, however, is not in. Marie tells Hack that she will keep trying, that she will not merely leave a message. When Aaron and Hack return from playing cards with Kitty and Yvon, there is an unsigned note on his dresser informing him that Dr. Bonifanti will telephone Dr. Egli and pass on my request to hurry along the report of his findings.

Two days later, in the afternoon on Friday, Marie locates the four of us playing cards in the dining room. She steps into the room and motions for Hack to approach her. He does, and by the time he reaches her side his hands are clammy and his legs weigh a ton.

"I have good news and bad news," she says. "You don't have cancer. But you need minor surgery."

She studies me. "Are you feeling all right?"

"Never felt better," Hack says.

[45]

Aaron, when Dr. Bonifanti arrives, is playing solitaire, and Hack is reading a "house" editorial, a position taken by the newspaper itself, published in a two-day-old *USA Today*. Kitty, minutes earlier, had dropped by to tell them that Joetta Fisher was hospitalized during the night. Fisher's heart had regressed into atrial fibrillation, an expression that Kitty pronounced slowly for Hack's benefit and explained that it meant her heart rhythm had become irregular.

Though it is Wednesday, her usual day to visit Cooper Greens, Hack had not expected to personally see Dr. Bonifanti. "You have prostatism," she says to him after perfunctorily greeting Aaron.

Hack stands and steps into his walker. "Prostat-*ism*, not prostat-*itis*? What in the heck is prostatism?"

"Your prostate's swollen and inflamed," Dr. Bonifanti says. "That's the clinical situation. It's squeezing your urethra. Before long you could experience a blockage of urine flow."

"I don't want that," Hack mumbles.

"No you don't. The medicine isn't helping, and unless your prostate is . . . shaved down a little, the backup of urine could damage your kidneys and bladder." She lets Hack ponder that possibility a moment and then says, "It could even be fatal."

"I'd rather not die, either," Hack says dully.

"Doctor Egli will do the surgery. He's done the same procedure many times. It's little different from–"

"Surgery? Hack interrupts, "That's, what, how a prostate gland is . . . shaved down? Wouldn't a little steel wool clean it up?"

Dr. Bonifanti shrugs. Hack cannot tell if she understands that he is being factious. She says, "In any case, he'll remove excess tissue by micro-laser surgery – through your urethral."

"Through my . . . penis?"

Dr. Bonifanti nods. "Minor surgery."

"Minor surgery. That's, what? Slashing away on someone else. Right?"

(That was Joe Luoma's definition of minor surgery, which explanation he offered every time the words "minor surgery" fissured a discussion or came up in print.)

Dr. Bonifanti is not amused. "You'll be sedated."

"It doesn't sound all that minor."

"They'll flush you with a catheter."

"Uh, how long will I be in the hospital?"

"It depends. Two, maybe three days. You have to void on your own before you leave. Are you on a blood thinner?

"Hell, I don't remember. Yes, I'm on Warfarin . . . I think it's called.."

"What, ah . . ." Hack begins, unsure of how to phrase his next question."What, ah . . . how does this . . . shaving procedure leave me? I mean . . . you know."

Dr. Bonifanti gives Hack a funny look, and Hack tells her that he is old but not dead. She still does not get it, and he adds, impatiently, "Will I still be chasing the ladies afterward?

"Oh, absolutely," Dr. Bonifanti replies quickly. Too quickly, it strikes Hack. "You may have dry orgasms. And in a few cases there's temporary impotency and incontinence. But it won't last."

"What in hell is a dry orgasm?" Hack asks suspiciously.

"Ejaculation into your bladder."

Hack sighs unhappily and says to Aaron, who has stopped playing cards and is listening intently to the conversation, "Exactly what I've always wanted – to join the Cooper Greens' romper set."

"I just might pass on this one," Hack says to Dr. Bonifanti.

"No," Aaron says, gathering his cards "He positively will not pass on this one, Doctor Bonifanti. I'll see to it, Marie and I."

"Tend to your knitting," Hack says to Aaron. Hack turns to Dr. Bonifanti: "I doubt he's taking his shots. "He goes in the bathroom and closes the door."

Aaron dismissively waves his hand. "I haven't missed one yet."

Aaron has overcome his dread of the needle, and from the confident way he said those words, Hack can tell he is as proud of overcoming that fear as he is of holding to his treatment schedule.

"Big deal," Hack says to Dr. Bonifanti, "he only started last week."

Dr. Bonifanti says to Aaron, "Cut back on sweets and stay on your diet. And exercise. I'll know from your blood work. Are you charting?"

Aaron, frowning crossly at me, insists he's adhering religiously to Dr. Bonifanti's orders.

"Well," Hack says, once Dr. Bonifanti has left, "I knew something had to be done."

"Yes," Aaron says. "And I'm going to see that it is."

"I'm mean to you," Hack says.

"And I mean to *you*," Aaron says.

Hack tells Aaron that he's a bigger pain in the butt than Helen ever was.

[46]

Tomorrow Dr. Egli will perform a "transurethral resection" of Hack's prostate gland. Hack told Kitty that he was having his prostate shaved down a little, and the next day she laid that transurethral mouthful on him.

Hack's surgery is schedule for 2:00 p.m., but for a reason that only the high priests of the Temple of Abattoir comprehend, he must report to the hospital at eight a.m.

Buddy, on this trip to Meadville, has other passengers, and Aaron and Hack are less inclined to exchange thoughts than on their last ride in the Cooper Greens' express. Being Thursday, the traffic is moderate. Now and then they pass a front yard decorated with two or three fully plumaged maple trees that are smattered with red- and yellow-tinted leaves, signs of an early Fall, according to one chatty passenger.

Hack is holding a brown paper sack on his lap, which contains a change of underwear, socks, a sweater, and a soft-cover edition of Tom Clancy's *Clear and Present Danger*. From Helen's last stay, Hack knows that the hospital will provide him a toothbrush, toothpaste, mouthwash, underarm deodorant, and maybe a few other accessory toilet articles. The aide completing Hack's registration explains to him that those items are stored in the top drawer of the nightstand. When Hack said to her that she forgot to mention Viagra, she straight-facedly reviewed her notes and said that it was not on the list.

Aaron, after carefully inspecting the contents of Hack's paper sack, looks at Hack and asks loudly, "Why the hairbrush?"

Hack will not shave again until he is back at Cooper Greens. Before they left, he gave Aaron his billfold, wristwatch, and wedding band for safekeeping. Aaron knows Hack has hidden twenty-some dollars in his socks-and-underwear drawer. Most of that stash will go for his Christmas present to Kitty. Hack's Medicare and Medicaid cards are in his breast pocket. Aaron has worked out other arrangements for his return to Cooper Greens, but he is tight-lipped about the details. Hack assumes he'll return in a taxi. Apparently he can afford to. Hack is touched that Aaron wants to be at the hospital when Hack comes to his senses as the anesthesia is wearing off.

The registrar assigns Hack a bed in a room for two on the hospital's third floor, and he is wheeled there by a volunteer, a man about his age. The other bed is empty but the covers have been thrown back and there are other signs that Hack will not have the room to himself. He is glad to see that the TV servicing that bed is tuned to the ESPN channel.

A woman wearing civvies brings Hack a folder of information about the hospital and jots down his answers to a number of administrative questions on a two-page form. An aide brings Hack a nightgown and tells him to change into it. A nurse takes his vitals, and later another nurse connects him to an IV machine.

Hack's hearing aids, expensive presents that he bought for himself while he was still living alone at his home in Snow Lake, fit entirely inside his ears. It is okay, the nurse tells him, to leave them in. His teeth are his own, that is, he does not plop them into a tumbler of colored water when he goes to bed.

The first nurse returns with a hypodermic syringe and injects Hack with a tranquilizer serum through a valve in the tube coming from the IV machine. She says it will relax him. Aaron does not move from his place in front of the window that he has been staring through almost since the minute they arrived in the room: Hack decides he is not as settled about the taking of shots as he let on earlier. Hack locates the remote control for the TV serving his bed, surfs to an ESPN station, and turns up the volume.

Hack notices that the program has changed, and he wonders if he had dozed off. Then he is certain that he did because Aaron is standing at the foot of his bed.

"How do you feel?" Aaron asks grinning.

"Okay."

More of his pearly whites show. "You're back, Tom."

"I'm back?"

Aaron's grin widens.

Hack hears a rustling sound to his right, and he glimpse a nurse standing at the foot of his roommate's bed. The privacy curtain is extended, so he cannot see the bed's occupant. He looks to Aaron for an explanation, and Aaron all but laughs. "You're back in your room!"

Hack looks around and, and Aaron says loudly, "Back in your room at the hospital!"

"Better not," Aaron says, stepping to the side of the bed when Hack tries to sit up.

"Well I'll be damned," Hack says, and he falls back asleep.

"A walk on the beach," Hack says to Aaron as he enters the room. "I figured you had left for Cooper Greens."

"I grabbed a sandwich," Aaron says. "How long have you been awake?"

"I don't know. Hours and hours."

Aaron rolls his eyes.

"A nurse took my temperature. What time is it?"

Aaron gestures at the clock centered on the wall across from the foot of the beds. "A quarter to six."

"Go home, Yank. I feel fine. Honest."

"I'm in no hurry. Besides, you'd probably relapse just to spite me. Want anything?"

"No thank you. Yeah, out of here."

"They told me it'd be three weeks," Aaron says casually, pretending he has caught sight of something in the window.

"Really?" Hack says. "Three weeks away from you'd be my first respite since . . . . When did you move in?"

"Likewise," Aaron says, turning back from the window.

"I don't have to pee, so I guess they have a Foley in?"

Aaron steps to a place near the side of Hack's bed, bends down, and tilts his head sideways. "There's a plastic bag over here that's filling up with ugly looking green fluid . . . something I'd wash the bottom of my car with. If I owned a car."

"It's not green. It's Aqua. My blood, remember, is royal blue."

Aaren nods contemplatively. "Hmm. Maybe we're blood brothers after all."

"Seriously, what color is it?"

Aaren bends down and looks again. "It's . . . a smidgen reddish."

"Uh-huh. Doctor Egli said I'd leak a little blood for a while."

Aaron gives Hack a crafty look, and Hack realizes he'd unintentionally punned on the word "leak."

"Well," Aaron says, not quite grinning, "he was right."

A nurse, a person that Hack had not seen before, enters the room and cheerfully addresses him by his first name. "Fine," Hack answers when she asks how he feels. She glances at the bag that is slowly filling with pink-tinted fluid and then spends almost a minute fiddling with the drip-rate valve on my IV apparatus. Satisfied, apparently, she attends to my roommate, whom Hack has yet to see or to hear speak. Aaron imitates a scooping motion near his crotch with his right hand to indicate that Hack's roommate is recovering from the same surgery Hack just went through.

The nurse completes her visit with the man in the next bed – addressing him as Jason – and leaves our room. Hack glances at Aaron, cuts his eyes at Jason's bed, and then looks back at Aaron. Aaron dismisses his gesture with a shrug. Hack manages a glare of some intensity and then says in an exaggerated manly voice, "Jason, I'm Tom Murtaugh. How you doin'?"

Jason does not answer for seconds but then, in a booming voice, he announces, "You're Tom Murtaugh! Well I'll be damned! Jason Wooley, here!"

"You're kidding!" Hack motions to Aaron to draw back the privacy curtain.

The man in the next bed does not resemble anyone Hack ever once knew. The Jason Wooley of his memory was a chisel-faced monument, a big man who was Gary Cooperish in build, complexion, and manner. The man in the next bed is heavy and seems to be anything but self-effacing.

Hack says, "My God, Jason. How long has it been? Fifty years?"

"Damn near, Tom."

Hack introduces Aaron, who is standing at the foot of Hack's bed smiling pleasantly. Hack explains to Aaron that he and Jason played baseball together, and he tells Jason that Aaron was an all-city, high-school basketball star in Philadelphia. "Back in nineteen ought eleven."

Aaron sniffles, but apparently Jason is not good with numbers, and he does not react.

Jason, impressed by Aaron's athletic credentials, sticks out his hand. Aaron hustles over and grabs it. Hack has to explain to Jason that Cooper Greens is a nursing home, not a residential development. He is a little sheepish explaining that to Jason.

Jason reminds Hack of the day their baseball team won the County League championship in a 1-0, extra inning game. Hack reminds Jason of the time they were playing a game when rain clouds gathered and lightening struck a transformer mounted on a utility pole standing some thirty feet behind the backstop. Aaron, once Jason and Hack quit congratulating each other over not being electrocuted on that day, says that he had better return to Cooper Greens.

"Hey," Hack says, "I really appreciate it, Aaron." Hack uncovers his right hand and candidly offers it to Aaron. "Now, you don't come back tomorrow. I'll be getting out of here directly. You work on that new macramé stitch you're having a time with."

Aaron looks at Jason, grins weakly, and shakes his head. "Nice to have met you, Jason," he says.

"Same old Murtaugh," Jason says. "Except, he used to have hair." Laughter booms from his side of the room.

"Is that right," Aaron says to Hack as he's leaving. "At one time you actually had hair?"

Hack tells Aaron, when he asks, that there is nothing that he needs, and Aaron leaves for Cooper Greens. Jason yells after him to hold the fort.

Hack and Jason are sitting in bed eating supper when Dr. Egli strides purposefully into the room. "Not too bad," he tells Jason after checking his plastic urine bag. He sounds pleased. "How do you feel?"

Jason says that he's beginning to feel some pain. Dr. Egli tells him he's arranged to have pain-relieving medicine available. Jason nods, "If I need it."

"Most likely you will. Let a nurse know."

Dr. Egli moves to Hack's bed and glances at the plastic bag underneath, which, Hack assumes, is slowly filling.

"I had to do a little more whittling on you," Dr. Egli ays, his manner a tad too jovial. He asks Hack as he did Jason, how he feels, and Hack tells him fine. Dr.

Egli says to Hack that he also qualifies to be comforted by pain-alleviating medicine.

The evening news program on NBC is not quite over when relatives and friends of Jason begin arriving in contingents of ones, twos, and threes. Hack's visitors consist of an aide who efficiently empties and flushes his out-take bag and a nurse who measures his vitals. Jason tells the nurse he wants a pain pill. Around nine thirty Hack also asks for pain medicine. During the night, Hack is awakened every hour or so by someone taking his vitals, but he falls right back to sleep. At six thirty – the darkness of night is fading – Hack finally awakes for good. He is hurting – it comes and goes – but not too badly.

It is late Saturday morning. Jason, with his wife's help, no doubt, has packed and left. Hack is on the telephone waiting for someone at Cooper Greens to answer the ring: the home's administrative offices are closed on weekends, and sometimes it's a while before the telephone gets answered. A woman sounding out of breath finally responds, and Hack asks her to transfer him to the Beechwood Drive nurse's station.

Being Saturday, Hack is surprised to hear Marie answer the telephone. "Stacy," she replies when he asks, "called in sick, and I'm covering four streets. How do you feel?"

Besides not sounding too happy, there is a hint of urgency in her delivery, so Hack is brief. "Fine," he says, "Is Aaron around?"

Just a minute, Marie says, and Hack faintly hears her tell someone to fetch Mister Blodgett.

Last night Hack called Aaron to say that he expected to be discharged tomorrow and that he'd call this morning with particulars. (Several days later, after Hack is back at Cooper Greens, he learned that both Marie and Aaron already knew that he would not be returning that Saturday.)

"About time," Aaron says when he picks up. "Everyone here knows you've been dogging it."

"Looks like it'll be Monday morning," Hack says, breathing a long dejected sigh. "Doctor Egli says there's still some bleeding."

"Monday's Labor Day," Aaron says, and then he quickly corrects himself. "No it isn't, Labor Day's next Monday."

"I can't keep track either."

"You want me to bring in your razor and shaving lotion?"

"No way, old man. The nurses adore my beard, think it's sexy."

"Adore? Ha. It's not your . . . fuzzy face. I told them you were loaded. Filthy rich."

"Yep," Hack says, nodding as if to authenticate his remark. "They probably think you're my butler. Do me a favor, please. Make clear my situation to Kitty."

Aaron assures Hack that he will update Kitty. "Seriously, how do you feel?"

"Not bad. It's . . . you know, there's still some pain. I'm still on something, and it helps. I guess."

On Monday, Dr. Egli decides that Hack has not yet healed enough to leave. He's of the same opinion on Tuesday, and it is Wednesday before he sees fit to sign Hack's discharge papers. Hack has to pee on his own before he lets him go. Urinating, Hack told Aaron, was as much pain as he had ever experienced – like voiding molten lead.

Hack returns to Cooper Greens late Wednesday afternoon sporting a six-day growth of whiskers. Kitty, the first time they're alone, orders him to shave it off – else, she warns, I am not to expect we'd be playing any double solitaire during my days of facial hirsute.

[47]

For weeks, beginning a day or so before Hack was hospitalized for prostate surgery, the afternoons have been hotter than the inside of a roofer's lunch pail in the summer. The front lawn is a massive quilt of tan and chartreuse checker-board squares. The Cooper Greens' residents would suffer heat prostration before trudging half way around the back parking lot. Governor Ridge has declared a number of counties, including Crawford, drought stricken, and he has banned residential lawn and garden watering in those counties. Farmers are worried.

It is Hack's second day back from the hospital, and when he urinates it still scalds his private parts. He sometimes passes slightly red-tinted urine. He left the hospital with a slight cough, otherwise he is physically, still a run-of-the-mill seventy-one year-old man, discounting his bad knees.

Milton Fruehoff, Raymond Richard's onetime roommate, died while Hack was hospitalized. His name is posted in the "tombstone" corner of the Cooper

Greens bulletin board, which is titled, "In Remembrance." It is where Hack chanced upon that expected but unwelcome news. Hack decided that Kitty forgot to tell him. Anyway, Fruehoff's name, along with his War II ribbons, were still pinned up yesterday evening. It was a solitary posting so Hack knew that nobody living at Cooper Greens had died since.

Aaron and Hack have returned to their room after eating lunch, and are playing cribbage on Aaron's bed. If their scoring pegs were horses running a race, Aaron's ponies would be thundering down the backstretch and Hack's nags would be plodding around the first turn; that is to say, Aaron, as he has every game so far, is kicking Hack's tail. Their bedroom door is barely open. If it was wide open they would be interrupted constantly by Aaron's female groupies. Hack tells Aaron if he'd remove his pearly teeth they could leave the door open. Aaron says it's his sparkling personality that pulls the chicks in, not his glittering ivories. Hack plays a card and tells Aaron that in his case teeth make the man. He plays another card, scores two points, and moves a peg again. Too bad, Aaron says, that shining baldness does not work for Hack with the same efficacy as sparkling teeth works for him. They have not played pinochle, Kitty, Yvon, Aaron, and Hack, since Kitty began writing her children's book.

While Hack is deciding on his next play, someone knocks on the door. It is a hard knock, different from the polite rapping of an aide or the quick, cursory tap of a nurse. The men look at each other and Hack says loudly, "Yes!"

The door flies open, and Lon Fuller, propelling himself unevenly with his cane, hobbles into the room. "Murtaugh!" he bellows in his usual bullhorn loudness, "I hear you been in the ol' hoosegow! Hello, Aaron!" Fuller's jowls quiver with every syllable of each word that he utters.

Fuller seldom speaks to Hack, and he has never addressed him by his name. For a moment Hack is confused, mostly from the simple fact of his being addressed by Fuller. But then he understands. "Uh, yes," he says. "I was indeed a patient in the hospital."

"Hospital, hoosegow, same difference," Fuller says. "You're locked up."

"Yeah," Hack says, glancing at Aaron for support, "that's exactly where I was."

Underscoring the importance of his next remark, Fuller's eyes narrow and he slightly cocks his head. "You know something? I have never spent one damn minute in a hospital."

"Never?" Hack says. "Not even in a sanitarium?"

Aaron, who had turned to greet Fuller, turns back. The pinched look on his face assures Hack that his sanity is in dispute.

"Nope," Fuller says. "*I* don't get sick. What were you in for, Murtaugh?"

"Parole violation," Hack says. He cannot help himself: some questions reach his ear with the impact of a scripted straight-line.

Fuller frowns and shakes his head. "For *what*?" he says.

Hack sighs heavily. "Better close the door," he says to Fuller.

After a pause, the hesitation of a man certain it is not his place to abide an order issued by the likes of a Tom Murtaugh, Fuller turns and pushes the door shut with his cane.

Hack cranes his neck for a quick look past Aaron, sees that the door is tightly shut, and says in a low voice to Fuller, "I had 'em removed. Both. I was double anesthetized, of course."

"Had both *what* removed?" Fuller says, a hint of anxiousness tainting his voice.

"You know *what*," Hack says. He shrugs offhandedly, but makes it clear he would rather not elaborate.

It's a second before Fuller replies. Frowning, but respecting Hack's obvious thirst for confidentiality, he lowers his voice. "Had both what removed?"

"You know," Hack whispers, "my nuts."

Fuller's eyes widen. "Jesus Christ! What in the holy hell was wrong with your nuts!"

Hack, as if he had been insulted, tilts back and stares dispiritedly at Fuller. "Nothing was *wrong*. I wasn't . . . sick. My surgery was strictly voluntary."

Fuller's frown lines deepen. "Voluntary! How do you mean, voluntary?"

"The VNP. You're not in it?"

"Not in what?"

Hack nods at Aaron. "Aaron signed up. Aaron, when's your surgery scheduled?"

Aaron's narrowed eyes tell Hack to leave him out of the conversation.

Shaking his head sympathetically, Hack says to Fuller, "Aaron doesn't like to talk about it."

"Doesn't like to talk about what?"

Hack checks the door again. Satisfied that it is still tightly closed, he says, "The VNP, the Voluntary Neutering Program. You're not enrolled?"

Fuller looks at Hack dumbly for a second. "No. I never even knew–"

"You do know that its Medicare approved?"

"I've never even heard of it."

"Well . . . the law was passed, oh, a year ago by Congress. And signed by Clinton. Senator Klosky voted for it. That wasn't exactly a given."

"Joe Klosky?"

No! Jose Klosky Fuentes. "Yes," Hack says, "our Man in Washington. Jose Klosky. A *few* Republicans are surprisingly compassionate, you know."

"That's why they get my vote," Fuller says, nodding with certainty. "Still . . . it sounds to me, Murtaugh, like you're actually talking about . . . castration?"

Hack gives his question a few seconds of silence. "Yes. Well . . . it is a *form* of castration. But, technically, it's merely neuterization."

"Yeah. But why in hell would any man want his balls cut off?"

Hack shakes his head disappointedly. "The program's not open to just any man. You have to be at least sixty-two and a citizen of the United States of America. We have a cross-border arrangement with Canada. Mexico wouldn't go along, though. You know how Catholics are about big families. I can't speak for other men, but for myself, I was always too horny."

Fuller grins cockily. "*That's* a problem?"

"For some men. Psychiatrists call it, SL, for Senility Lust. It's a well-studied mental condition of elders, one of only a trillion psychoses recognized as couch-treatable by the Union of American Psychiatric Episcopates. Cooper Greens isn't exactly Shangri-La, but I'm not about to spend my last years in prison for the boffing of one of our aides. Aaron feels the same way. Do you remember Joe Luoma? (Of course Lon Fuller remembers the man with whom he had a fight in the dining room.) He passed away here. The older Joe got, the meaner he got. That's why he enrolled – afraid he'd kill someone. He died a week to the day before he was scheduled for the surgery. That's the other main reason men enroll in the Hostility Abatement program."

Aaron stands suddenly and says he has to run an errand. Making his way around Fuller, he walks rapidly from the room. Fuller watches him suspiciously.

Hack looks compassionately at Fuller. "Aaron's uncomfortable talking about it."

"Well, hell," Fuller says turning back from confirming that Aaron had closed the door. "Do you blame him?"

Hack considers Fuller's question before he answers: "Um . . . I think it's indicative of a certain immaturity, the sign of a man who has not quite grown up yet. You know, Aaron's only five feet four–"

Fuller interrupts Hack. "It's this way, Murtaugh . . . ." He finishes his thought after a long pause; his frown lines have totally vanished: "I'm passing on this one. I'd certainly like to join, but, ah, I've got this serious blood problem."

"Well then it doesn't matter anyway," Hack says. "The VNP won't accept men with a venereal disease."

Fuller's eyes dart back and forth impatiently while he waits for voices in the hall to fade away. "I *don't* have a venereal disease!" he hisses.

Hack shrugs. "These days, it's not that big a deal. Hasn't been since penicillin was invented."

"I *don't* have VD," Fuller repeats, his voice now sounding like steam escaping from a leaking boiler.

Hack says soothingly, "I shouldn't have jumped to that conclusion, Lon."

"That's right," Fuller says. "You should not have."

"It's a mea culpa on me," Hack says shaking his head.

Fuller's frown lines return. After a few seconds he says, "Have you noticed any difference?"

"Any difference? How do you mean?"

"You know. Do you still . . . piss in a urinal? I mean . . . do you still sometimes go on your feet?"

"Oh heavens, no. Not on my shoes. Of course not."

For a second, Fuller is confused, and then he says, "I meant . . . *standing up*."

"Oh, I see what you mean. No, no, I never sit down just to pee. Nothing like that. Besides, the doctor has me on a Testosterone Supercede diet. I don't feel any different in that respect."

Fuller's blustery self-assurance returns. "Still, I'm passing on this one, Murtaugh."

"I understand. Aaron will be disappointed. But I fully understand."

"Aaron. Why would he . . . ."

"It's just the way he is. He respects you enormously."

Fuller nods. "Anyway, I'm skipping this one."

On his way out of the room Fuller tells Hack to remind Aaron that he is still waiting to get him in a cribbage game. After a pause he adds, "No big hurry." After another few seconds of thinking it over he apparently decides it would be better if *he* called on Aaron. "I'll look him up," he promises.

Aaron returns, scolds Hack for egregiously disrespecting Fuller, and insists that he is toying with his own health.

"Naw," Hack says. "He never caught on. Though he did act a bit upset when I told him about you and Edith. You know, about you two regularly meeting on Thursdays out by First Energy's main gas meter."

Aaron chuckles. "He'd kill me if that were true."

They begin a new game of cribbage, and after two hands, with Hack ahead for once; somebody again knocks on their door.

"Not decent!" Hack yells.

"Tom," a woman replies, "this is Birdie Yoder. I need to see you and Aaron."

"Hell," Hack says softly to Aaron, laying his hand down. "Do you concede?"

Aaron brushes aside my question with a tiny grunt.

"Give me a minute," Hack yells.

Birdie Yoder has not spoken to Hack since the day she, Harris, and Dekker interrogated Hack about Kitty's fight with Lorrie Hoover, and Hack is not sure what to expect. They lay the cribbage board and their cards on Aaron's dresser. Hack moves to the side of his bed, and Aaron opens the door.

Birdie is all smiles. "Good morning," she says, walking briskly into the room. "How are you gentlemen doing today?"

Okay, both men answer cautiously: a caller from an administrative office is seldom a bearer of good tidings.

"Why I'm here," Birdie begins, taking up a position in front of our bathroom doorway, "is to offer advice on creating a living-will – if you're interested. I've been checking our records, and I cannot find one in either of your files."

"I don't have one," Hack says to Aaron, addressing him as if he were asking the question.

Aaron shakes his head. "Neither do I."

"I've brought forms," Birdie says. "If either of you is interested."

Aaron tells Birdie that he is definitely interested, and she hands him a two-sheet, multi-subject form titled Advanced Directives Declaration. Hack tells that in his case it does not much matter, but he takes a form anyway. As Hack and Aaron are reading, she explains in a few obviously memorized sentences, how a living-will works. The gist of what she says is that a living-will directs that all measures supporting life will be ended if the signer is fast dying of a defined, incurable medical condition.

Aaron stops reading the form and says, "I'll bring this by your office later. If that's okay."

"That's fine," Birdie says, her smile cranked up again. She looks at Hack, and he tells her that in his case he can't see where having a living-will will matter. Uncertain of how to respond, Birdie nods, works up a smile, waves, and walks from the room.

Their cribbage game is interrupted again, this time by Marie, who sharply knocks on the door. As usual, she barrels in before either man answers her knock.

"What if I was naked?" Hack says crossly.

"I'd break-up laughing," she says. "I just got a call from Stacy. Three residents–"

"Stacy?"

Struggling to hide her impatience, Marie reminds Hack that Stacy is her counterpart for Ash and Poplar streets. "She said three of her patients have asked about a Medicare neutering program that you claim to have signed up for. What in . . . is that all about, Murtaugh?"

"Oh, nothing, Hack says. "Aaron was giving Lon Fuller a hard time earlier and in his usual thoughtless way he implicated me."

Since spending most of his waking hours with Aaron, Hack has become pretty good at faking a hang-dog face, and he shows Marie a good one.

[48]

Hurricane Floyd, peaking as a Category Four Atlantic Ocean storm, has been front-page news for a week. The day before yesterday, after turning northward from a point off the shore of South Carolina, it swept through eastern Pennsylvania, New Jersey, and eastern New York, sometimes dumping as much as a foot of rain in a mere hours. Aaron, once the storm began churning north, all but affixed his nose to the TV. Hack does not get worked up over remote, localized disasters, especially when the victims are people he could not possibly know. Besides, he has watched TV broadcasts of storm disasters many times, and the main difference among them, in his mind, is where the destruction takes place.

Hack has reasonably recovered from his prostate surgery, but he cannot seem to shake the sniffles that he caught in the hospital. He even spits up a little blood now and then. It takes longer to get over colds when you're elderly, actually, Hack reminds himself, everything takes longer when you're old – except falling asleep. At some point, elders stop wearing shoes that don't simply slip on, shirts and blouses that button in the front, and jackets that don't zip closed.

This morning Kitty stopped by Hack's and Aaron's room and left a copy of yesterday's *USA Today,* one that she had mooched from somewhere. Near the bottom of the front page is a small, thick-bordered notice reminding readers that today is a Jewish holiday.

Since Aaron is consumed with watching the flooding on TV, Hack decides to visit Larry Goldberg. As far as he knows Larry (Laurenz) is the only Jew living at Cooper Greens. He and Homer Lott share a room. Larry is form-and-fit interchangeable with most of the men living at Cooper Greens: bent at the waist, hair – the smidgen he has left – silky white, rheumy eyes, and a plain but oversized nose. He settled into Cooper Greens a couple years before Hack had moved in. Hack's father liked him. Larry is not as old as Hack's father would have been if he was still alive, but he is likely twenty years older than Hack.

Larry and his wife owned and operated a turkey ranch situated on the outskirts of Linville, another nearby borough. He and his parents fled Germany in the late thirties as Hitler and the Nazis were beginning to treacherously dominate the politics of the "Fatherland." The Goldbergs reached Linville by way of Palestine, Canada, and Buffalo, New York. All considered, Larry has an impressive command of the English language though he often pronounces the English v as the letter w and the English w as a v. Sometimes, too, he utters a hasty "Ja, ja" after impatiently waiting to comment on the dilatory verbalizing of another resident. Larry's parents eked out a living in Palestine by raising and selling chickens. Larry is a quiet, thoughtful man, popular and well-liked. (But probably scorned by Bob Ford and a few others of Ford's disposition. Hack doesn't know.) Marginally ambulatory, Larry usually navigates the halls in his wheelchair, which is a fancy rig with balloon tires and relatively thick padding.

The door to Goldberg's room is open, and Hack, before knocking, peeks inside. Larry and his wife are sitting side-by-side on the edge of his bed watching TV.

"Tom Murtaugh!" Larry blurts out when he sees Hack. "You step right in here!"

"No," Hack says, "I only want to say hello and wish you well."

The words have not left Hack's lips before Larry's wife is on her feet insisting that he sit in her place on the bed. Hack knows her name from seeing it on a roster, but he cannot remember it, nor can he tell it from Larry's pronunciation: Grazyna, maybe? Grazina? She is eighty years old or near to it. Hack coaxes her to return to where she was sitting on the bed, but she refuses, insisting that she was about to leave anyway.

Larry and his wife hug warmly. Backing from the room, she waves to both of us.

"How long have you folks been married?" Hack asks Larry.

"Fifty-two years," he says, after he finishes waving goodbye to his wife. "How are you doing, Thomas?"

"Usual. Yourself?"

"I could complain, but vhat good does it do."

Hack tells him that he has learned how to play chess, something he did not mention the last time they talked.

"We'll play sometime," Larry says, sounding as if he's issuing an order. "You vill likely defeat me."

"Oh sure," Hack says grinning.

They are silent for a moment, each searching for a subject to talk about: senility and gender, are truthfully all the two of them have in common.

"Hey, Larry," Hack says, breaking the silence."Help me to understand something. Why do I feel funny about calling you a Jew? I mean, I have to say, 'Larry is Jewish.' I can't say, 'Larry is a Jew.' It sounds . . . you know like I'm disrespecting you. Like I'm calling you a Hunky or something"'"

Our eyes meet, and his seem to briefly penetrate my soul. He sighs and props his chin on his fist but does not answer.

Hack again breaks the silence. "Somehow my saying 'Larry is a Jew' seems to be . . . derogatory."

Again Larry doesn't answer.

"But surely calling a Jew a Jew isn't . . . degrading. Is it? I don't get it."

After another long moment Larry says, "Thomas, I know this. The problem is not with the verd Jew."

Hack lets his remark sink in. "So . . . you think it's *my* problem? The way I say it?'"

"Do you think Jews are . . . bad people?"

Hack draws back. "No, of course not. I don't think that. Hell, if anything . . . ."

Larry smiles kindly. "It does not distress me to say, 'Thomas is a Christian,' or, 'Thomas is a Catholic.'"

"I know. But . . . you listen to any talk show on TV and the host or another guest almost never says, 'So-so is a Jew.' The ethnicity of a person, if addressed at all, comes out as 'So-so is of the Jewish faith.' Never 'He or she is a Jew.'" Sometimes the guest may say that he's Jewish, even say 'I'm a Jew.' But . . . I don't know. There's a kind of . . . phony bluster to the way he or she says it. Do you know what I mean?"

"Yes," Larry says. "I have seen that. And I don't have an answer, not off the top of my head."

Homer Lott, Larry's roommate returns and without a word enters the bathroom.

Larry, raising his voice, says, "Vhen did you learn to play chess, Thomas?"

Hack spins his walker around to where he can step into it. "Higgins taught me. Carl Higgins. He was my roomie for several months last year."

"I remember Mister Higgins. His vife was a Ro-Day-O performer?"

Hack chuckles. "You could say that."

Larry couldn't keep the humor from his eyes. "She vore a coat of many colors, eh?"

Lott emerges from the bathroom and begins puttering around in a drawer of his dresser. Both men watch him for a few seconds, and then Hack tells Larry that Aaron is probably waiting for him to go to lunch.

When Aaron and Hack return to their room after eating lunch, Larry is sitting in his wheelchair staring out of their window. After he and Aaron exchange pleasantries. He says to Hack, "Ve did not finish our discussion this morning, Thomas."

Hack says, "I guess not."

Aaron glances at Hack and Hack returns a subtle "Whatever?" look to let Aaron know he can either stay or leave. Aaron says he has an errand to run, and he tells Larry that he'll see him later.

Larry bids Aaron farewell and says to Hack, "Tom, I have thought about your question. Here's vhat I think. We all have tiny prejudices, me, you, Aaron – everyone. Some are more jaundiced-eye than others. They become lodged in our minds even though we don't mean it to happen. So we cover up these childish biases by being super polite."

"Super polite. How do you mean?"

"Take the word niggardly. You know vhat it means?"

"Yeah, it means you're a tight-wad."

"Exactly. And that's all it means. Would you use it in front of Aaron?"

Hack answers after a long moment, "Probably not."

"Exactly. See my point?"

"I guess. Only I wouldn't use 'niggardly' more on account of I'd be afraid Aaron wouldn't know what it means."

"So. When you conwerse with Aaron you are careful to never use words that he may not understand?"

"No. I don't even think about it . . . usually."

"Usually," Larry says, nodding. "See what I mean?"

"Kind of," Hack says exaggeratedly shrugging his shoulders once. Only, Hack doesn't at all see what Larry means.

"Good," Larry says. "Also, in English a simple declarative sentence . . . for example, `Larry is a Jew,' or `Thomas is a Catholic,' or . . . `Aaron is a black man comes close to being an accusation. Doesn't it seem that vay to you?"

"A little. But . . . what difference does it make? It's only words."

Larry disdainfully disagrees, "Thomas, *nothing uttered*, is only words."

"I know. I didn't really mean that."

Larry stares unblinkingly into my eyes. "Anyway," he says, "that is how I see the answer to your question. Vhat do you think?"

"I think I'm in over my head."

"You think about it, Thomas. Please."

I will, Hack answers.

Larry's wandering gaze pauses to take in the scene outside our bedroom window. "It's a vonderful time for a walk. The best time. Just once more I would like to stroll down one of our beautiful country lanes with my sweet G_____, see the leaves that have turned, and smell the apples that have fallen on the ground. The leaves are turning early. I wonder if the apples will ripen late this year because of the dry summer. Do you know, Thomas?"

No, Hack tells Larry, that he does not know, that, that it was a reach for him to master running a lathe let alone understanding the wisdom of Mother Nature. Larry laughs, he and Hack exchange friendly parting remarks, and he wheels from the room.

In a week, the major league baseball season will end and the playoff games will begin, which is why Hack likes this time of the year. Larry would have thought he was a knuckle-dragging chimp if he had mentioned that fact to him, so Hack didn't bring it up. The Cleveland Indians won their division almost a month ago, and the regular starters, when they played, only half tried to win, and Hack has not lately followed the scores.

The major league baseball season ended a week ago Sunday. In the American League, the Cleveland Indians, Texas Rangers, and New York Yankees won their respective divisions; the Boston Red Sox were the wild-card team, the team with the best won-lost record that did not win a division title. Hack's Indians, though heavily favored, lost to the theoretically subpar Red Sox in the fifth and deciding game of the first round of playoffs. Hack was so consummately upset that Aaron never once heckled him over it. Aaron's team, the Phillies, finished in third place in their division, 26 games behind the first-place Atlanta Braves.

[49]

Saturday, October 23rd. It is a cool morning and the wind, when it stirs at all, barely amounts to a light breeze. Once the temperature reaches forty degrees, Aaron and Hack leave the building to begin their daily walk. The fog is dense and they cannot see the vehicles creeping along on the road fronting Cooper Greens. The weather forecast, however, calls for a sunny day, with temperatures in the low sixties. The Cooper Greens' lawn, mostly perennial rye, has recovered from the summer drought and once again is a lively green – though of varying shades. Many of the deciduous trees, except for the oaks, have shed their leaves. The nearby forests, as usual about this time of year, are becoming darker, even a tad spooky.

The staff of Cooper Greens, joined by all able residents, has decorated the inside and the outside of Cooper Greens for Halloween. They have monsters lurking in nooks waiting to assail passers-by; the halls are creepy with cobwebs; feathery ghosts flit about, partially disemboweled freaks of nature lie supine in open caskets; doors lead to grottos that promise a club-wielding, cave-man reception; human skeletons beckon; and so forth. The outside is only a little less decorated. Local residents pack Rolling Greens the evening of Open House. Cars fill the front yard and dozens are parked haphazardly in the adjacent open fields.

In one of the open caskets, the eyes of the occupant are shown rolled back into its skull leaving sockets replete with bulging white orbs. The occupants' macabre visage reminded Hank of a few minutes of crudeness on his part at our luncheon some two weeks ago. Will MacElroy, a blind resident, ate with Aaron and Hank. Leading him to their table, Hank lightly pressed his hand on Will's coffee cup and water tumbler, cubed his meat, and described the kind and location of the food on his plate.

Will is smart, and he is talkative. Midway through their meal, he mentioned something that could be interpreted as a bigoted slur. (It wasn't, but never mind.)

Lightly tapping his arm, Hank, in a low but audible voice, says, "Keep in mind, Will, that you are black, too."

Aaron stifles a guffaw by transmuting a sudden expulsion of air into a cough.

Will's jaw drops, and he tilts his head toward Aaron. "No, I'm not," he says softly.

"You didn't now?" Hank says. "I'm so . . . terribly sorry."

It was a good second before Will offered a rebuttal: "Mother would have told me."

"Maybe," Hank says, "but you know Mothers. They'll tell their children anything. Mine told me I was handsome. I learned the hard way in grade school that I was rat-face ugly. So I'm not surprised she told you that you were white."

Will, of course, before too long caught on, and all of us chortled our way to another subject. Will hasn't eaten with Hack and Aaron since. And Hack wishes he had never kidded him.

Hack is still coughing, sometimes bringing up blood, so Dr. Bonifanti will be seeing him on Wednesday, her usual day to visit. Both Kitty and Aaron have been after Hack to make an appointment.

[50]

The Dallas Cowboys play the Philadelphia Eagles on TV tomorrow, Sunday, at one o'clock. Ordinarily, Hack would watch that particular football game only if he was encased in a body cast, immobilized in a hospital bed, and unable to work a TV remote control.

Football, as a spectator sport, in Hack's opinion, is okay but he much prefers baseball. He hates NBA basketball, a sentiment he keeps from Aaron, not only because Aaron was damn good at basketball as a kid but also because the game, especially at the pro level, is dominated by free-lancers, albeit each and every one is a superbly talented athlete. Hack does like watching the clever execution of scoring plays involving two or more teammates. If he was running the NBA, a pass that led to a basket would count as a point, making the scoring shot add up to three points. And dunking the ball would cost the responsible player's team a turnover. He does not much like three-point shooting – distant shots – either. He argues that long, deep shots that go in the basket are more luck than skill, and he cites statistics to prove it. Where, he questions, is the athleticism involved in launching the ball toward an 18-inch hoop from a distance of twenty-four feet or more?

To the extent that Hack follows football, he is a Pittsburgh Steelers fan. Teams in the National Football League play sixteen games a year. At Cooper Greens, if the residents are lucky, they get to see four or five Steelers' TV games each football season, depending, in part, on marketing-influenced constraints that Hack never did understand.

The Dallas Cowboys team, which has a national following, is on TV damn near every Sunday. It is beyond Hack, why it is that certain sport franchises – the New York Yankees is another – attracts fans who do not know a bowling ball from a volley ball let alone the difference between a football red-dog and a stadium hot dog. Hack presumes that some people just never get over the hunger to fit in.

Last year the Eagles, Aaron's team, was a pitiful lot. And so far this season they're all of that. They won by one point in their opening game against the last-place Arizona Cardinals team, however, and Aaron, being a typical die-hard football fan, believes that this year the Eagles can beat anyone, including the Dallas Cowboys. Last year the Cowboys made the playoffs, as they usually do, by twice plucking the tail of the Eagles and beating every other team in their division at least once.

This last week, several times at great length, Hack explained to Aaron why the Eagles could not beat a Cuban conga drum, let alone defeat the Dallas Cowboys, even if every member of the team had mallets for hands. Aaron contemptibly disagreed, of course, and he even went so far as to suggest that they make a friendly bet on that game's outcome.

Hack agreed, enthusiastically, and proposed that they wager fifty cents on the score at the end of each quarter of play and a dollar on the final score of the game, all washes going Hack's way since he initiated the idea of betting. Aaron flummoxed Hack, argued that he could not bet for money as gambling was the Devil's playground. As an afterthought, he said that Bingo was the only exception. Hack should have been suspicious right then, but he wasn't.

Hack told Aaron that he was open to suggestions. And as a last resort – his bad knees proscribing the "push-a-peanut-by-nose penalty" for losing the bet – Hack came up with the cockamamie notion of the loser paying off the bet by singing a song in the dining room during lunch on the Monday after the game. Hack can sing. Nobody ever asks him to sing, but he can sing a little, if the range of notes is flat as west Texas acreage. Aaron, on the other hand, could not carry a tune in a wash tub with help from a team of Olympic weightlifters. So, Hack right away argues for his suggestion, confident that the Cowboys would not lose. The form of payment established, they agreed that it would also suitably humble for the loser to stand by his table during lunch on the Monday after the game and sing two stanzas of the children's ditty, *Three Blind Mice*.

They are still bickering over the point spread midway into the NFL pre-game show. The Cowboys are nine-point favorites, and Aaron insists that Hack add nine points to the Eagles score before determining the winner of the game. "No way," Hack says, giving as his reason the Cowboys' handicap of playing before the notoriously unruly Philadelphia Eagle fans.

At ten minutes before game-time Aaron inserts a blank tape into his new VCR and adjusts its front-panel controls. "It'll start recording at exactly one o'clock," Aaron says matter-of-factly, rising from his kneeling position. "Likely," he adds, "I'll need a tape of the game to claim my winnings."

Aaron has fabricated a cardboard Do-Not-Disturb sign as a joke, and after hanging it on our exterior door knob he closes the door. They have darkened the room by draping Hack's bedspread over the window: the sun has burned away the morning fog and has left the afternoon mid-summer bright. Both men have a can of diet pop handy. Yesterday, while Hack was out of their room, someone – no doubt a woman resident – brought Aaron a big bag of Rold Gold brand pretzels, which he and Hack will pass back and forth once the game begins.

"Somebody's asleep at the switch," Hack says, as suddenly, interrupting a Budweiser commercial, Pat

Summerall, the game's play-by-play announcer, begins telling viewers that a lad named Ty Detmer will start the game at quarterback for the Eagles.

"No," Aaron says, "that's the VCR. My old one did the same thing, interrupted whatever was playing when it came on in the record mode and paused a bit before passing on the announcer's voice. I have no idea why. Maybe they all do it."

"Is this Detmer kid any good?" Hack asks.

"You'll see," Aaron answers cockily.

The teams line-up for the kick-off, and shortly it dawns on Hack that he is looking at a game about to begin in Texas Stadium, the Cowboy's home field. "I thought they were playing in Philadelphia?" he mumbles.

Aaron, concentrating hard on the TV, dismisses Hack's concern with a slight shrug of his shoulders.

A Cowboys' running back catches the kick-off on the goal line and returns the ball to the twenty-four-yard line, where he is tackled hard and fumbles the ball. An Eagle player recovers the ball, and Aaron goes joyously bonkers.

Aaron quiets down, and Hack says, more seriously this time, "No kidding, I really thought they were playing in Philadelphia."

Aaron, his attention still fast on the game, mumbles something to the effect that he knew Hack's screen door did not always latch.

The Eagles convert the Cowboys' miscue into a touchdown and extra point, making the score 7-0, Eagles. It is less than two minutes into the game. Aaron taunts Hack by singing the *Three Blind Mice* song – to the tune of God only knows what. Aaron, Hack realizes, absolutely has no sense of either rhythm or pitch.

"What were you singing?" Hack asks when he finishes. "Or, were you . . . praying to Allah?"

Aaron removes his hand from in front of his mouth, placed there to spare Hack the embarrassment of his vast enjoyment. "Just reminding you of how the song goes,." He says.

Hack scoffs. "The game has just begun. We didn't bet on who scored first."

The Eagles kick off, and six plays later, including a long forward pass play, the Cowboys tie the game. "Pay close attention," Hack says to Aaron, and he sings a stanza of *Three Blind Mice*.

At half time, the score is 14-10 in favor of the Eagles. The Cowboys are a second-half team, Hack tells Aaron. Aaron says he's not worried, and he fetches himself another can of diet pop. He offers to bring Hack one, but Hack tells him if he drinks another can he'll have to watch an image of the game on their bathroom mirror while sitting on the pot. Hack suggests that he pay for his second drink, but Aaron says that his offer is merely an attempt to predispose him, Aaron, to mercy in the face of what he assures Hack will be the Cowboys' certain shellacking.

While he was out of the room, Susan, their weekend nurse's aide, took Hack's vitals and then waited for Aaron to return so she could take his. She said she did not follow football but admitted to knowing who Troy Aikman was. Like most NFL quarterbacks, Aikman, the Dallas Cowboys' quarterback, is a handsome guy. So far, Susan has been our only visitor, so maybe Aaron's home-made Do-Not-Disturb sign is working. Susan snaps off our ceiling light, which she had turned on when she entered the room, and leaves, shutting the door on her way out.

At the end of three quarters of play, the Eagles are ahead, 21-13, and Hack again has to suffer through Aaron's weird attempt to sing. Worse, the Eagles, the whole third quarter, clearly outplayed the Cowboys. And Hack is becoming antsy.

"Here's where the Cowboys get down to nut-cracking time," Hack says confidently as the fourth quarter begins. And, in fact, the Cowboys on their next series of downs tie the game on a seven-yard touchdown run by their all-pro running back, Emmitt Smith. A Cowboy player, an infrequent receiver, catches a bullet-like, two-point conversion pass from Aikman.

"What else is on?" Hack says. "This game's over."

"We'll see," Aaron says.

And they did. That is, they watched as Aikman, the Cowboys' veteran, all-pro quarterback, was intercepted twice, ultimately allowing the Eagles to win the game 31-21.

"Ho hum," Aaron says at the final whistle. "Another day at the office. I knew I wouldn't need those nine points. How's that song go again, is it . . . 'Three blind mice . . .' or is it 'Three sightless rodents' . . . I've forgotten."

"I hate those damn Cowboys," Hack says glaring hard at the TV.

[51]

Monday, October 25th. While the Cooper Greens diners are seated and waiting for an aide to bring their lunches, Hack stands, uses the dining-room table to steady himself, clears his throat, and sings two stanzas of the song *Three Blind Mice*. When he finishes, Kitty and Yvon wildly cheer. A few other diners also understand that Hack is supposed to be making a fool of himself, and they follow the lead of Kitty and Yvon. Everyone else, at least the residents who can halfway hear, sit with flabbergasted looks. Hack compliments himself, decides that his playing the lead in scenes that could whisk away the forbidding solemnity of some residents was the way to invigorate all of Cooper Greens.

"Aaron," Hack announces loudly to the room before he sits back down, "was supposed to join in. Only, he chickened out."

Aaron vigorously shakes his head.

Hack tells the room that they will practice tonight and try again tomorrow.

"I have to admit, Old Guy," Aaron says, as they trudge back to their room, "you didn't sound all that bad."

"I know," Hack says, "I could have made a good-living singing solo."

"Yeah," Aaron counters, "and I could have made good money playing center on an NBA basketball team."

Kitty did not leave Hack and Aaron a copy of a newspaper this morning, and a few steps away from the dining room they turn from Ash Street onto Chestnut, where Hack tells Aaron that he's going to swing by the lobby and pick up a *Beacon*.

"No," Aaron says grimacing. "I'll go. I have business on the way. I'll get us a copy." Aaron hurries off, and Hack does not see him until a half hour later when he walks into their room shaking his head. "I couldn't find a newspaper anywhere," he says.

Knowing that several residents get the *Beacon* – often subscribed to in their name by a relative – Hack says, "Not even a *Beacon*?"

Aaron perplexedly says, "Not even a *Beacon*. I checked everywhere. One will turn up. How about me thrashing you in a game of cribbage?"

After losing yesterday's bet, Hack is not overly excited about engaging Aaron in any kind of contest, let alone one Aaron will likely win. While Hack is making up his mind, Kitty walks into the room. It is her custom, as it is Marie's, to lightly knock on the door frame and then march on in. They say their hellos, and then Hack says to her, "No paper today?"

Kitty glances at Aaron. "I didn't see one. I heard that part of Meadville was without power last night. Maybe the *Tribune* presses were down."

Wondering about the reason for her visit, Hack says to her, "You doing all right today, Kit?"

"I just wanted you to know, that as a singer you're . . . another Boots Crosby."

Pretending to believe that he has been hugely complimented, Hack clamps his lips together and nods vigorously. "Aaron wonders why it is," Hack says, "that I never sang professionally."

Aaron exasperatingly looks away.

"You know," Kitty says to Hack, "I never heard *Three Blind Mice* sung as a roundelay before. Have you?"

Hack has to think a moment. "You mean, as a 'Row, row, row your boat' song? No, not that I recall."

"I'll bet it works," Kitty says, and she begins singing the words to *Three Blind Mice*. When Kitty finishes the fourth line of the first verse, Hack joins in. And when Hack reaches the fourth line Aaron joins in. Then Kitty and Hack cannot finish because they cannot stop laughing at Aaron's version of the melody. In fact, they laugh so hard that Hack begins coughing, and it's a while before he stops.

"Get something for that, Tom," Kitty commands him when he finally quits hacking.

"I've been after him," Aaron says shaking his head. "Sometimes he brings up blood."

"Keep on his butt," Kitty orders.

Kitty leaves, casually remarking on her way out, that she understands why it is that Aaron thinks Hack is a good singer. She means, of course, that Aaron himself is so bad that he makes Hack sound good.

Tuesday, October 26th. Back from eating breakfast, Hack is waiting in front of the Beechwood Street nurse's station for Marie to show-up when he glimpses a folded newspaper sticking out of a wastebasket that has been pulled from under the counter – probably for emptying. Billie returns before Marie. Hack asks, and she hands him the newspaper. It is a copy of yesterday's *Morning Beacon*. Deciding he can put off his business with Marie, Hack tucks the paper in the front of his trousers and heads for his room. Aaron, when Hack arrives, is writing a letter.

"Lookee here!" Hack says, pulling the paper from the front of his trousers and tossing it on his bed. "Yesterday's *Beacon*."

Aaron stops writing. He stares at the paper as it slowly unfolds. "Both sections?"

"Yep," Hack answers backing onto his bed.

Hack starts reading, and Aaron begins snickering. Hack glances his way. Aaron stops snickering and morphs into an animal with a face that reminds Hack of a cartoon of Lewis Carroll's grinning Cheshire cat.

"Nothing," Aaron mumbles, answering Hack's look.

Hack reads further, and Aaron begins snickering again.

Hack looks at Aaron suspiciously. "You're writing about me losing our bet, aren't you?"

Aaron finally stops snickering. "My goodness no," he says. "Would I do that?" Aaron's reply is ambiguous – exactly, Hack decides, as he intended.

After another few seconds Aaron lays his pen down, buries his head in his hands, and begins quietly shaking with laughter.

Hack watches for a moment and then says, "The deuce you're not."

"No I'm not," Aaron says, laughing so hard that he is barely lucid.

Aaron stops laughing, and Hack resumes reading. Hack finishes the first part of the paper, picks up the sports section, and Aaron begins snickering again. Shaking his head, Hack dismisses Aaron's behavior as barely pubescent. Hack finds the page where Sunday's NFL games are briefly summarized in short, column-wide boxes. He reads the one covering the Steelers-Bills game. Hack had meant to skip over the box covering the Cowboys-Eagle game, but the little headline catches his eye.

"Hey," Hack says, audibly, but mostly to himself, "they got the score wrong for the Cowboys-Eagle game."

Aaron's snickering intensifies. "How's that?" he asks, wedging his question in between snickers.

"The paper has it thirteen ten, not thirty-one twenty-one. I guess the typographer screwed up."

Aaron finds this remark to be far and away the funniest thing Hack has uttered since he moved here.

"What's so funny?" Hack asks suspiciously.

Aaron stops laughing and takes a deep breath. "Nothing," he says. If anything, he concentrates harder on his letter.

The write-up of the Cowboys-Eagles game totally misses the mark. Hack reads through it again and every couple sentences he mumbles a comment such as, "What the hell?" "Who's Doug Pederson?" and "That ain't *right*."

And then it hits him. "Blodgett!" Hack screams. "You horse's ninny! You sewer rat!"

Hack wads the newspaper and throws it at Aaron. His laughter out of control, Aaron falls from his chair onto the floor and assumes the supplicating posture of a praying Muslim – except he gleefully slaps the floor with both hands and does not stop.

"That was rotten" Hack says, when Aaron finally comes up for air. "And you claim to have once been a church deacon? From here on, Pal, it's every man for himself, World War Three right here in Cooper Greens B1006."

"If I die tomorrow," Aaron says, "I'll pass happily on to my reward."

"You'll be lucky to see another sunrise," Hack huffs. "What game did we really watch?"

After another uninterruptible laugh, Aaron says, "The second Cowboys-Eagles game of 1996."

Hack says, "You had it on tape, huh?"

Aaron vigorously nods.

"Who all knew about your underhanded little trick?" Hack asks.

Aaron's eyes close to a narrow opening. He's trying to recollect something, Hack is supposed to infer. "Oh, only. . . Kitty, the nurses and aides, the residents, all of management . . . my daughters . . . ."

[52]

Hack's cough has worsened, has become more than the constant barking of a chain-smoker, to which status, in his mind, he had devalued his respiratory problem. Furthermore, his breathing is shorter, and he is having chest pains that he can no longer discredit as stomach gas or a touch of pleurisy. Aaron chides Hack for frequently smoothing the part of his shirt covering his chest.

Aaron has been puttering about in their room since he and Hack returned from breakfast. Hack doubts that he knows what he is doing, but Aaron does know: he wants to be in their room when Dr. Bonifanti arrives.

Hack is sitting on his bed reading Tom Clancy's *Clear and Present Danger* – going through the motions, really – waiting for Dr. Bonifanti. "What in the hell are you messing with?" he says to Aaron.

"None of your business Old Guy," Aaron says. "Read your book."

"How can I read with you stinking it up in here?"

"A skunk smells his own hole first," Aaron says. "How about a game of cribbage?"

"No. You cheat. Move your pegs when I'm not looking. Otherwise, we'd be playing right now."

After a while Aaron stops fidgeting and sits quietly on his bed; his back is to Hack. Evidently, he wants Hack to think he is contemplating his next activity. A few minutes of his idleness and Aaron abruptly leaves the room. He ducks back fifteen minutes later with – surprise! – Dr. Bonifanti and Marie leading the way into their room.

Stepping rapidly past Aaron, Dr. Bonifanti, without the slightest hint of a greeting to Hack, says to him, "You're coughing?"

Hack does a fast burn. "If you don't have time for me today Doctor, come around *next* Wednesday."

"I have time," Dr. Bonifanti says, no more flustered than if Hack had complimented her. "How long have you been coughing? When did it start?""

Marie, standing behind Dr. Bonifanti, slightly shakes her head. Hack is not looking her way, but he can tell she's sending him a message. Instead of turning away – his anger lessened by Marie's signal – Hack tells Dr. Bonifanti that he has have been coughing for a month. Dr. Bonifanti looks at Hack's throat and ears, listens to his chest and back through her stethoscope, and goes over his vitals with Marie.

"You've been coughing blood?" she asks Hack.

After a moment, he says, "A couple times."

Dr. Bonifanti glances at Aaron, and he nods once strongly.

Looping the stethoscope over her neck, Dr. Bonifanti crosses her arms. "When," she asks, "was the last time your chest was x-rayed?"

"Truthfully. " Hack says, "I don't remember."

"You used to be a heavy smoker?" Knowing that Hack once smoked three packs of cigarettes a day – it's recorded in his chart – Dr. Bonifanti is stating a fact, not asking a question.

"Years ago."

Dr. Bonifanti says to no one in particular, "I want to see a film."

Hack mumbles that he was afraid that's what she'd say. "What's you're thinking?"

Dr. Bonifanti does not answer Hack's question. "You sound hoarse."

Aaron nods grimly. Hack again asks Dr. Bonifanti why she wants to X-ray his lungs, and she again ignores his question.

"For God's sake, Doctor" Hack says softly. "You can write it on a damn shit-house wall for all I care. I'm seventy-one years old."

After a moment, Dr. Bonifanti says, "I want to rule out a tumor." The expression on her face is pensive. "My office will set up an appointment and call Marie."

"Dammit," Hack says to Aaron after Dr. Bonifanti leaves, "I really didn't care to hear that."

"No," Aaron says, "I didn't either. But most likely it's just a little sac of fluid in one of your lobes."

"I hope so," Hack mumbles. But he is sure in his heart, Aaron thinks, that the source of his problem is not just a "little fluid."

Aaron steps to where he can see out the window. "It isn't that bad out," He says. "Why don't we take our walk? There's still time before lunch."

"Might as well."

They dress for the cool weather.

Circling the nurse's station, Hack and Aaron pass Kitty. "You're late this morning," she says, a funny look on her face.

"A little," Aaron answers.

Kitty remembers Hack's appointment. "What'd Doctor Bonifanti say?"

Hack slightly shrugs. "Not much."

Come by and see me later, Kitty says. Her look tells Hack that he damn well better stop by her room.

Returning from lunch, Hack reminds Aaron that Kitty is expecting him. "No napping," he adds, as they separate at the doorway to their room. It irks Hack that Aaron can take a long nap in the afternoon and still sleep like a baby all night long.

Once, while they were lying down after lunch, Hack told Aaron that he never owned a dog that slept as much as Aaron. The sleep of a man with a clear conscience, Aaron replied. Or no conscience, Hack countered. A *clear* conscience, Aaron said, his voice trailing off. Hack disagreed, and a minute later they were both sound asleep.

[53]

Hack greets Kitty by asking how her children's book is coming. She writes on it every morning; her dedication equals Hack's effort to accumulate notes for this book. Sometimes she works right through lunch. Hack and Kitty do not see each other as often as they used to, and they have not bedded down together since the week before Hack's operation. But that is Hack's fault: there is still some kind of decoupling between his fantasies and his plumbing, and he is afraid he'll be embarrassed if Kitty attempts to treat him.

"Slowly," Kitty says, assessing Hack's question in the matter of the progress of her book. "I can't seem to focus on a target age group. So far, I've written a story for eight-year-olds who'd have to be wiser than the Magi, the trio that brought Jesus gifts honoring his birth."

"Three rag-heads guided by a star," Hack mumbles casually.

Kitty does not like Hack's characterization of the men who visited the newborn baby Jesus, thinking, no doubt, that as a devout Catholic he should not be making fun of biblical gospel. Hack, referring to Kitty's difficulty of settling on an age for her readers, says, "I can see where that *would* be a problem."

Hack's hand goes to his chest, and he begins to cough. Kitty's eyes focus anxiously on his face, and when he stops coughing she says, "You did see Doctor Bonifanti?"

Hack throws up his hands impatiently. "*Yes*. But not much came of it. I have to get my chest X-rayed."

"She say why?"

"Not really." Hack remembers Aaron's off-hand diagnosis: "I may have sacs of fluid . . . ."

Her eyes slightly enlarge, and she nods. "That's . . . rather common."

"I guess so."

"Did you hear about Maureen?"

"Maureen?"

"Maureen Post. The third shift nurse for Walnut–"

"I know who you mean. I haven't seen her since Raymond died."

"She's no longer an employee of Cooper Greens."

Hack does not say anything. Kitty, he knows, could no more hold back gossip than a kid's leaky balloon can hold in air.

"The night before last, Lil Monnin caught her getting it on with a guy in the PT room. You know that fanny strap machine? The one that shimmy's the hell out of you?"

"The one that shakes your butt all over the place?"

Kitty grins. "They were . . . experimenting. And they were"– Kitty, using her fingers, sets her next phrase in quotes –"improperly attired for the intended use of that machine."

"Stark naked," Hack says.

Still grinning, Kitty nods. "From the waist down. The guy tripped on his pants and fell face down trying to run off."

"Interesting," Hack says, "that you'd know so much about the subject."

"Hearsay," Kitty replies.

Hack looks at her accusingly. "Right. Who'd you say caught them?"

"Lil Monnin. She called Security. Lil has her own telephone, remember."

"Maureen," Kitty says, "used to work for Lil."

Hack says, "Like to know what it reminds me of?"

"Do I have a choice?"

"Reminds me of the time Dick Gamble and I were hunting frogs with our BB guns and ran into this couple going at it across the creek on the other bank. They weren't–"

"French Creek?"

"No. Actually, a branch of the old Erie Canal. Nobody fished it, 'cause there weren't any fish in it – maybe some carp. Anyway, they were not kids, either. The girl had coal black hair that fell nearly to her ass. Did you know Gamble?"

"Dick Gamble? I don't think so."

"Ol' Gamble plunked lover boy right in the butt with his BB gun."

Kitty snickers. "What happened?"

"Nothing, really. I mean, nothing happened to us. The guy didn't know where the shot came from. I wish I had a film of him trying to get his pants on. He was very well endowed. He let us know that whoever we "asshole sons-a-bitches" were he would "get" us.

Kitty shakes her head.

"Lil," Hack says, "should have stuck to her knitting."

"Yeah," Kitty says indifferently. "I've got to get back to work." Waving at the empty bed in her room, she adds, "Stick around. You can suggest synonyms."

Hack climbs onto the spare bed and Kitty hands him her dictionary. When Hack wakes up fifteen minutes later Kitty is scribbling furiously on a new tablet, and he no longer has her dictionary. Kitty does not notice when Hack quietly leaves the room.

The note on Hack's dresser, in Marie's hand, says that Hack is scheduled for a chest X-ray at ten a.m. at the Meadville Medical Center – departing from Cooper Greens at eight thirty. The sentence, ordering him to be on the Cooper Greens shuttle bus at eight thirty, is underlined. Hack tells Aaron of his appointment, and Aaron says he'll ride along, says he wants to see what's left of the Fall colors. Hack reminds him that he better not miss his insulin shot, and Aaron says he will take one before we leave and again after we return. He is now a full, insulin-dependent diabetic: diet, exercise, and pills no longer offset his body's insufficient production of that hormone. Hack talks Aaron out of accompanying him to the hospital.

The X-ray technician, a short, jolly, heavy-set black woman, thirty years old, at most, takes four pictures of Hack's chest while he is standing and four more, two while he is lying on his back and two while he is lying on his side on one of those cold, plastic-topped hospital tables. Hack asks Jean – the name on her badge – if she normally takes that many x-rays, and she answers tiredly, "Whatever the order calls for." She voluntarily tells Hack that the hospital's resident radiologist will read the films and fax a report to Dr. Bonifanti.

"How long will that take?" Hack asks.

"Two days, sometimes three."

"You can't tell me anything?"

"No, Mister Murtaugh. I check focus. Look for blurring."

"Okay. Then, just let me look, too."

"I can't do that either."

"I can't see X-rays of my own chest?" Hack says sharply.

"You can see them, Mister Murtaugh, but I cannot be the one who shows them to you."

"Why not?"

She shrugs. "I only work here, Sir."

Hack puts on his shirt while Jean is looking at his films in another room. When she returns, he says, "You're a good woman. Are you married?"

"No I'm not," she answers cheerfully.

"Want to get married?"

"Maybe."

"How about to me?"

"Are you rich?"

"I don't have a pot or a window."

"So. You want me to marry down, is that it?"

Hack makes his way to the door, Jean holds it open, and he tells her as he's leaving, "You're too old for me, anyway." She is not listening and does not see Hack's grin.

When Hack reaches the hospital lobby, Buddy, Cooper Greens' van driver, is waiting.

People say the worst part is waiting to hear. It isn't, not by a damn sight. The worst part is hearing the bad news.

Dr. Bonifanti, followed by Marie, enters our room. Marie gives Hack a somber glance and closes the door. Aaron is writing a letter. It later occurs to Hack that Aaron was only waiting for Dr. Bonifanti to arrive, a prearrangement scheduled by Marie, he is sure. Hack lays aside Tom Clancy's *Clear and Present Danger*.

"There's a spot on your left lobe, Thomas," Dr. Bonifanti says. "It's a tumor. That's . . . all it can be. There may be smaller ones."

From her tone of voice, Hack could tell that she meant the probability of other tumors existing was one-hundred per cent.

Hack closes his eyes and very slowly nods; he had expected as much. "Damn it," he says softly.

"It may be benign," Dr. Bonifanti says. "But I'm not optimistic."

"Neither am I. Why in the hell . . . ."

Dr. Bonifanti waits for Hack to finish his thought, but he just shakes his head.

"I've ordered more X-rays, and we'll go from there."

"Meaning?"

"Meaning, we'll know more after seeing the films – and after a biopsy. Doctor Michalak will be working from the malignancy perspective. His specialty is oncology."

"And if it's . . . cancerous, then what?"

"If it is, and we don't know that yet, "Doctor Michalak will develop a treatment plan . . . depending upon the histology of the tumor. Its stage . . . maturity, size, and so on."

"Treatment involving what? Surgery? Radiation?"

"Possibly both. Chemotherapy's another possibility. Cancer treatment has come a long way, Tom. But let's not get ahead of ourselves."

"Whatever," Hack says. He glances at Marie and then at Aaron. Marie's eyes fly from his face to the back of Dr. Bonifanti's head. Aaron nods without really nodding.

Dr. Bonifanti offers to write Hack a prescription for a mild tranquilizer. He tells her that that will not be necessary. "Just like in the movies," he adds, striving to sound lighthearted. "It only hurts when I laugh."

Dr. Bonifanti and Marie leave together, and Hack says to Aaron, "Well . . . you can't win 'em all."

"We're going to win this one," Aaron says. "Nothing's a given yet."

They did not 'win this one,' however. The cells drawn by a CT-guided biopsy extractor confirmed the worst, that the spot on Hack's lung was indeed malignant.

Hack visited Kitty after he heard. She read to him from her soft-cover Health and Medical Guide book. With treatment, he has about one chance in seven of living five more years. He grins mockingly, internally, at his one-time hope of significantly leveraging to higher spirits the collective temperament of the residents of Cooper Greens.

[54]

Hack takes one chemotherapy pill a day for four days, and then thirty days later he takes four pills over another four-day period. Dr. Michalak is hazy about the total number of treatments, an indefiniteness that does not at all thrill Hack.

Anticancer drugs attack body cells, including those in the stricken person's digestive tract, and it was three days after Hack took his last pill of the first treatment before he could keep food down. When he was not dry-puking in the direction of a bedpan on the floor by the bed, he was folded up tightly in bed irritably scorning anyone who tried to coax an agreeable word from him. Hack had forgotten how miserable it is to suffer the dry pukes: his last brush with that malaise of non-stop, unproductive vomiting occurred on a troop transport ship sailing for Korea in December of 1952. Anyway, Hack stopped collecting notes for this book, and he did not resume – and when he did his effort was random and haphazard – until almost a week after his next treatment replica.

Hack lost all his hair, which is a bit like saying he lost all his money, because he had damn little of either. Kitty and Aaron noticed, and so did Marie; no one else did. He also lost fourteen pounds, no less than ten from his face, he thinks. War is hell, true enough, but chemotherapy is a close second. In battle, you hope to survive. When you're on chemo, you wish the hell you'd die.

Hack, to himself, admits that Aaron is more patient with him than Helen was. Hack tells himself again that the son-of-a-gun is an undercover saint. Once Hack told Aaron that he would propose if Aaron was not so blamed ugly. Aaron laughed and said that, aged, bald-headed, honkies, thank goodness, turned him off.

Today is the first time Hack has left his room in a week, even to bathe. Cooper Greens has two rooms equipped with motorized bathing tubs that whirl and tilt and do everything but uniquely douche a person's external genital parts. In fact, they probably do that, too. The last phase is an optional whirlpool cycle.

"Our first real snow," Hack says to Kitty. "I like winters, always have. I used to trap muskrats in the winter. We got two dollars and fifty cents for a rat – big money back then when a cheeseburger cost fifteen cents. And pop was a nickel."

The two of them are alone in Kitty's room. Hack is lying on his side on her spare bed looking at the landscape outside – or gazing wistfully at the scenery, as Kitty would have told it. Kitty is working on her children's book and no doubt wishing the hell Hack was somewhere else. Since that first replication of his medicine, she has generally given him a wide berth.

"I don't like them at all," kitty says, remarking on her disenchantment with snowy seasons. Her pen never stops making rapid little up-down strokes.

Hack says, "About an inch, I'd guess. But, it's still coming down – a little."

She slightly nods.

Hack comments impassively on the ghostly white sycamore tree rising almost alone from the dark stand of maple and oak trees across the road from Cooper Greens, the tree Kitty has named Methuselah. Kitty looks up, smiles pleasantly, and says, "Bare ruined choirs where late the sweet birds sang." Hack has no idea of what the hell she means by that. And he decides not to ask, to deprive her of the self-satisfaction of explaining the meaning. It was probably, he projected, the only thing she would have interrupted her writing for.

"'Where late the sweet birds sang,'" Hack says amicably. "I guess you heard that Dirt Jamison died? Last night in his sleep."

Kitty's eyebrows bob slightly, but she does not look up.

"He was a damn good mechanic," Hack says, looking away from the scene outdoors.

"He must have been," Kitty mumbles.

"That's probably the way you'll remember me," Hack says. "Tom was a good tool maker, but otherwise gross."

Kitty sighs and stops writing. "No, Tom. I'll remember you as Don Juan Tenorio reincarnated. Now would you please *shut* the hell up!"

"Sorry."

Hack sits up and pretends for a few seconds that something new and interesting outdoors has caught his attention. His equilibrium restored, he steps into his walker.

"Give me a minute," Kitty says.

"I can make it all right," Hack says. But, Kitty stops writing and heads for her bathroom. On the way she warns Hack with a threatening look to stay put.

They pass Marie on their way to Hack's room, and she tells Kitty to let her know if I get to acting up, that if I do she will "take me to the woodshed." Kitty's manner is pleasant, but all the same Hack knows that his sometimes ill-tempered behavior of late is the reason for her sweet, whip-cream words.

"Marie's been trying to get me alone in a linen closet ever since I moved in," Hack says loudly to Kitty.

Ordinarily, Marie would have responded by asking Hack if he had just received a new bong in the mail, or something to that effect, but she merely rolls her eyes.

Aaron, when they reach his and Hack's room, is standing and pointing the remote controller at the TV.

After a moment he clicks it off. "More snow coming," he says.

"Good," Hack says, "What's for lunch? I'm starved."

Aaron starts for our bulletin board but stops when Kitty says that we're having Swiss steak.

"Honest?" Hack says skeptically. "Steak for an entree? Must be a holiday."

"And you eat all of it, too," Kitty warns Hack.

"I'll try," Hack murmurs.

They make their way to the dining room. Hack takes a bite of the meat, chews it thoroughly and swallows, takes another bite, chews it thoroughly and swallows. And then up-chucks both bites into his hand and onto his dinner plate.

[55]

This year the commemoration of the birth of Jesus Christ falls on a Saturday, exactly nine months after the Annunciation. Dr. Michalak has considerately moved the start of Hack's third cycle of chemotherapy treatment back to the Monday after Christmas. Hack was scheduled to take the first pill today, the twenty-second. He cannot decide if falling five days behind schedule will not matter, in terms of his healing, or just will not matter, period. Anyway, that thinking illuminates the way Hack's mind has worked since learning he had cancer.

Hack's weight is down to one hundred sixty-two pounds, from one hundred seventy eight. It has been two weeks since he took his last chemo pill, however, and he feels fairly good. He is weak and the room spins if he moves his head abruptly, but the vertigo, or whatever it is, soon fades away, and he no longer feels sporadically nauseous. Dr. Michalak told him that after the first repetition it gets easier, and Hack concludes that Dr. Michalak is right. Still, Hack tells himself, it is not a walk on the beach, not like the day before the start of Lent. Hack is not certain why it is that he's losing weight. Yes, he knows that he is not eating as much, but he thinks there is more to it, that somehow the food he does eat is not fully converting into energy, fat, and nutrients as it should. Besides, he feels certain that he passes too much of the good stuff – when he passes anything – as waste.

Aaron still hikes around the building every morning. Near the halfway point of his route, the one they walked (Hack clomped) together for nearly a year, Hack can see him from their bedroom window. Aaron always stops and waves and Hack waves back. Once Hack forgot Aaron was outside walking, and when he remembered to look, Aaron was trying to get his attention by prancing around as if he was daft.

Aaron is tirelessly sympathetic. Hack is not ignorant enough to think it has anything to do with his blackness, but he sometimes wonders. Aaron has received Christmas boxes from Jolene, Carolina, and Maragold (yes, M-a-r-a-gold), and nineteen Christmas cards, which he stood on his dresser, arranged in order of inherited importance – or whatever. He showed Hack the ones from his daughters. Both Jolene and Carolina write glowingly of Hack in their greetings. They did not mention his illness, but he could tell that Aaron has let them know that cancer is engorging his lungs. Hack has still not received a Christmas card from Danny, his brother in Dallas. He sent one to Danny's family, but, figuring it wouldn't matter, he did not mention his sickness.

Christmas morning. It snowed last night, layering a sooty base of snow with an inch or so of fluffy white flakes, and making the scene outside Hack's and Aaron's room endlessly serene. Hack can make out the occasional white-and-green of a tall evergreen tree in the solid black wall of deciduous trees that borders the far back edge of the arable acreage behind Cooper Greens.

Aaron, returning from breakfast, insists that Hack help him open his Christmas boxes. As Hack had supposed, there are presents for him from Jolene and Carolina, hard-cover editions of Tom Clancy's *The Cardinal of the Kremlin* and *The Sum of All Fears*. Both books are annotated inside with assurances that the four of them would be eating out together again come Summer.

Not having any children, Helen and Hack were not big on celebrating Christmas. They went to Mass the night before, exchanged presents before nine o'clock on Christmas morning, ate breakfast, dallied around, and spent the afternoon at her folk's home. They gave gifts – judiciously selected by Helen – to her nieces and nephews and sent a check for twenty-five dollars to each of Danny's three kids, to Hack's two nephews and one niece.

After Mom passed away, Helen cooked Christmas dinner for Hack and Pap, and Helen's sisters and their kids would swing by to see Pap. Hack assumes he'd be more sentimental about Christmas if he and Helen had had children. All the same, he is deeply touched by his presents from Aaron's daughters, by their well-intentioned, but what he knows in his heart is a futile promise of the four of them ever again enjoying another lunch together.

Hack misses Helen, of course, but hardly worse than any other day.

Aaron puts away his presents and cleans up the mess that he and Hack had made opening them. He says to Hack, "Feel like eating out today?" Aaron means, of course, does Hack feel like walking to the dining room to eat.

"I think so. Let's give it a try."

In truth, for the last week Hack has been strong enough to make it to the dining room, but he is so damn hollow-eyed and haggard looking that he hates for others to see him. Whoever wrote, "Vanity thy name is woman," was only half right.

Because relatives and friends will dine today with residents, dinner will be served in two shifts, at noon and at one o'clock. Hack is certain the dining room will be less crowded at one o'clock. Aaron agrees and sees to it that they are scheduled for the second seating. (A celebratory Christmas dinner was served to Cooper Greens' sponsors, supervisory staff, and the residents helped prepare that meal, at three o'clock on December 16th.)

They take their seats in the dining room at a table where Kitty and Yvon are waiting. The room and tables are decorated in Christmas favors, but neither excessively nor, frankly, in Hack's opinion, in a very appealing way. They're served turkey and fixings, and for dessert a slice of pumpkin pie topped with a spoonful of whipped cream. The turkey helpings are obviously cut from a whole bird, not from a turkey roll, and the topping on the pie is real whipped cream. Hack is thinking that the kitchen help had to have busted their butts for this one. To the constant urging and then excessive approval of his dinner companions, Hack eats every bite on his plate except the cornbread dressing, a staple of southern and military cooking that he never cottoned to. Aaron is not served any of the sweet dishes, which omission he pretends, by gesturing, is more evidence of racial discrimination.

At fifteen minutes after two, as they are eating, six women and six men, twelve smiling, rosy, winter-chafed faces, walk into the dining room and form up as a three-row choir. They sing *Deck the Halls with Boughs of Holly, Jingle Bells*, and *The Twelve Days of Christmas*, all lively, cheerful songs. Larry Goldberg and his wife G___ are sitting by themselves two tables away, and Hack cannot help but notice that Larry synchronously mouths almost every word of every song. Hack recalls that he never sang more than three lines of *The Twelve Days of Christmas* without getting mixed up, even when he was fifty years younger.

Besides being Jewish, Larry is eighty-some years old – hardly the cornerstones of a foundation for knowing and recalling the lyrics of Christmas songs. As Hack watched, he decided that he would someday soon ask Larry if Jews believe in a life after death. He hopes they do, but he is uncertain. He had not much cared to know before. Larry, Hack is sure, would quote the Talmud, if an afterlife is mentioned in that resource.

The first day of the year 2000 came and passed without a single Y2K calamity, anyway none that swirled around Hack. At the stroke of midnight, eastern America time, on the last day of the twentieth century, all computers world-wide were forecasted to misinterpret 2000 as 1900, the earth was supposed to stop spinning and wobbly depart the sun's gravitational pull for the gravity of another star. Or the planet would implode, explode, unplode, or whatever. Two days before this was to happen, Hack took the fourth pill of his third treatment, and on that January 1st he would have greeted – welcomed – a crashing end to the world.

[56]

It is bitter cold outside and so windy that tree limbs are flailing about as if they were still dressed in wind-catching summer leaves. A. J. and Aaron are in their room writing. Aaron has not hiked around Cooper Greens for two days. Twice he has curiously looked in Hack's direction, but Hack pretends not to notice. Aaron is undoubtedly penning a letter to one of his daughters; Hack is composing his obituary. Hack has not conceded anything – just being practical. In fact, his weight seems to have stabilized at one hundred fifty-four pounds and his hair, on the sides and in the back where it used to grow, is slowly coming back; it is wispy and curlier than it was before Hack began chemo.

Old folks read obituaries. Hack never used to, not unless Helen showed him one covering the death of a person they knew. Now, looking for a recognizable surname – that perhaps might briefly remind him of better times – Hack reads them every day. At seeing some names, Hack's natural competitiveness seems to reflexively dominate his reaction, leaves him with the weird feeling that somehow he has bested that person in the game of life. Maybe it is just the chemo enfeebling his brain; he is unsure.

Over the last few years Hack has read dozens of *Morning Beacon* obituaries. He knows the opening phrasing, and if he had not spent twenty minutes puzzling over the spelling of his mother-in-law's maiden name, a long wyz Lettish surname meaning 'cultivator of land', he could have written his own inside an hour.

He polishes what will be a final version of his obituary, folds the paper once in the middle, sharpens the crease, and hands it to Aaron. "Maybe you should read this," he says to Aaron blandly.

Aaron unfolds the sheet, and when he finishes reading, Hack says, "Now don't start in. I meant to write one a year ago."

Aren looks up but says nothing.

Hack says, "I had a hell of a time writing Helen's. Please just see that mine gets to the *Beacon*."

Aaren slowly folds the sheet back up and wordlessly lays it on his dresser.

"Kind of sad, isn't it? Hack says, "I mean, sad because we never had kids and I didn't amount to a blade of grass. When I'm gone, it'll be like I never existed, as if I was stillborn or something."

"God formed man of the dust of the ground," Aaron says, shaking his head as if dressing Hack down. "He didn't mean for all of us to be heroes – or smart, or whatever. You're a damn good man, Thomas, and that's what matters."

"He sure as hell never singled me out," Hack mumbles, distracted at Aaron's rare use of profanity.

Hesitantly, Aaron asks Hack if he intended to give a copy to Kitty. "Likely she'll be around long after we're both gone." Aaron manages a tiny grin.

"No," Hack says, after a moment. "She'll re-write every damn line. Give it to Marie, if it comes to that."

"If you're sure . . . ."

"Yes. I'm sure. And something else, Aaron. In the bottom right-hand drawer of my dresser is an envelope addressed to me – from a Joe Luoma. Joe died before you moved in, and I didn't know how to disposition his letter; probably I should have deep-sixed it. It's . . . more or less a last-will. You can read it if you want, but I honestly wouldn't. I'm not throwing in the towel, not yet, but if I do cash out would you please give the letter to Kitty? And, keep the home fires burning – I mean keep up the jolly. Promise me."

"I will," Aaron finally says, unconvincingly.

"I'm to be buried in a grave next to Helen. Dickey's funeral home gets me. They already have a casket that I bought. It's exactly like Helen's. There's a thousand-dollar burial CD in my name in the Western Reserve National Bank in Snow Lake. For my embalming and . . . whatever. Cooper Greens is aware of all these things. I know *you'll* make sure it gets done right. If there's a little left over, you're welcome to it. I'll leave a note to that effect. Only . . . hell, we both know Cooper Greens will get it. I'm going to be buried with Helen."

And for the second time since Helen's death, the tears seep from Hack's eyes, and he cannot stop the flow.

Epilogue

I promised Tommy I would write this epilogue for *Cooper Greens*. He said, "You can tie up loose ends."

Loose ends? What loose ends? I would have kidded him, suggested that *The Bluing of Cooper Greens* wasn't exactly Tolstoy's *War and Peace*, only he was so feeble when he finally asked me to pen these last words that I didn't have the heart. I spent all last week reading the author's draft, which mainly consists of the sifting and winnowing of Hack's hand-written notes, the hundreds that the author was privy to maintain.

Tommy drew his last breath sometime before the first light of dawn three days ago. He had virtually quit eating four days prior, and he hadn't swallowed a drop of water, juice, or any other liquid the last couple of days. His passing was anything but a surprise to those of us mindful of his true condition.

Marie told me of his death before breakfast. She said that Janet, working graveyard, had checked him hourly through the night and found him permanently resting in peace at 5:20 a.m. I knew that Janet would do more than just peek in every now and then, that she would make sure he was dry and warm, roll him to new positions, moisten his lips, and coo comforting words all the while she was doing those things. Except for his labored breathing, Tommy was passably comfortable to the very end. I think God mercifully waited until he had finished writing the Preface to this book.

Tommy and Aaron kept Cooper Greens in constant, rousing, unsettled turmoil; I helped them arrange and carry out some of their pranks. Unfortunately, with Tommy's passing, those days are gone forever: Tommy started things, was the spark that ignited the fire that often as not swept through a whole wing of Cooper Greens.

I watched with Aaron, as Tommy was buried next to Helen, his enduring love. Their gravesites were situated three feet apart, side-by-side under the spread of a weathered apple tree. The old tree's few remaining leaves, dry and without scent, seemed to look out on Snow Lake – where a few rowboats, each guided by a lone, huddled fisherman, were rising and falling with the lake's small waves. The air that morning was chilly.

Heirlooms to pass on? His seventy-five dollar Seiko quartz watch – to Aaron. That is all.

A devout Catholic, Tommy believed without reservation that his soul would survive his body's demise and be reconstituted by God in Heaven. Personally, I have my doubts. If Tommy's right, though, he'll certainly reconnect in the hereafter with his beloved Helen.

I truly was never his beloved. Still I liked the son-of-a-gun immensely.

Catherine Proctor

ABOUT THE AUTHOR

Hugh McClintock, the author of Cooper Greens, spent months in nursing homes – not as an observer, but as a resident. To get in, he allowed himself to be hit by a car as he was walking across a street. But for Hugh, no sacrifice is too great. While recovering, he observed happenings seldom seen by outsiders. Cooper Greens, he assures, is not a feel-good story about old folk facing the end-game of life; it is, however, an honest, humorous account of their circumstances.

Hugh earned a BA at Allegheny College and a BSEE at Carnegie Mellon University. He held sundry engineering jobs and several everyday duties until he retired. A widower, he lives in Meadville, Pa.

www.ingramcontent.com/pod-product-compliance
Lightning Source LLC
Chambersburg PA
CBHW071643090426
42738CB00009B/1413